GOLD-PLATED
POLITICS

GOLD-PLATED POLITICS

RUNNING FOR CONGRESS IN THE 1990S

SARA FRITZ AND DWIGHT MORRIS

LOS ANGELES TIMES

Congressional Quarterly Inc.
Washington, D.C.

Copyright © 1992 Congressional Quarterly Inc.
1414 22nd Street, N.W., Washington, D.C. 20037

Printed in the United States of America

Book design: Kaelin Chappell
Cover design: Ben Santora

Library of Congress Cataloging-in-Publication Data

Fritz, Sara, 1944-
    Gold-plated politics : running for Congress in the 1990s / Sara
Fritz and Dwight Morris.
        p.   cm.
    Condensed ed. of: Handbook of campaign spending / Sara Fritz and
Dwight Morris.
    Includes index.
    ISBN 0-87187-858-5
    1. Campaign funds--United States--Handbooks, manuals, etc.
2. United States. Congress--Elections, 1990--Handbooks, manuals,
etc. I. Morris, Dwight, 1952- . II. Fritz, Sara, 1944-
Handbook of campaign spending.   III. Title.
JK1991.F74   1993
324.7'8'0973--dc20   92-32153
                                                                            CIP

For all their love and support throughout this project,
this book is dedicated to James A. Kidney and Jenifer Ellen Morris

Contents

List of Tables and Boxes

Tables

Boxes

Preface

U ntil now, campaign spending has been ignored in the study of American politics. Political scientists, journalists, and even proponents of campaign finance reform held the view that it made no difference how campaign money was spent. If they focused on the role of money in politics, they concentrated on contributions.

It was simply assumed that politicians used their campaign contributions for all of the usual things: television ads, bumper stickers, billboards, yard signs, phone banks, and sample ballots. That assumption was never challenged, in part, because it was virtually impossible for political analysts to penetrate the mountains of paper reports on campaign spending filed each year with the Federal Election Commission (FEC).

What we expected to uncover by looking through all those FEC reports were questionable or improper expenditures by political candidates. While we were not disappointed on that count, we also uncovered a wealth of information that sheds new light on many issues that have been debated about politics in recent years, including the decline of the two-party system, the rising cost of campaigns, and the role of technology in politics.

This book is based on a database compiled by the authors and others while working in the Washington, D.C., bureau of the *Los Angeles Times*. It is the product of about two years of work and a considerable financial expense by the *Times*.

We analyzed 437,753 separate expenditures reported to the FEC by 972 candidates who sought congressional office in 1990. Copies of each FEC report were obtained by the *Times,* and every expenditure was entered into the database under 1 of 220 different categories. While we relied primarily on the candidates' own descriptions of their expenditures, we sought to contact every campaign for an explanation of all ambiguous entries in which the candidate spent more than a few thousand dollars. While most campaigns were very cooperative, some members of Congress and their employees refused to explain their vaguely reported campaign expenditures.

In House races, this book covers all expenditures during the two-year cycle beginning January 1, 1989, and ending December 31, 1990. In Senate races, it covers the six-year cycle beginning January 1, 1985, and ending December 31, 1990. We made no effort to report on the campaign expenditures of senators who were not up for reelection in 1990. In cases where special elections were held during the cycle to fill House vacancies, the book contains data from the special election as well as the subsequent primary and general elections.

Our findings come at a time when members of Congress are trying to decide how to reform the campaign finance system. They also come at a time when Americans are questioning whether politicians are committed more to their own careers than to the well-being of the nation. We hope this book will cause Americans to be concerned enough to demand serious, substantial reform of the campaign finance system. We also hope it will cause members of Congress to opt for a full-scale overhaul of the system, rather than a few cosmetic changes.

We are journalists. It is not our purpose to side with Republicans, Democrats, Common Cause, or Ralph Nader or to endorse any particular approach to campaign finance reform. In fact, we have never seen a reform proposal from any source that would satisfy our concerns.

Our intention in writing this book was nonpartisan and nonideological. We wanted to point out problems in the campaign finance system that have been ignored. We also wanted to encourage political scientists, journalists, and others interested in politics to study the full impact that special-interest money is having on American democracy.

We would like to emphasize that except in a few cases we are not accusing any member of Congress of doing anything illegal. By and large, most members of Congress are guilty of nothing more than participating in a widely accepted system of conduct. At the same time, we believe many of the practices outlined in this book should be illegal.

Acknowledgments

For their strong support of this project, we are deeply grateful to the management of the *Los Angeles Times:* Publisher David Laventhol, Editor Shelby Coffey III, Managing Editor George J. Cotlier, Assistant Managing Editor Martin Baron, National Editor Norman C. Miller, Washington Bureau Chief Jack Nelson, Deputy Bureau Chief Richard T. Cooper, and Angela Rinaldi, manager of book development.

This book could never have been written had it not been for the long hours, night, and weekends Murielle E. Gamache, Stephanie Grace, Desiree Williams, and Debbie Szpanka spent researching the expenditures and coding the data. For their assistance in writing the book, we thank Richard S. Dunham, Eric Woodman, and Lisa Hoffman. For their encouragement and patience, we are grateful to our family members: Jenifer Morris, James A. Kidney, Mary Kathleen Kidney, and Daniel McCarthy Kidney II. For their advice and counsel, we are grateful to our good friends: Cheryl Arvidson, Karen Tumulty, David Lauter, and Art Pine, as well as many others in the Washington Bureau of the *Los Angeles Times.*

A special thanks to Tom McLean of Data Tabulating Service, who put up with our demanding schedule and frequently stayed up all night to compile or make changes in the database, and to the staff of Data Tabulating Service, who provided us with rapid and, above all, extremely accurate data entry and verification: Carmen Hughes, Nancy Houston, Jimmy Owensby, Darlene Lyons, and Rachelle Pitts. For technical assistance, we thank Phil Ruiz.

A Guide to the Tables

The analysis of individual races that follows is based on an examination of all 437,753 separate expenditures reported to the Federal Election Commission (FEC) by 972 candidates who sought congressional office in 1990.

Copies of each campaign's financial reports were obtained from the FEC by the *Los Angeles Times*. Each expenditure was entered into the database under 1 of 220 different categories. To ensure that the categorization was accurate, we contacted officials of each campaign that spent more than a few thousand dollars and asked for clarification of all vaguely reported expenditures. We also inquired about the duties of every consultant employed by the campaign.

While most campaigns were extremely cooperative, some were not. In cases where neither the candidate nor the campaign employees provided sufficient information, we contacted the consultants directly. In all, we conducted more than 700 interviews with candidates, campaign staff, and consultants.

In calculating expenditure totals, transfers between authorized committees, payments of debts from prior election cycles, contribution refunds, and loan repayments have been excluded in order to avoid double counting expenditures. All debts to vendors reported at the end of the 1990 cycle have been included.

The expenditures were subsequently assigned to one of eight major spending categories. Five categories were broken further into specific areas of spending. The following is a description of the categories and the types of items included in each.

OVERHEAD

Office furniture/supplies: Furniture and basic office supplies, telephone answering services, messenger and overnight delivery services, monthly cable TV payments, newspaper and magazine subscriptions, clipping services, payments for file storage, small postage and photocopying charges, office moving expenses, and improvements or upkeep of the office (including office cleaning, garbage pickup, repairs, plumbers, and locksmiths).

Rent: Monthly rent and utility payments for campaign offices.

Salaries: Salary payments and employee benefits, including health insurance. In addition to payments specifically described as salary, this category includes regular payments to those people who performed routine office tasks, which were frequently misrepresented in campaign finance reports as "consulting." Whenever a housing allowance was part of a campaign manager's compensation package, it was considered to be salary as well.

Taxes: All federal and state taxes paid by the campaign, including income taxes paid on the campaign's investments and payroll taxes.

Bank fees: Interest payments on outstanding loans, annual credit card fees, and check charges.

Lawyers/accountants: Fees paid for their services as well as any other expenses incurred by the campaign's lawyers and accountants.

Telephone: Purchases of telephone equipment (including cellular phones and beepers), monthly payments for local and long-distance service, installation fees, repairs, and reimbursements to staff for telephone expenses.

Campaign automobile: All payments for the purchase or lease of a campaign vehicle, maintenance, insurance, registration, licensing, and gasoline.

Computers/office equipment: All payments related to the purchase or lease of office equipment, such as computer equipment and software, typewriters, copiers, FAX machines, telephone answering machines, televisions, radios, and VCRs. Repair and warranty costs were included.

Travel: All general travel expenses, such as air fare and hotels, as well as rental cars, taxis, daily parking, and entries such as "food for travel."

Restaurant/food: Meeting expenses (for example, steering committees, campaign committees, state delegations) and other food costs not specifically related to constituent entertainment, travel, or fund raising.

Fund Raising

Events: All costs related to fund-raising events, including invitations, postage, planning meetings, travel costs, room rental, food and catering costs, liquor, flowers, bartenders, follow-up telephone calls, in-kind fund-raising expenses, general reimbursements to individuals for fund raising, tickets to sporting or theater events that served a fund-raising purpose, and fees paid to consultants who planned the events.

Direct mail: All costs related to fund raising via the mail, including the purchase of mailing lists, computer charges, postage, printing, consultant fees, and consultant expenses. Mailings that served a dual purpose, both to raise funds and inform voters, were included in this category.

Telemarketing: All expenses related to a telephone operation designed to raise money, including consulting fees, list purchases, and computer costs. Campaigns use the terms *telemarketing* and *phone banking* loosely. Some items identified as telemarketing in campaign reports to the FEC were found to be inaccurately identified.

Polling

All polling costs, including payments to consultants as well as in-kind contributions of polling results to the campaign.

ADVERTISING

Electronic media: All payments to consultants, separate purchases of broadcast time, and production costs associated with the development of radio and television advertising. In most cases, payments to media consultants for other purposes were excluded.

Other media: Payments for billboards; advertising in newspapers, journals, magazines, and publications targeted to religious groups, senior citizens, and other special constituencies; as well as program ads purchased from local charitable and booster organizations.

OTHER CAMPAIGN ACTIVITY

Voter contact mail: All costs associated with the strictly promotional mailing undertaken by campaigns, including artwork, printing of the brochures or other mailed material, postage, the purchase of mailing lists, as well as consultant fees and consultant expenses.

Actual campaigning: Filing fees and costs of petition drives, announcement parties, state party conventions, campaign rallies and parades, campaign training schools, opposition research, printed campaign handouts, posters, signs, buttons, bumper stickers, speech writers and coaches, get-out-the-vote efforts, election-day poll watchers, and all campaign promotional material (T-shirts, jackets, caps, embossed pencils, pens, nail files, potholders, etc.). Fees and expenses billed by campaign management firms and general consultants for services unrelated to advertising, fund raising, and voter contact mail are also included. In cases where it was impossible to isolate advertising, fund-raising, and other expenses incurred by these consultants, the entire consulting fee was included here.

Staff/volunteers: All food expenses for staff and volunteers, including phone bank and get-out-the-vote volunteers. These expenses included bottled water, soda machines, monthly coffee service, and food purchases that were specifically for the campaign office. Also included were recruitment of volunteers, gifts for staff and volunteers, and staff retreats.

CONSTITUENT GIFTS/ENTERTAINMENT

Meals purchased for constituents, the costs of events that were designed purely for constituent entertainment (for example, a local dominos tournament), constituent gifts of all kinds, flowers, holiday greeting cards, awards and plaques, and costs associated with the annual congressional art contest.

DONATIONS

To candidates (both in-state and out-of-state): Direct contributions to other candidates as well as the purchase price of fund-raiser tickets.

To civic organizations: Contributions to charitable organizations, such as the American Cancer Society, as well as local booster groups, such as the Chamber of Commerce and local high school athletic associations. Includes the purchase of tickets to events sponsored by such groups.

To political parties: Contributions to national, state and local party organizations, including tickets to party-sponsored fund-raising events.

UNITEMIZED EXPENSES

Candidates are not required to report expenditures of less than $200, and many do not list them on their FEC reports. This category also includes expenditures described in FEC reports merely as "petty cash," unitemized credit card purchases, and all reimbursements that were vaguely worded, such as "reimbursement," "political expenses," or "campaign expenses."

CHAPTER 1

Political Campaigns
Why Do They Cost So Much?

It is not good for this country that the cost of campaigns
continues to skyrocket. It is not good that the average cost to
successfully run for the Senate has gone from $600,000 when I
first came to the Senate thirteen years ago all the way to $4
million. It is not good. . . . Where is it all going to end? Is the
sky the limit?

Sen. David Boren, D-Okla., May 23, 1991

I n the same anguished tones used to decry the federal deficit or the
high cost of health care, today's politicians lament the rising cost
of political campaigns. Over the past decade, the money spent in
congressional campaigns has more than doubled. Senate incumbents
complain that they must raise an average of $12,000 a week during
their six-year term to be ready for a reelection campaign. In California, a candidate running for the Senate must be prepared to raise at
least $20 million. It is no longer unusual for incumbent House candi-
dates—even those without opposition—to spend between $500,000
and $1 million on their reelection.

Politicians tell us they are helpless to control these rising costs,
which they invariably blame on the high price of television advertising. The television stations, they say, bleed politicians dry by charging
them more than other advertisers. They cite other uncontrollable
costs, such as the exorbitant fees charged by political consultants, the
high price of fund raising, and the cost of air travel.

Ostensibly, these rising costs are to blame for forcing most of
our nation's politicians to turn to special-interest groups to finance
their elections and, as a result, to enter into an unspoken agreement
to use their office to defend the interests of those who help finance
their campaigns. Without these burdensome expenses, the politicians
claim, they could escape the ethical dilemma posed by financing elections with huge sums of special-interest money.

In fact, it is simply not true that high campaign costs are beyond the control of the politicians. Campaign spending is growing in response to the ever-increasing availability of campaign contributions, not because of rising costs.

More than half the money spent in the 1990 congressional elections went for purchases that were virtually unrelated to contacting voters. Of all the money spent by House incumbents, 55 percent was invested in races by those with little or no opposition. In short, campaign funds are not being used primarily for campaigns.

Even television costs, which have long been blamed as the root cause of escalating campaign costs, accounted for only a fraction of what candidates spent from their campaign treasuries in 1990. On average, House candidates spent only 23 percent of their money on radio and television advertising. In fact, 127 incumbents spent nothing at all on either radio or television advertising; another 55 incumbents spent less than $10,000. For Senate candidates, radio and television costs averaged 35 percent of the campaign budget.

The truth is that Congress is awash in special-interest money and incumbents simply have created a variety of new ways to gild the electoral process in order to make use of it. If less money were available, candidates would still be able to communicate effectively with the voters—even on television.

Perhaps the most persuasive proof of the needless excesses of the current system is the continued success of a few members of Congress who spend very little money on their campaigns—even in contested elections or marginal districts—such as Reps. Andrew Jacobs, Jr., D-Ind., William S. Broomfield, R-Mich., and Glenn Poshard, D-Ill. The records of these incumbents disprove the contention that big spending is a necessary element of modern politics.

This book offers the first comprehensive study of spending by political candidates. In the past, journalists, political scientists, and reformers have focused on the growing dependency of candidates on special-interest money and the undue influence that big contributors exert on policy making. Little or no attention has ever been paid to what is our primary focus: how the electoral process itself has been distorted by big money.

In this book, we look closely at what money in politics actually buys and how it has radically transformed the process of electing public officials. In our view, the current patterns of campaign giving and campaign spending are far more responsible for the failures of the

U.S. electoral process than many of the factors normally cited by political scientists, such as the influence of television or the decline of the two-party system.

Money from special interests has enabled most incumbent members of Congress to create their own state-of-the-art, permanent political machine—an apparatus that makes them almost entirely independent of the two-party system and frees them from some of the parochial influences of their own districts or states.

To maintain these high-tech, personal political organizations, incumbents spend hundreds of thousands—even millions—of dollars on elections in which they have little or no opposition. By and large, campaign costs are driven by the urge to build a political empire, not by the seriousness of the opposition.

Nor do members of Congress abide strictly by rules that prohibit them from spending campaign funds on themselves and their families. We found dozens of entrenched incumbents who spent large sums from their campaign treasuries to enhance their personal lifestyles with fancy automobiles, high-priced restaurant meals, resort vacations, country club memberships, and expensive office furniture.

In the 1990 election cycle, congressional candidates reported raising nearly $472 million in campaign contributions and spending about $446 million. As large as those figures are, they do not take into account the hundreds of millions of dollars in "soft money" contributions that escaped federal law by being funneled through state and national party accounts. Nor do they include large, unreported contributions that went to congressional candidates through voter registration groups, charitable trusts, legal defense funds, and a variety of other fund-raising gimmicks.

In many races in 1990, candidates spent sums of money that just a few years earlier would have been unthinkable in a congressional election. The average House incumbent spent more than $390,000 to be reelected (see Table 1-1); the average senator spent more than $4 million (see Table 1-2).

In the year's most expensive race, Sen. Jesse Helms, R-N.C., and Democrat Harvey B. Gantt spent a total of nearly $26 million. In New Jersey, Republican Dick Zimmer and Democrat Marguerite Chandler set a record for a single House race by spending a combined total of $2.6 million. Fifteen House candidates, including three incumbents who had no serious opposition, spent more than $1 million each.

After the election, four senators had surpluses in excess of $1 million in their campaign treasuries; fourteen had surpluses exceeding $500,000. More than one-quarter of the House members had campaign surpluses in excess of $250,000; seven had surpluses exceeding $1 million.

Big spending was by no means confined to the hotly contested races. The burdens of campaigning had nothing to do with the decision of Rep. Martin Frost, D-Texas, to spend nearly $600,000 in an election in which he had no opponent. Rep. Joseph P. Kennedy II clearly did not need to invest more than $826,000 to defeat Republican challenger Glenn Fiscus, who spent lss than $5,000. Nor did Sen. Joseph R. Biden, Jr., D-Del., have to spend $21.99 per vote in an election that was never seriously contested. Rep. Jim Kolbe, R-Ariz., could have prevailed with less than the $323,000 he spent to defend against an impoverished opponent who was jailed during the campaign for writing a bad check.

While challengers were scrambling for cash—often spending their own money to mount campaigns—most incumbents had no trouble meeting whatever fund-raising goal they set for themselves. Virtually every weeknight in Washington, D.C., the National Democratic Club, the Ronald Reagan Center, the Capitol Hill Club, and various popular restaurants near the Capitol were booked with an endless schedule of fund-raising parties held by members of Congress. Indeed, even though incumbents often complained about the rigors of fund raising, these parties were so numerous and so predictable that members of Congress had come to view them as a necessary chore of daily life.

"I don't find it that onerous," confided Sen. John C. Danforth, R-Mo. "You just go down to the Ronald Reagan Center, stand around for two hours, shake hands, and collect $50,000 to $100,000."

Money has become so plentiful that some members of Congress seldom bothered to ask their own constituents for contributions. In fact, many members prided themselves on being able to raise money all over the country. In 1990, it was not unusual for a representative from Illinois to hold a fund-raising party in Los Angeles or New York City.

Many ideologues on the left and right have effectively used direct-mail fund-raising techniques to build themselves a national network of like-minded contributors to finance their campaigns. Rep. Robert K. Dornan, R-Calif., got so much of his money from a nationwide list of donors that he could boast of having a "constituent" in every district.

Money has been easy for congressional candidates to come by, in part, because of the growth of political action committees, or PACs. In sheer numbers, PACs grew from 608 in 1974 to 4,677 in 1990. Total giving by PACs to congressional candidates grew from $12.4 million in the 1974 election to $159 million in 1989-1990. The growth in spending by individual PACs is demonstrated by the giving history of the Democratic Republican Independent Voter Education Committee—DRIVE—the Teamsters' Union PAC, which contributed only $141,500 to federal candidates in 1978 but gave $2.3 million in 1990.

But PACs were not solely responsible for making campaign cash more readily available to politicians. In fact, the importance of PAC contributions to the campaign finance system has been overstated by reform groups, such as Common Cause. As PAC funding has acquired a bad reputation over the past few years, candidates have increasingly turned to their original source of funds: rich, individual donors. In 1989-1990, congressional candidates raised $159 million from PACs and about $164 million from individuals who gave $200 or more.

Frequently, politicians who rely primarily on money from wealthy individuals, instead of PACs, claim that they have escaped the clutches of special interests. But like PACs, most big individual donors are motivated to give money to politicians because they want something in return—a tax break, a policy change, or a better deal with a federal agency. Indeed, they are often the same executives who contribute money to candidates through corporate PACs.

In the 1970s, when the Watergate scandal exposed many of the evils of the existing campaign finance system, people were shocked by the huge checks that President Richard M. Nixon had collected from wealthy business executives—such as the $25,000 check from Archer Daniels Midland Corp. chairman Dwayne O. Andreas that was found in a bank account belonging to Watergate burglar Bernard L. Barker.

In response to Watergate, Congress enacted legislation in 1974 to encourage special-interest groups to form PACs and to prevent wealthy individuals from buying influence with big donations. Under the law, individuals could not give more than $2,000 to any candidate or more than $25,000 total in any year.

By 1990, the safeguards written into the law had been eroded to the point where wealthy influence-seekers such as Andreas were once again making contributions ranging as high as $100,000 or $200,000. The era of Watergate-style campaign financing had returned.

Rich individuals such as Andreas have succeeded in circumventing the federal contribution limits in two ways: (1) by collecting or "bundling" together many checks from friends, relatives, and like-minded business associates, or (2) by contributing to "soft money" accounts maintained by the local, state, and national parties, which can accept checks for unlimited amounts.

Without meaningful limits on contributions, campaign spending has grown precipitously, altering the nature of the American electoral process and turning it into something it never was intended to be.

Big money flows primarily to incumbents, thereby reducing competition in elections. Of the 405 House races in 1990 involving an incumbent, only 30 percent involved challengers who had enough money to be considered even remotely competitive.

Of course, a few underfunded challengers won against the odds, usually because scandal tarnished the incumbent or a third-party candidate siphoned off votes. Democrat Paul Wellstone of Minnesota performed the miracle of the year by defeating Sen. Rudy Boschwitz, an entrenched Republican incumbent who outspent him by more than five to one.

The overwhelming lesson of the 1990 congressional election, however, was that big money still virtually ensures victory for an incumbent. Sen. Bill Bradley, D-N.J., and Rep. Newt Gingrich, R-Ga., might never have been reelected had it not been for the big spending advantage they had over their challengers.

With very few exceptions, incumbents raised far more money than challengers. Even a hot political phenomenon such as David Duke, the former Ku Klux Klan leader who challenged Sen. J. Bennett Johnston, D-La., before running unsuccessfully for governor and president, could not raise the large sums of money that Johnston had access to.

Big money from special interests freezes out challengers not only because so much money is needed to communicate with the voters, but also because challengers cannot compete with the massive organizational advantage that incumbents have carefully created for themselves with years of free spending in their districts. Using the massive amounts of money available to them, many members of Congress run their campaigns like energetic small businesses, complete with full-time employees, well-appointed offices, an impressive stock portfolio, regular newsletters, frequent social events, free gifts, high-priced consultants, a generous travel budget, and expensive lawyers and accountants on retainer.

Less than 40 percent of all the money spent by congressional incumbents during the 1990 election cycle was devoted to communicating with voters through the traditional methods: advertising, mailings, rallies, and the like. Instead, the bulk of the spending went to cover the costs of building their political organizations: overhead, consultants, and fund raising (see Tables 1-3 and 1-4).

Take the example of Sen. Phil Gramm, R-Texas. Not only did he outspend his opponent $12.2 million to $1.3 million, but he also had an excess of $4 million in the bank when it was all over. At its peak, Gramm's campaign employed fifty people and maintained a permanent office in Dallas and satellite offices in Houston, San Antonio, East Texas, the Texas Panhandle, and El Paso. The total expenditure for Gramm's campaign overhead alone was more than $2.7 million.

Likewise, Rep. Sam M. Gibbons, D-Fla., who ran unopposed in 1986 and 1988 and received less than 60 percent of the vote only once since being elected in 1962, spent nearly $826,000 in 1990 against a Republican challenger who raised and spent less than $5,000. He maintained two campaign offices throughout the entire two-year cycle—one in Washington, D.C., and the other in his hometown of Tampa, Fla. In addition, he paid one of the nation's leading media consultants, Squier/Eskew Communications, nearly $48,000 to develop five television spots, only three of which actually ran. The total cost of Gibbons's broadcast advertising campaign was nearly $230,000.

First elected in 1978, Rep. Bill Thomas, R-Calif., had seen his winning percentage fall below 70 percent only once in six previous reelection bids. Yet, while his 1990 Democratic challenger could muster only $2,095 for the race, Thomas spent nearly $500,000 on his campaign. Like a number of his California colleagues, Thomas turned over his campaign almost entirely to a general consulting firm, Western Pacific Research of Bakersfield, Calif. Western Pacific received almost $210,000 of the money Thomas dispensed. Thomas also gave away more than $116,000 of his campaign funds, much of it to support other Republican candidates.

Rep. John D. Dingell, D-Mich., chairman of the House Energy and Commerce Committee and another firmly entrenched incumbent, raised nearly $844,000 in preparation for his contest with a Republican challenger who ultimately spent less than $3,800. Dingell spent liberally and inundated his constituents with gifts and cards— $7,700 for Christmas cards, nearly $8,000 for gifts, $2,800 for calendars, nearly $4,000 for flowers, and more than $3,800 for meals.

The campaigns of Gramm, Gibbons, and Dingell epitomize the unrestrained spending that is possible for influential incumbents with access to limitless amounts of money from special interests. But such spending is not nearly as unusual as sometimes portrayed. These are simply blatant examples of a pattern that is now deeply ingrained in the American political system (see Tables 1-5 and 1-6).

The true costs of machine building can best be seen in races where there was no challenger. In 1990, the average unopposed House member spent $250,000 and the three unopposed senators spent an average of $668,000, most of it simply to maintain their personal organizations.

Rep. Les Aspin, D-Wis., spent almost $800,000 in 1990 despite running unopposed. While more than 60 percent of his spending was devoted to overhead and fund raising, Aspin spent more than $51,000 on gifts and entertainment for constituents. Another $44,858 was donated to various candidates, civic groups, and Democratic party organizations.

It is often said that incumbent members of Congress amass huge campaign war chests just to scare away potential challengers. What is seldom said is that incumbents do not just sit on their money—they actually spend it in ways that make it virtually impossible for a challenger, even a well-funded one, to compete.

What challenger can compete with an incumbent who has spent thousands of dollars every year on gifts, parties, and other benefits for the most politically active and influential people in their district? What challenger can out-organize an incumbent whose campaign payroll exceeds fifty people? What challenger can raise more money than an incumbent whose permanent fund-raising apparatus churns out contributions every day of every year?

While politicians and pundits lament the decline of strong political parties in the United States, they seldom recognize the role special-interest money plays in minimizing the influence of national Republican and Democratic leaders. Despite growth in the House and Senate party committees, money from these organizations plays a relatively small role in congressional elections.

When office-holders have all the electoral advantages that special-interest money can buy, they have no real need for their party and no true respect for party discipline. They can vote however they please on most issues, knowing that their party leaders have no control over the real organization that ensures their reelection. They can supplant the party in their home states by distributing money from their own campaign accounts to local and statewide candidates they expect will be beholden to them. In most cases, they not only do not rely upon the party, but state party leaders actually come to them begging their financial support for registration and get-out-the-vote efforts.

Big money may even be altering the original rationale for having a Congress. The Founding Fathers viewed the House as a place where conflicting views of different regions of the country would be expressed. But if a member of Congress from Illinois raises most of his campaign funds from donors in Washington, D.C., New York, and Los Angeles, he is less likely to continue identifying with the needs of voters in Illinois. The drafters of the Constitution did not envision a day when members of the House would—as Dornan does—have a "constituent" in every congressional district in the nation. Because of these giving patterns, today's Congress is divided more by conflicts between competing economic interests than by regional differences.

Furthermore, big money has enabled some members of Congress to live and work in a lavish style that creates a sense of entitlement among them and separates them from the common folk. In 1990, Rep. C. W. Bill Young, D-Fla., used his campaign funds to buy a $30,000, light blue Lincoln Continental. Sen. Strom Thurmond, R-S.C., doled out $733,000 from his campaign war chest for college scholarships and two endowed chairs that will carry his name into posterity. Rep. Carroll Hubbard, Jr., D-Ky., paid $3,000 from his campaign funds to commission an artist to paint a portrait of his father. As these expenditures indicate, some campaign coffers are regarded as slush funds to be used by incumbents for whatever purchases meet their fancy.

When it comes to spending campaign cash, virtually nothing is off limits. While the House and Senate ethics codes prohibit members from spending campaign funds on themselves, the Federal Election Commission seldom questions reported expenditures that appear to be purely personal. The FEC checks the candidates' spending reports for inconsistencies and omissions, but does not audit them regularly. In many cases, we found members of Congress spending campaign funds for purposes that had no plausible link to politics. We found cases where candidates masked the true nature of their expenditures, either by making vague entries on their FEC reports or by funneling the disbursements through private corporations that were closely related to their campaigns. We strongly suspect that some of that money ended up in the pockets of members of Congress or their employees.

Whenever members of Congress convert campaign funds to personal use, aren't they betraying those citizens who contribute $25 or $50 from their pocket every two years to support their favorite congressional candidate?

There continues to be a persistent attitude among members of Congress that the money belongs to them and that they need not account to anyone when spending it. Indeed, we heard that attitude expressed by an aide to Rep. Charles A. Hayes, D-Ill., who responded to our inquiries about the campaign spending by saying: "You are asking entirely too many questions!"

In recent years, senior members of Congress have been permitted to pocket their campaign funds when they retire. If they died, the money became part of their estate. But beginning in 1993, members of Congress will no longer be permitted to convert their campaign money into personal retirement accounts.

Public disclosure of campaign spending does little to discourage candidates from spending the money in any manner they see fit. While the news media can easily obtain computerized records of campaign contributions from the FEC, reporters and political scientists must plow through dozens of filing cabinets full of spending reports in order to determine how the money is being spent. Until the *Los Angeles Times* decided to devote considerable resources to this project, no news organization or public interest group in the United States had ever attempted a comprehensive study of campaign spending

As currently organized, the FEC exists only to ratify ever-increasing distortions in the system of campaign financing. The commission is not only to blame for failing to crack down on profligate spending by congressional candidates, it is also responsible for allowing the political system to be flooded with so much special-interest money in the first place. In the FEC's own records, we found more than sixty people who appeared to have made contributions in excess of the $25,000 annual limit, including one Chicago resident who contributed nearly four times the amount allowed by federal law. Yet the commission had taken no action against them.

Money has so completely changed the political system that only a few members of Congress have resisted the temptation to build vast organizations with the hundreds of thousands of campaign dollars available to them. But it is possible to succeed in politics today without spending large sums of money.

Jacobs, for example, won reelection in 1990 by spending less than $15,000 against a better-funded opponent. He spent less than all other members of Congress, except Rep. William H. Natcher, D-Ky. Yet Jacobs has never been a particularly secure incumbent. In his twelve successful House races prior to 1990, he received less than 55 percent of the vote three times and was even swept out of office for one term during Richard M. Nixon's 1972 presidential landslide.

In fact, many of those members of Congress who have dared to hold down their spending have found that voters are impressed by their frugality. Poshard, who was reelected despite his decision to hold spending to no more than $100,000, said he felt his position was "on the cutting edge" of electoral politics.

Ironically, one of the most articulate critics of the system, Rep. Anthony C. Beilenson, D-Calif., has long represented one of the richest sources of campaign cash in the nation—the people of Beverly Hills. Even when his opponent spent vast sums to defeat him, he did not respond in kind. "Some of my colleagues spend a lot more money than they need to," he said. Beilenson's political survival calls into question the rationale for the permanent campaign. If Beilenson and a few other like-minded incumbents can get reelected year after year without spending huge sums of money, then there should be no reason for many other entrenched members of Congress to be amassing large campaign treasuries.

Sen. John McCain, R-Ariz., whose role in the Keating Five influence-peddling scandal has made him sensitive to these issues, argues that members of Congress raise campaign funds under false pretenses. "Campaign funds should be used for campaign purposes," he said. "I do not go out and ask people to provide me with campaign funds so I might attend a funeral or send flowers or take a constituent to dinner or any other form of recreation that has sometimes been indulged in with campaign funds."

Beilenson and McCain represent a small minority. Even many critics of the system, such as Sens. Hank Brown, R-Colo., and David L. Boren, D-Okla., continue to go along with the majority by raising and spending vast sums of money from special interests. While Boren refuses to accept PAC money, he continues to take money from individuals who represent the same interests.

Of course, there is no question that politicians need to raise and spend money to get elected. In 1990, no one could blame House incumbents for being nervous about the tough races that might lie ahead of them after redistricting in 1992. Still, only 30 percent of the House races involving incumbents were truly contested. There was no logical reason why an entrenched incumbent such as Gibbons would spend so much money on his reelection, except that the money was available to him.

Unlike many reformers, we do not think that special-interest money can be eliminated from the electoral process. We do not quarrel with those incumbents in contested races who feel the need to raise substantial sums of money to defend their seats on election day. Nor are we suggesting that the vast majority of members of Congress are spending their campaign funds in nefarious ways.

Nevertheless, after considering the data in this book, it is hard to escape the conclusion that the costs of elections have been unnecessarily and greatly inflated by the easy availability of special-interest money and by spending that goes far beyond the purpose of directly appealing for votes.

Whenever Congress debates the ills of the campaign finance system, members dredge up a variety of shop-worn reform proposals, including a ban on PAC contributions, public financing of congressional elections, and cut-rate television time. No one ever proposes to eliminate expenditures made for purposes only vaguely related to elections.

Until Congress restricts campaign spending to campaign purposes, the electoral process will always be heavily skewed toward the incumbent. As long as incumbents can spend hundreds of thousands—even millions—of dollars year after year to build an unshakable, permanent political organization that effectively takes the place of the party, challengers will be at a severe disadvantage and political parties will not thrive. True reform will require members of Congress to dismantle the one thing they prize most: their gold-plated, permanent political machine.

Table 1-1 What Campaign Money Buys in the 1990 House Races: Average Expenditures

Major Category	Incumbents in				Challengers in			
	Total	Hot Races[a]	Contested Races[b]	Unopposed	Total	Hot Races[a]	Contested Races[b]	Open Seats
Overhead								
Office furniture/supplies	$ 9,206	$ 11,238	$ 8,716	$ 7,066	$ 4,117	$ 6,480	$ 2,124	$ 11,843
Rent	6,650	8,902	5,996	4,571	2,662	4,070	1,474	7,960
Salaries	34,898	48,287	30,346	24,306	17,127	28,827	7,258	61,542
Taxes	11,433	14,671	10,462	8,527	2,255	3,722	1,017	10,792
Bank fees	1,003	1,225	973	704	149	206	100	1,241
Lawyers/accountants	8,450	11,587	6,977	7,048	483	800	216	2,974
Telephone	6,593	10,034	5,486	3,703	4,113	6,990	1,686	16,209
Campaign automobile	3,347	4,030	2,420	4,650	363	457	284	1,601
Computers/office equipment	6,733	8,032	6,291	5,707	2,051	3,111	1,157	7,227
Travel	16,247	18,415	15,107	15,603	3,051	4,823	1,556	12,053
Restaurant/food	3,488	3,064	3,455	4,294	243	389	120	810
Total Overhead	**108,049**	**139,485**	**96,229**	**86,179**	**36,614**	**59,876**	**16,992**	**134,255**
Fund Raising								
Events	49,217	55,514	46,249	46,430	7,895	13,295	3,341	38,529
Direct mail	18,249	25,965	17,582	6,952	3,009	5,634	796	14,549
Telemarketing	1,588	2,450	1,345	771	827	1,807	0	4,192
Total Fundraising	**69,053**	**83,928**	**65,176**	**54,154**	**11,732**	**20,736**	**4,136**	**57,269**

Polling	11,178	20,193	8,419	3,229	3,615	6,204	1,430	23,435
Advertising								
Electronic media	76,109	148,223	55,056	9,860	36,168	67,876	9,421	203,778
Other media	11,594	15,588	11,404	5,332	5,413	7,804	3,396	15,663
Total Advertising	87,703	163,811	66,460	15,192	41,581	75,680	12,817	219,441
Other Campaign Activity								
Voter contact mail	37,825	65,795	27,546	17,739	18,395	30,119	8,505	64,880
Actual campaigning	28,097	40,712	22,687	21,092	16,472	25,286	9,037	50,061
Staff/volunteers	1,006	995	826	1,501	97	143	58	416
Total Other Campaign Activity	66,929	107,502	51,059	40,332	34,964	55,548	17,600	115,356
Constituent Gifts/ Entertainment	6,741	5,840	6,160	9,810	21	36	9	374
Donations to								
Candidates from same state	5,226	3,552	6,426	4,875	49	59	41	354
Candidates from other states	4,325	3,060	5,078	4,471	3	6	0	319
Civic organizations	5,490	4,214	6,397	5,245	114	162	73	582
Political parties	11,451	9,726	12,830	10,710	133	152	118	738
Total Donations	26,492	20,552	30,731	25,301	299	379	232	1,993
Unitemized Expenses	14,243	15,834	12,591	15,932	4,406	5,904	3,143	11,383
Total Expenditures	$390,387	$557,145	$336,825	$250,128	$133,231	$224,363	$56,359	$563,507

Note: Totals are for the entire two-year cycle.

[a] Races where incumbent garners 60 percent or less of the vote.
[b] Races where incumbent garners more than 60 percent of the vote.

Table 1-2 What Campaign Money Buys in the 1990 Senate Races: Average Expenditures

	Incumbents in				Challengers in			
Major Category	Total	Hot Races[a]	Contested Races[b]	Unopposed	Total	Hot Races[a]	Contested Races[b]	Open Seats
Overhead								
Office furniture/supplies	$ 67,630	$ 101,314	$ 42,791	$ 36,673	$ 27,228	$ 41,137	$ 14,245	$ 25,155
Rent	52,251	84,775	27,174	26,185	20,493	30,448	11,201	16,181
Salaries	310,123	497,018	190,577	74,401	194,840	304,004	92,953	167,218
Taxes	144,161	231,607	81,321	58,040	58,062	83,090	34,702	52,754
Bank fees	7,246	14,467	1,921	611	2,239	2,791	1,723	331
Lawyers/accountants	43,752	64,142	32,515	11,719	8,779	15,848	2,181	9,584
Telephone	66,443	108,982	37,793	17,828	43,416	70,332	18,295	34,374
Campaign automobile	13,304	15,940	9,427	17,644	2,959	4,039	1,951	2,288
Computers/office equipment	83,404	129,477	56,172	17,464	21,077	28,907	13,769	24,357
Travel	163,950	212,093	140,160	78,714	60,673	90,643	32,701	53,296
Restaurant/food	11,930	12,899	11,396	10,411	3,422	3,319	3,519	5,080
Total Overhead	**964,194**	**1,472,714**	**631,247**	**349,688**	**443,188**	**674,559**	**227,241**	**390,619**
Fund Raising								
Events	349,141	527,971	249,834	70,808	123,457	156,824	92,315	112,043
Direct mail	836,786	1,625,723	274,788	42,503	155,435	225,071	90,442	70,484
Telemarketing	79,057	122,190	58,512		48,172	96,691	2,887	11,352
Total Fundraising	**1,264,985**	**2,275,884**	**583,135**	**113,311**	**327,064**	**478,585**	**185,644**	**193,879**

Polling	132,406	216,177	81,659	16,823	36,387	59,914	14,428	46,072
Advertising								
Electronic media	1,336,206	2,271,196	766,715	56,959	673,191	1,046,221	325,029	650,390
Other media	29,166	30,552	34,715	4,892	29,491	51,190	9,238	11,776
Total Advertising	1,365,372	2,301,748	801,430	61,851	702,682	1,097,412	334,267	662,165
Other Campaign Activity								
Voter contact mail	88,928	85,436	114,544	11,496	51,522	88,080	17,401	140,460
Actual campaigning	151,854	230,078	107,335	33,885	100,914	137,719	66,562	99,765
Staff/volunteers	3,956	3,673	3,912	5,103	458	445	469	1,633
Total Other Campaign Activity	244,721	319,184	225,762	50,455	152,888	226,232	84,433	241,857
Constituent Gifts/Entertainment	30,038	24,365	36,325	27,889	649	786	521	1,159
Donations to								
Candidates from same state	2,502	2,619	2,958	500	397	221	560	1,046
Candidates from other states	4,079	2,242	5,288	6,275	431	214	633	
Civic organizations	28,878	6,158	57,800	7,170	579	561	595	1,446
Political parties	24,549	26,325	22,762	24,587	1,440	1,127	1,733	1,158
Total Donations	60,008	37,344	88,808	38,532	2,847	2,124	3,521	3,650
Unitemized Expenses	39,597	55,404	32,463	9,241	20,906	30,734	11,734	19,371
Total Expenditures	$4,101,338	$6,702,823	$2,480,857	$667,820	$1,686,616	$2,570,358	$861,790	$1,558,772

Note: Totals are for the entire six-year cycle.

[a]Races where incumbent garners 60 percent or less of the vote.
[b]Races where incumbent garners more than 60 percent of the vote.

Table 1-3 What Campaign Money Buys in the 1990 House Races: Expenditures by Percentage

Major Category	Incumbents in				Challengers in			
	Total	Hot Races[a]	Contested Races[b]	Unopposed	Total	Hot Races[a]	Contested Races[b]	Open Seats
Overhead								
Office furniture/supplies	2.36	2.02	2.59	2.82	3.09	2.89	3.77	2.10
Rent	1.70	1.60	1.78	1.83	2.00	1.81	2.62	1.41
Salaries	8.94	8.67	9.01	9.72	12.85	12.85	12.88	10.92
Taxes	2.93	2.63	3.11	3.41	1.69	1.66	1.80	1.92
Bank fees	.26	.22	.29	.28	.11	.09	.18	.22
Lawyers/accountants	2.16	2.08	2.07	2.82	.36	.36	.38	.53
Telephone	1.69	1.80	1.63	1.48	3.09	3.12	2.99	2.88
Campaign automobile	.86	.72	.72	1.86	.27	.20	.50	.28
Computers/office equipment	1.72	1.44	1.87	2.28	1.54	1.39	2.05	1.28
Travel	4.16	3.31	4.49	6.24	2.29	2.15	2.76	2.14
Restaurant/food	.89	.55	1.03	1.72	.18	.17	.21	.14
Total Overhead	**27.68**	**25.04**	**28.57**	**34.45**	**27.48**	**26.69**	**30.15**	**23.82**
Fund Raising								
Events	12.61	9.96	13.73	18.56	5.93	5.93	5.93	6.84
Direct mail	4.67	4.66	5.22	2.78	2.26	2.51	1.41	2.58
Telemarketing	.41	.44	.40	.31	.62	.81	.00	.74
Total Fund Raising	**17.69**	**15.06**	**19.35**	**21.65**	**8.81**	**9.24**	**7.34**	**10.16**

	2.86	3.62	2.50	1.29	2.71	2.77	2.54	4.16
Polling								
Advertising								
Electronic media	19.50	26.60	16.35	3.94	27.15	30.25	16.72	36.16
Other media	2.97	2.80	3.39	2.13	4.06	3.48	6.03	2.78
Total Advertising	22.47	29.40	19.73	6.07	31.21	33.73	22.74	38.94
Other Campaign Activity								
Voter contact mail	9.69	11.81	8.18	7.09	13.81	13.42	15.09	11.51
Actual campaigning	7.20	7.31	6.74	8.43	12.36	11.27	16.03	8.88
Staff/volunteers	.26	.18	.25	.60	.07	.06	.10	.07
Total Other Campaign Activity	17.14	19.30	15.16	16.12	26.24	24.76	31.23	20.47
Constituent Gifts/Entertainment	1.73	1.05	1.83	3.92	.02	.02	.02	.07
Donations to								
Candidates from same state	1.34	.64	1.91	1.95	.04	.03	.07	.06
Candidates from other states	1.11	.55	1.51	1.79	.00	.00	.00	.06
Civic organizations	1.41	.76	1.90	2.10	.09	.07	.13	.10
Political parties	2.93	1.75	3.81	4.28	.10	.07	.21	.13
Total Donations	6.79	3.69	9.12	10.12	.22	.17	.41	.35
Unitemized Expenses	3.65	2.84	3.74	6.37	3.31	2.63	5.58	2.02
Total Expenditures	100.00	100.00	100.00	100.00	100.00	100.00	100.00	100.00

Note: Totals are for the entire two-year cycle.

[a] Races where incumbent garners 60 percent or less of the vote.
[b] Races where incumbent garners more than 60 percent of the vote.

Table 1-4 What Campaign Money Buys in the 1990 Senate Races: Expenditures by Percentage

Major Category	Incumbents in				Challengers in			
	Total	Hot Races[a]	Contested Races[b]	Unopposed	Total	Hot Races[a]	Contested Races[b]	Open Seats
Overhead								
Office furniture/supplies	1.65	1.51	1.72	5.49	1.61	1.60	1.65	1.61
Rent	1.27	1.26	1.10	3.92	1.22	1.18	1.30	1.04
Salaries	7.56	7.42	7.68	11.14	11.55	11.83	10.79	10.73
Taxes	3.51	3.46	3.28	8.69	3.44	3.23	4.03	3.38
Bank fees	.18	.22	.08	.09	.13	.11	.20	.02
Lawyers/accountants	1.07	.96	1.31	1.75	.52	.62	.25	.61
Telephone	1.62	1.63	1.52	2.67	2.57	2.74	2.12	2.21
Campaign automobile	.32	.24	.38	2.64	.18	.16	.23	.15
Computers/office equipment	2.03	1.93	2.26	2.62	1.25	1.12	1.60	1.56
Travel	4.00	3.16	5.65	11.79	3.60	3.53	3.79	3.42
Restaurant/food	.29	.19	.46	1.56	.20	.13	.41	.33
Total Overhead	**23.51**	**21.97**	**25.44**	**52.36**	**26.28**	**26.24**	**26.37**	**25.06**
Fund Raising								
Events	8.51	7.88	10.07	10.60	7.32	6.10	10.71	7.19
Direct mail	20.40	24.25	11.08	6.36	9.22	8.76	10.49	4.52
Telemarketing	1.93	1.82	2.36	.00	2.86	3.76	.34	.73
Total Fund Raising	**30.84**	**33.95**	**23.51**	**16.97**	**19.39**	**18.62**	**21.54**	**12.44**

Polling	3.23	3.23	3.29	2.52	2.16	2.33	1.67	2.96
Advertising								
Electronic media	32.58	33.88	30.91	8.53	39.91	40.70	37.72	41.72
Other media	.71	.46	1.40	.73	1.75	1.99	1.07	.76
Total Advertising	**33.29**	**34.34**	**32.30**	**9.26**	**41.66**	**42.69**	**38.79**	**42.48**
Other Campaign Activity								
Voter contact mail	2.17	1.27	4.62	1.72	3.05	3.43	2.02	9.01
Actual campaigning	3.70	3.43	4.33	5.07	5.98	5.36	7.72	6.40
Staff/volunteers	.10	.05	.16	.76	.03	.02	.05	.10
Total Other Campaign Activity	**5.97**	**4.76**	**9.10**	**7.56**	**9.06**	**8.80**	**9.80**	**15.52**
Constituent Gifts/Entertainment	**.73**	**.36**	**1.46**	**4.18**	**.04**	**.03**	**.06**	**.07**
Donations to								
Candidates from same state	.06	.04	.12	.07	.02	.01	.06	.07
Candidates from other states	.10	.03	.21	.94	.03	.01	.07	.00
Civic organizations	.70	.09	2.33	1.07	.03	.02	.07	.09
Political parties	.60	.39	.92	3.68	.09	.04	.20	.07
Total Donations	**1.46**	**.56**	**3.58**	**5.77**	**.17**	**.08**	**.41**	**.23**
Unitemized Expenses	.97	.83	1.31	1.38	1.24	1.20	1.36	1.24
Total Expenditures	**100.00**	**100.00**	**100.00**	**100.00**	**100.00**	**100.00**	**100.00**	**100.00**

Note: Totals are for the entire six-year cycle.

[a]Races where incumbent garners 60 percent or less of the vote.
[b]Races where incumbent garners more than 60 percent of the vote.

Table 1-5 What Campaign Money Buys in the 1990 House Races: Total Expenditures

Major Category	Incumbents in				Challengers in			
	Total	Hot Races[a]	Contested Races[b]	Unopposed	Total	Hot Races[a]	Contested Races[b]	Open Seats
Overhead								
Office furniture/supplies	$ 3,691,532	$ 1,427,202	$ 1,734,393	$ 529,937	$ 1,115,739	$ 803,513	$ 312,226	$ 734,277
Rent	2,666,506	1,130,567	1,193,148	342,791	721,444	504,721	216,722	493,544
Salaries	13,994,258	6,132,450	6,038,878	1,822,930	4,641,378	3,574,519	1,066,859	3,815,614
Taxes	4,584,646	1,863,271	2,081,863	639,513	611,100	461,586	149,515	669,106
Bank fees	402,112	155,601	193,688	52,822	40,265	25,568	14,697	76,964
Lawyers/accountants	3,388,649	1,471,527	1,388,493	528,629	130,922	99,157	31,765	184,416
Telephone	2,643,806	1,274,291	1,091,808	277,707	1,114,535	866,740	247,795	1,004,978
Campaign automobile	1,342,100	511,753	481,597	348,750	98,506	56,699	41,807	99,283
Computers/office equipment	2,700,007	1,020,114	1,251,864	428,028	555,898	385,802	170,096	448,097
Travel	6,515,231	2,338,654	3,006,348	1,170,228	826,774	598,086	228,688	747,298
Restaurant/food	1,398,673	389,131	687,489	322,053	65,808	48,195	17,612	50,230
Total Overhead	**43,327,520**	**17,714,562**	**19,149,569**	**6,463,389**	**9,922,368**	**7,424,586**	**2,497,782**	**8,323,807**
Fund Raising								
Events	19,735,950	7,050,221	9,203,489	3,482,241	2,139,648	1,648,550	491,098	2,388,771
Direct mail	7,317,707	3,297,505	3,498,767	521,436	815,573	698,607	116,966	902,043
Telemarketing	636,678	311,128	267,711	57,839	224,046	224,046	0	259,894
Total Fund Raising	**27,690,336**	**10,658,854**	**12,969,966**	**4,061,515**	**3,179,267**	**2,571,203**	**608,064**	**3,550,708**

Polling	4,482,219	2,564,567	1,675,454	242,198	979,553	769,351	210,202	1,452,999
Advertising								
Electronic media	30,519,832	18,824,274	10,956,067	739,491	9,801,518	8,416,641	1,384,877	12,634,241
Other media	4,649,030	1,979,717	2,269,412	399,901	1,466,951	967,720	499,230	971,125
Total Advertising	**35,168,862**	**20,803,992**	**13,225,478**	**1,139,392**	**11,268,469**	**9,384,361**	**1,884,108**	**13,605,366**
Other Campaign Activity								
Voter contact mail	15,167,953	8,355,959	5,481,601	1,330,393	4,985,073	3,734,810	1,250,264	4,022,535
Actual campaigning	11,267,076	5,170,366	4,514,781	1,581,929	4,463,926	3,135,512	1,328,414	3,103,760
Staff/volunteers	403,329	126,384	164,390	112,555	26,187	17,672	8,516	25,805
Total Other Campaign Activity	**26,838,358**	**13,652,709**	**10,160,772**	**3,024,877**	**9,475,187**	**6,887,993**	**2,587,194**	**7,152,100**
Constituent Gifts/ Entertainment	**2,703,323**	**741,704**	**1,225,882**	**735,737**	**5,788**	**4,447**	**1,341**	**23,179**
Donations to								
Candidates from same state	2,095,510	451,129	1,278,788	365,592	13,327	7,297	6,030	21,957
Candidates from other states	1,734,398	388,576	1,010,464	335,358	750	750	0	19,750
Civic organizations	2,201,518	535,189	1,272,952	393,377	30,811	20,144	10,667	36,091
Political parties	4,591,703	1,235,195	2,553,264	803,244	36,174	18,804	17,369	45,775
Total Donations	**10,623,128**	**2,610,089**	**6,115,468**	**1,897,572**	**81,061**	**46,995**	**34,066**	**123,573**
Unitemized Expenses	5,711,438	2,010,954	2,505,553	1,194,931	1,194,029	732,038	461,991	706,012
Total Expenditures	**$156,545,183**	**$70,757,431**	**$67,028,141**	**$18,759,611**	**$36,105,722**	**$27,820,974**	**$8,284,748**	**$34,937,744**

Note: Totals are for the entire two-year cycle.

[a]Races where incumbent garners 60 percent or less of the vote.
[b]Races where incumbent garners more than 60 percent of the vote.

Table 1-6 What Campaign Money Buys in the 1990 Senate Races: Total Expenditures

Major Category	Incumbents in				Challengers in			
	Total	Hot Races[a]	Contested Races[b]	Unopposed	Total	Hot Races[a]	Contested Races[b]	Open Seats
Overhead								
Office furniture/supplies	$ 2,164,158	$ 1,418,391	$ 599,076	$ 146,691	$ 789,603	$ 575,921	$ 213,682	$ 150,931
Rent	1,672,034	1,186,854	380,442	104,738	594,292	426,277	168,015	97,084
Salaries	9,923,933	6,958,252	2,668,079	297,602	5,650,357	4,256,058	1,394,299	1,003,308
Taxes	4,613,140	3,242,491	1,138,491	232,158	1,683,796	1,163,260	520,536	316,525
Bank fees	231,869	202,538	26,888	2,443	64,922	39,080	25,842	1,989
Lawyers/accountants	1,400,073	897,985	455,212	46,876	254,599	221,877	32,721	57,505
Telephone	2,126,168	1,525,750	529,104	71,314	1,259,067	984,647	274,420	206,245
Campaign automobile	425,720	223,167	131,978	70,575	85,816	56,550	29,266	13,730
Computers/office equipment	2,668,941	1,812,677	786,407	69,857	611,227	404,693	206,535	146,142
Travel	5,246,394	2,969,299	1,962,240	314,855	1,759,521	1,268,999	490,522	319,776
Restaurant/food	381,770	180,584	159,542	41,643	99,241	46,460	52,781	30,480
Total Overhead	**30,854,200**	**20,617,989**	**8,837,457**	**1,398,754**	**12,852,441**	**9,443,821**	**3,408,620**	**2,343,715**
Fund Raising								
Events	11,172,507	7,391,598	3,497,676	283,233	3,580,248	2,195,530	1,384,718	672,257
Direct mail	26,777,167	22,760,121	3,847,036	170,010	4,507,626	3,150,990	1,356,636	422,903
Telemarketing	2,529,833	1,710,661	819,173	0	1,396,986	1,353,677	43,309	68,113
Total Fund Raising	**40,479,507**	**31,862,379**	**8,163,885**	**453,243**	**9,484,860**	**6,700,197**	**2,784,663**	**1,163,273**

Polling	4,236,992	3,026,483	1,143,219	67,290	1,055,220	838,797	216,423	276,430
Advertising								
Electronic media	42,758,594	31,796,751	10,734,005	227,837	19,522,538	14,647,100	4,875,438	3,902,339
Other media	933,304	427,724	486,012	19,568	855,234	716,661	138,573	70,653
Total Advertising	**43,691,898**	**32,224,474**	**11,220,018**	**247,406**	**20,377,773**	**15,363,761**	**5,014,011**	**3,972,992**
Other Campaign Activity								
Voter contact mail	2,845,700	1,196,098	1,603,618	45,984	1,494,138	1,233,120	261,018	842,759
Actual campaigning	4,859,322	3,221,097	1,502,684	135,541	2,926,498	1,928,066	998,431	598,587
Staff/volunteers	126,603	51,424	54,768	20,412	13,273	6,231	7,042	9,796
Total Other Campaign Activity	**7,831,073**	**4,468,580**	**3,160,675**	**201,818**	**4,433,743**	**3,167,251**	**1,266,492**	**1,451,142**
Constituent Gifts/ Entertainment	961,224	341,116	508,552	111,557	18,825	11,006	7,819	6,953
Donations to								
Candidates from same state	80,079	36,662	41,417	2,000	11,500	3,100	8,400	6,275
Candidates from other states	130,522	31,390	74,032	25,100	12,500	3,000	9,500	0
Civic organizations	924,094	86,218	809,196	28,680	16,782	7,855	8,927	8,679
Political parties	785,566	368,544	318,672	98,350	41,768	15,777	25,992	6,947
Total Donations	**1,920,261**	**522,814**	**1,243,317**	**154,130**	**82,550**	**29,731**	**52,819**	**21,901**
Unitemized Expenses	1,267,099	775,654	454,480	36,965	606,286	430,276	176,010	116,223
Total Expenditures	$131,242,807	$93,839,528	$34,731,999	$2,671,281	$48,911,864	$35,985,007	$12,926,857	$9,352,630

Note: Totals are for the entire six-year cycle.

[a] Races where incumbent garners 60 percent or less of the vote.

[b] Races where incumbent garners more than 60 percent of the vote.

CHAPTER 2

Incumbents and Reelection
The Gold-Plated, Permanent Political Machine

On the outskirts of Winston-Salem, N.C., a modest, well-kept building stands as a monument to the current system for financing political campaigns.

In 1986, Rep. Stephen L. Neal, D-N.C., purchased the building for $125,000 to serve as his permanent campaign headquarters. He then began paying himself rent from his campaign treasury, which also financed numerous improvements on the property. In essence, he was buying the building for himself with campaign funds.

Neal's campaign building typifies the excesses of campaign spending that occur in an era when contributions are so plentiful that incumbents can devote hundreds of thousands of dollars to creating a gold-plated, permanent political machine that will operate at full tilt in off-years as well as in election years, even if no serious challenger ever steps forward.

BUILDING A POLITICAL EMPIRE

Well-funded members of Congress now approach the task of staying in office as if they were starting up a real estate or insurance business. They write business plans, install sophisticated computers, carry large payrolls, and worry about investments. "These are multi-million dollar or at least many multithousand dollar small businesses," said consultant Peter Fenn, whose firm, Fenn & King

Communications of Washington, D.C., advises many congressional campaigns.

In his book, *The United States of Ambition,* author Alan Ehrenhalt noted that modern politicians are usually self-appointed, ambitious professionals whose primary strength is entrepreneurship. "People nominate themselves," Ehrenhalt wrote. "That is, they offer themselves as candidates, raise money, organize campaigns, create their own publicity, and make decisions themselves. . . . Candidates do not win because they have party support. They do not win because they have business or labor support. They win because they are motivated to set out on their own and find the votes." *

The transformation in American politics that Ehrenhalt describes could never have occurred without a windfall of millions of dollars of special-interest money to these politicians. Special-interest money is the venture capital for today's political entrepreneurs. Without that money, and the political organization that it buys, many members of Congress would be unable to sustain themselves in politics because they lack a natural constituency, party support, or an overriding cause to galvanize the voters.

Overall, congressional candidates spent nearly $108 million—or about 26 percent of their campaign funds—on campaign overhead in the 1990 cycle. Most of this money went to support and perpetuate their permanent political organizations (see Table 2-1). In fact, 56 percent of the money spent in the 1990 elections had little or nothing to do with what has long been considered the main task of a member of Congress seeking reelection: appealing directly to the voters.

Politicians sometimes claim that they raise large sums of money just to scare off potential challengers. As Craig Tufty, administrative assistant to Rep. Fred Grandy, R-Iowa, said: "If you look like a 900-pound gorilla, people won't want to take you on."

But that notion has created the false impression that unopposed candidates simply hoard their funds, never actually spending them. To the contrary, very few incumbent members of Congress—not even those who have gone unopposed for many years—decline the opportunity to spend most of the money available to them. Potential challengers are often less discouraged by the size of an incumbent's campaign

---

* Alan Ehrenhalt, *The United States of Ambition: Politicians, Power, and the Pursuit of Office* (New York: Times Books/Random House Inc., 1991), 17.

war chest than by the political empire an incumbent has built with the money.

Neal's permanent office is one example of the empire-building scheme that successful incumbents have engaged in. But many incumbents maintain thriving permanent political machines without actually taking Neal's bricks-and-mortar approach. Other common attributes of a thoroughly modern congressional political campaign include:

- *A well-paid, professional staff.* In 1990, salaries, benefits, and taxes represented twelve percent of the costs of the average congressional campaign. In some cases, congressional employees served double duty by collecting salaries from both the government and their bosses' campaigns (see Table 2-2).

- *Big entertainment budgets.* Most successful incumbents provide gifts, parties, sports and theater tickets, flowers, greeting cards, restaurant meals, and other perquisites for their most influential constituents. On average, House incumbents spent nearly $7,000 on these activities; Senate incumbents averaged more than $30,000.

- *A generous travel budget.* For many incumbents, their travel budgets include thousands of dollars spent on chartered airplanes as well as commercial flights. Overall, members of Congress spent nearly $11.8 million from their campaign treasuries on travel during the 1990 election cycle, including travel expenses for campaign aides and family members (see Table 2-3).

- *High-paid political consultants.* Some campaigns are run entirely by consultants; others simply hire consultants for specific tasks. Either way, the tendency of congressional candidates to rely heavily on consultants has spawned a thriving industry that earned $188.1 million from congressional candidates alone during the 1990 election cycle.

- *Lawyers and accountants.* Many members of Congress keep a lawyer or an accountant, or both, on retainer to give advice and prepare the financial reports they must file regularly with the Federal Election Commission (FEC) (see Table 2-4). Incumbents who get into legal trouble generally use campaign funds to pay their legal fees, even if the matter has nothing to do with an election.

- *Donations.* By sharing their own campaign contributions with other politicians, political organizations, and civic groups, members of Congress enhance their own stature in the community and the Congress. In the 1990 cycle, members of Congress made donations totaling more than $12.5 million from their campaign coffers.

- *A full-time fund-raising apparatus.* Whether they rely on fund-raising parties, direct mail, or telemarketing, most members raise money constantly—not just in election years and not just in preparation for a particular opponent. On average, House incumbents spent 18 percent of their campaign money on fund raising and senators spent 31 percent.

- *Investments.* With millions of dollars in their campaign coffers, members of Congress earned considerable income from investing their political funds. Some also reported losses from unwise investments. Rep. Dan Rostenkowski, D-Ill., reported paying $26,255 to Salomon Brothers for "a decrease in market value" of an investment.

With these tools, members of Congress build permanent organizations that sustain them in office by providing a visible presence in the community, a close link to state and local leaders, a constant source of revenue, and a clearinghouse for political correspondence.

Some would argue that a permanent campaign organization serves a laudable public purpose by enabling members of Congress to be involved in district politics, even while they are working in Washington, D.C. But, of course, that is the primary function of their district congressional offices, for which they receive taxpayer funding. In truth, a permanent campaign organization makes them more firmly entrenched and less likely to look to their party for assistance.

The first objective of a permanent campaign organization is to build a strong network of influential supporters in the state or district that the incumbent represents. Yet members of Congress chose to attain that objective in different ways, creating a variety of permanent campaign organizations.

In the 1990 election, perhaps the most elaborate permanent political organization belonged to Sen. Bill Bradley, D-N.J., who spent $8.4 million on campaign overhead, fund raising, and polling. Bradley's telephone bills alone amounted to nearly $251,000—or about as much as many House candidates spent to get elected. He spent $225,986 to buy a mainframe computer and terminals and $171,000 for computer software licenses. By any measure, Bradley's $12.4 million reelection budget would be the envy of any small business entrepreneur.

In the House, Majority Leader Richard A. Gephardt, D-Mo., had a model, $1.4 million permanent campaign organization. He maintained offices in both St. Louis and Washington, D.C., kept eleven consultants on retainer, and employed at least four year-round workers.

The most remarkable aspect of these organizations is that they were often built by incumbents completely without regard to the likelihood of having an opponent on election day. In 1990, the average unopposed House member spent about $140,000 on overhead and fund raising and the three unopposed senators spent an average of $463,000 on those costs.

Rep. Joseph P. Kennedy II, D-Mass., maintained a $1,093-a-month office with seven employees, even though there was little likelihood he could be challenged successfully in the election.

Many members of Congress built their political machines strictly around fund raising, either by maintaining massive lists of regular contributors or by holding frequent fund-raising parties that brought supporters together on a regular basis. The campaign of Rep. Robert K. Dornan, R-Calif., was based on a nearly $1 million direct-mail operation run by Response Dynamics of Vienna, Va., which churned out frequent, hyperbolic appeals for money from the maverick representative. Likewise, Sen. Jesse Helms, R-N.C., and Reps. Ronald V. Dellums, D-Calif., and William E. Dannemeyer, R-Calif., built their political organizations on direct-mail lists.

It is equally common for members of Congress to build their political organizations around social events, as Rep. Dean A. Gallo, R-N.J., has done since he was first elected in 1984. It seemed as if Gallo was always throwing a party for his supporters—a fancy gala, a golf outing, an evening at the Meadowlands racetrack, or an organized trip to a Jets-Giants football game.

Many permanent organizations were based on "congressional clubs," which usually offered special benefits to supporters who contributed a minimum amount, anywhere from $19.90 to $1,000. Rep. E. Clay Shaw, Jr., R-Fla., provided his congressional club members with regular newsletters, policy briefings, and even specially designed lapel pins patterned on the seal of the House of Representatives.

While some permanent campaign organizations were run by the campaign staff, others were directed by a general campaign consultant. That was the case with Minority Leader Robert H. Michel, R-Ill., whose campaign was headquartered in the Peoria, Ill., office of consultant MaryAlice Erickson, the highest paid campaign management consultant in the 1990 elections. For $243,670, she ran Michel's campaign on a day-to-day basis while also running other campaigns in the state.

In bygone days, candidates for Congress had little need for elaborate political organizations of their own with year-round offices, staff, and the rest. Instead, they relied on their local party organizations to provide a headquarters, a cadre of volunteers, contributions, advice, signs, buttons, sample ballots, phone banks, get-out-the-vote drives, and whatever else was needed to get reelected.

In some places in Pennsylvania, Illinois, Michigan, New York, and Minnesota, the party was still playing a significant role in congressional elections in 1990, sometimes providing campaign headquarters, sample ballots, and posters touting the entire ticket. Frequently, the districts where the party was a force in the election were represented by old-style members of Congress, such as Michael R. McNulty, D-N.Y., who had been groomed for office by the party.

Yet wherever the local or state party provided these services, it also extracted large financial contributions from the candidates in exchange. The only genuine party support that most members of Congress got—if any—was usually a contribution from one of the congressional campaign committees located in Washington, D.C.

In most places, the local party has given way to the political machines of individual politicians. As Rep. Stephen J. Solarz, D-N.Y., succinctly put it: "Nobody I know of relies on the party structure in their home district to get them elected or reelected."

In fact, many candidates complained bitterly that instead of being supported by their party, they themselves had become the sole support for their state and local parties, which no longer had a strong rank-and-file membership. Sen. Howell Heflin, D-Ala., for example, gave $179,200 to Victory '90, the state coordinated Democratic party campaign to get out the vote, because other Alabama officer-holders were resisting.

Rep. Joe L. Barton, R-Texas, who was first elected in 1984 to represent a predominantly Democratic district, has used his campaign funds to single-handedly build a GOP organization in his district. In 1990, he ran up a phone bill of nearly $43,000, mostly to operate a phone bank that was designed to elect Republicans in three counties on the outskirts of Dallas and Fort Worth. In addition, he contributed about $22,000 to local Republican candidates, including GOP nominees for judge, county clerk, county commissioner, and state representative.

No less than $5.5 million of the money spent by congressional candidates in the 1989-1990 cycle was donated to various party organizations. That total does not include payments to parties for specific services such as get-out-the-vote activities and sample ballots.

Because members of Congress are permitted to keep as much money as they want in their treasuries from election to election, investments are not only an important part of most permanent campaigns, but a potential source for conflict-of-interest as well. There is no legal requirement that members of Congress must disclose precisely how their campaign funds are invested, as they must do with investments of personal funds. Thus, incumbents could make large, secret investments of campaign funds in corporations and industries over which they hold sway.

In 1990, some members raised as much money from investments as they did from fund raising. Rep. Larry J. Hopkins, R-Ky., earned $104,464—or 51 percent of his total receipts—in interest on his campaign account. But campaign money can be squandered through bad investments as well. Rep. Bill McCollum, R-Fla., reported nearly $44,000 in investment losses.

Among congressional incumbents in virtually every state, the permanent campaign organization was a bipartisan phenomenon, even though Republicans seemed to receive more assistance from their party. "The Republican party is more active in raising money and supporting their candidates, which has led to a greater degree of party discipline," observed Rep. Henry A. Waxman, D-Calif. "On the Democratic side, there's more of an entrepreneurial approach."

In some cases, members of Congress themselves did not realize how the costs of maintaining a permanent political operation had eliminated any possibility of running an old-fashioned, low-cost campaign.

In March 1990, Rep. Pete Stark, D-Calif., pledged to spend only what was necessary to pay for filing fees, bookkeeping, and "some housekeeping fees." But the costs of his permanent campaign caused him to spend a total of more than $300,000—nearly three-fourths of it on overhead and fund raising.

Likewise, Sen. Nancy Landon Kassebaum, R-Kans., vowed that she would hold her 1990 reelection expenditures to no more than her 1984 election costs, when she spent about $400,000. But when she made that announcement in 1989, she apparently was unaware that her campaign had already spent about $151,000, making it virtually impossible to keep her commitment. In the final analysis, she spent $519,843.

Once members of Congress have their hometown networks in place, ambition often drives them to draw on those political organizations to help establish a national reputation for themselves or to move up in the hierarchy in Washington, D.C. In recent years, some members of Congress have contributed heavily from their own campaign treasuries to other members whose support they needed to win important committee chairmanships or positions in the party leadership. In 1990, for example, Rep. Steny H. Hoyer, D-Md., distributed $55,000 to other Democrats in preparation for his unsuccessful quest for the position of House Democratic whip.

In fact, aggressive, well-run permanent political organizations are essential to House members who contemplate running for the Senate or to senators who aspire to be president. In the 1990 election cycle, Sen. Joseph R. Biden, Jr., D-Del., spent nearly $2.5 million. But much of Biden's spending was not directed at the voters of Delaware. Instead, he invested a substantial portion of his Senate campaign funds in a failed bid for the Democratic presidential nomination in 1988.

Beyond whatever practical purpose a permanent political organization serves, members of Congress also get a feeling of pride and enjoyment from it. As political scientist Norman J. Ornstein noted, members of Congress maintain their permanent political organizations as if they were vintage Rolls Royce automobiles—all carefully polished, well-oiled, and full of high-test gasoline. They like to drive them, whether or not they have anywhere to go.

"If you are a politician, you can't say that you've worked and slaved and got your Rolls Royce and now you're just going to let it rust away," Ornstein said.

CAMPAIGN HEADQUARTERS

Not too long ago, if members of Congress had their own campaign headquarters at all, they were normally located in abandoned storefronts in the low-rent part of town. On the day after the election, the campaigns were disbanded and the offices were closed.

Today, many incumbents have moved uptown to respectable, permanent offices with carpeted floors, upholstered furniture, and computer terminals at every desk. In fact, members often maintain permanent campaign headquarters in the same high-rent office building where their government-financed, district congressional office is located.

In the 1990 election cycle, candidates for Congress spent more than $6.2 million to rent campaign offices, many of which remained open from election to election (see Table 2-5).

A permanent campaign headquarters is said to be a virtual necessity for the majority of incumbents who maintained computerized lists of supporters and contributors. Not only must the lists be updated frequently, but campaign computers and records are not supposed to be kept in any government offices provided for members of Congress. This type of organization is particularly valuable to those incumbents who raise money through direct-mail solicitations.

"With the direct-mail fund raising, we need to keep our lists clean, and it's easier to keep a part-time operation running than to constantly stop and start," explained Mary Lu Nunley, who worked for Rep. Jim Kolbe, R-Ariz. "Plus, it's cleaner. By having a phone number outside the congressional office it keeps the [congressional employees] out of the campaign."

A permanent campaign headquarters also is seen as a way of preventing the campaign from mixing politics with official duties, which is discouraged under House and Senate rules but often occurs anyway. "While this increases the cost of our campaigns, I think it's important to clearly separate congressional and campaign activities," said Rep. Sam M. Gibbons, D-Fla.

Whether necessary or not, a permanent campaign headquarters is for many members of Congress the pulse of their political life. "The campaign office stays in close contact with elected local officials and with the town party chairs," explained Rep. Christopher Shays,

R-Conn. "I keep my political organization to make sure I don't forget my own base or lose touch with my own party."

In the Senate, Bradley set the pace for expenditures on office space by moving to a $10,000-a-month campaign office six months before election day. Bradley spent $263,601 on rent and utilities, more than any other candidate, and $384,659 on office supplies and furniture. Virtually all this money was spent before Bradley ever realized he was in a tough race.

Other senators with high rent and utility bills were Rudy Boschwitz, R-Minn., $141,727; Phil Gramm, R-Texas, $131,697; John Kerry, D-Mass., $129,192; and Mark O. Hatfield, D-Ore., $124,316.

In the House, those who invested most heavily in campaign headquarters were Neal, $54,100; Helen Delich Bentley, D-Md., $48,037; Gephardt, $40,480; Thomas J. Downey, D-N.Y., $40,030; Constance A. Morella, R-Md., $33,565; and Ray Thornton, D-Ark., $33,402.

Neal paid more than any other House member for an office, even though he contends he was not overcharging the campaign for using his building. While his desire for a permanent office was understandable, considering the tough reelection campaigns he has waged, it is hard to see why he needed to spend more for rent than incumbents in high-rent metropolitan areas.

According to Neal's special assistant, William Connelly, the North Carolina Democrat bought a building for his campaign headquarters because office space was scarce in Winston-Salem, N.C., at the time. He said Neal's objective was to rent the space for just enough to cover his expenses on the property. In 1989 and 1990, Neal received more than $33,000 in income from his campaign for rent, which just about covered the costs of his mortgage, insurance, and taxes on the property. In addition, the campaign paid $6,895 for repairs and upkeep on the building (see box, page 37).

Whenever the $2,167-a-month rent began to exceed Neal's costs, he said, the North Carolina Democrat either stopped collecting rent for a few months or returned money to the campaign. As a result, he reported $18,000 in uncollected rent and a $7,500 rebate to the campaign in the 1990 cycle.

Neal's rental arrangement appeared to be patterned on the House ethics committee's findings in a 1987 case involving former Rep. William H. Boner, D-Tenn. In that case, the committee ruled that it was not against House rules for Boner (who by that time had been elected

Expenditures for Stephen L. Neal's Building

	Expenditures
Rent	$33,673
In-kind rent	18,000
Total rent	**$51,673**
Lawn service	1,978
Utilities	1,602
Air conditioner	1,230
Door repair	969
Heating oil	759
Clean carpets	130
House/garden cleaning	80
Plumbing repairs	80
Water and sewage	67
Total upkeep and utilities	**$ 6,895**

mayor of Nashville) to rent to his campaign a building that he owned because he had been able to show that he personally earned no more from the deal than the cost of his mortgage and upkeep on the property.

At the same time, the ethics committee noted: "The money gained from the lease of this building will be applied toward Rep. Boner's ownership interest in it. Eventually, he will own the building. In effect, he is using campaign funds to buy the building for himself." *

Likewise, Neal appeared to be using campaign funds to buy a building for himself. Fred Wertheimer, president of Common Cause, said he viewed Neal's rental arrangement as improper. "That's converting campaign money to personal use," he said.

In Maryland, Bentley's campaign helped to finance a building pur-

* Committee on Standards of Official Conduct, U.S. House of Representatives, Staff Report in the Matter of Representative William H. Boner, December 1987, U.S. Government Printing Office, 11.

chased by her friends and campaign workers. In 1989, her campaign moved into a $2,000-a-month building in Timonium, Md., that had just been purchased by a partnership including her campaign treasurer, Margaret E. Mullen, another paid campaign worker, and other people closely allied with Bentley. Rent on the new headquarters exceeded by nearly $600 a month the amount she paid for her previous office in the same neighborhood, which was torn down to make way for a fast food restaurant.

Bentley not only paid a considerable amount of rent for the building, but her campaign also funded a number of expensive improvements: $5,800 in masonry work; $7,000 for electrical work, including $1,200 of rewiring needed before her computers could be installed; $4,200 for plumbing repairs; $800 to install a burglar alarm system; and $425 for carpeting.

Mullen denied that Bentley was using her campaign funds to enhance a financial investment by friends. "There's nothing at all wrong with it," insisted Mullen, a close friend of Bentley who also received a salary from the campaign.

In 1989 and 1990, the campaign of Rep. Elton Gallegly, R-Calif., paid nearly $20,000 to rent space in a building that he owned with his wife Janice and another couple. Rep. Jack Fields, R-Texas, rented an office for $300 a month from his family's cemetery, Rosewood Memorial Park. Rep. Arthur Ravenel, Jr., R-S.C., rented from a real estate firm he once owned but gave to his six children.

Rent of $400 a month, plus utilities, was paid to Rep. Richard Ray, D-Ga., by his campaign for the use of 288 square feet, or 40 percent of the space, in an apartment in a duplex building owned by Ray in Columbus, Ga. Whenever Ray returned to his home district, he used the apartment home for lodging. The FEC okayed this arrangement in a 1988 letter to Ray.

Although it was not unusual for senators and some House members to have offices both in their home towns and also in downtown Washington, D.C., Rep. Barbara Boxer, D-Calif., may have been the only one who had an auxiliary campaign office that was neither in Washington nor in her district. In July 1990, she signaled her intention of running for the Senate by opening a small office in Los Angeles, more than 400 miles from her Marin County-North San Francisco district. She paid the rent with her House campaign funds.

"The office gave Barbara and [me] someplace to go to make calls when we were in the area meeting people," explained Ed McGovern, Boxer's 1990 House campaign manager. "We set up the office in anticipation that Barbara would win reelection to the House and we were exploring the possibility of running for the Senate."

While challengers complain bitterly about the advantages that incumbents enjoy as a result of special interest money, it does not take long after being elected to take on the adornments of incumbency. After surviving his first reelection bid, Rep. Steven H. Schiff, R-N.M, decided to experiment with a permanent office too. "It seemed reasonable just to leave it open," Schiff said.

Campaign Staff

It is not unusual for a Senate candidate to be one of the best employers in town.

In 1990, Bradley reported having nearly forty full-time people on his payroll on election day. His campaign manager, Nicholas Donatiello, was receiving a paycheck of $2,380 every two weeks. All told, Bradley's payroll costs for the six-year cycle totaled nearly $1.3 million.

Although Sens. Gramm and Tom Harkin, D-Iowa, were less generous with staff salaries, they employed even more workers than Bradley. They each spent more than $700,000 on salaries, but reported having more than fifty people on each of their campaign payrolls.

In the House, the biggest payrolls belonged to the campaigns of Gephardt, $196,191; John Bryant, D-Texas, $186,519; Chet Edwards, D-Texas, $179,155; Jolene Unsoeld, D-Wash., $176,929; Rosa DeLauro, D-Conn., $173,712; and Kennedy, $173,621. Two unsuccessful challengers were among the top employers in 1990: Hugh D. Shine of Texas with $177,449 in salaries and Marguerite Chandler of New Jersey with $167,807.

Most campaigns had only one or two employees in the off-year, usually a treasurer, a secretary, or a person who maintained the computer lists. Often, the only campaign employee in the off-year was a person who also served on the district congressional staff. In California, for example, Dellums's campaign activities were left entirely in the hands of H. Lee Halterman, his district legal counsel, who kept some campaign records in the representative's congressional offices in the Oakland post office building.

Frequently, campaign employees were called "consultants," even if they were expected to work regular hours like any ordinary employee. By calling them consultants, members of Congress escaped paying payroll taxes and other benefits for them. Ordinary entrepreneurs are not permitted to avoid paying taxes in such circumstances.

An Internal Revenue Service (IRS) spokesman, Wilson Fadley, said his agency monitors the records of political campaigns as it would for those of any employer, but he was unable to cite any case on the public record in which a member of Congress was called to task by the IRS for improperly paying employees as consultants. Campaign attorneys say the IRS does not vigorously monitor campaign records.

In Vermont, Socialist candidate Bernard Sanders was cited by the state Department of Employment and Training for improperly paying his employees as consultants. State officials were satisfied when he agreed to put his consultants on the campaign payroll.

Closer to the election, campaigns hired more employees, including more members of the congressional staffs. Usually, this included the administrative assistant or chief of staff and the press secretary from Washington, D.C., who took a leave of absence from the government payroll and relocated in the district for most of the election season. Some workers were carried on both the congressional and campaign payrolls simultaneously.

Some members of Congress ran their campaigns almost exclusively with the assistance of congressional employees. In Massachusetts, Rep. Kennedy reimbursed twenty of his congressional employees for campaign work. Of the ten people who drew salaries or consulting fees from the campaign of Rep. Henry J. Hyde, R-Ill., eight were also employed in one of his congressional offices. In Georgia, Sen. Sam Nunn reimbursed several dozen of his Senate employees from campaign funds, including Chief of Staff Charles E. Harman, who got more than $32,000 in salary and expenses during the 1990 cycle.

While congressional employees are prohibited from doing campaign work on government time, they are not restricted from doing it on their own time—weekends, evenings, and holidays. Senators are permitted to designate employees in their government offices to accept campaign checks. These loopholes open the the way for abuse. While a few members of Congress were scrupulous about separating campaign and official work, others were less so. Even among members of Congress who observed the rules, it was common for them to require congressional staffers to work in the campaign as a condition of employment in Congress.

David Coggin, chief of staff to Rep. Ron Packard, R-Calif., acknowledged that campaign work was a part of his job description. "I'm the third chief of staff here, and with all of us it's been the same—you take your vacation and run the campaign," he said.

Indeed, some congressional employees were paid handsomely for their campaign work. Rep. C. Christopher Cox, R-Calif., paid his chief of staff, Robert J. Sutcliffe, $35,000 from campaign funds, in addition to his $82,500 government salary. Cox denied that the payments were intended to make up for the loss of salary that Sutcliffe experienced when he left a lucrative law practice to join Cox's congressional staff. In Florida, McCollum paid $75,000 to his congressional chief of staff, Vaughn S. Forrest, who was also collecting an annual salary in excess of $80,000 from the federal government.

Sen. Ted Stevens, R-Alaska, rewarded twenty-three of his Senate employees with checks from the campaign ranging between $400 and $6,000 just six days before Christmas in 1990. It looked as if Stevens paid his employees a Christmas bonus from campaign funds, but Tim McKeever, Stevens's campaign treasurer, insisted that the money was reimbursement for work performed by Stevens's Senate employees during his successful reelection campaign. "That's just when we got around to [paying] it," he said.

In the House, members have long been forbidden to use campaign funds for official purposes, and thus it would be unethical for them to pay a congressional employee from campaign funds unless that employee actually worked on the campaign. In the Senate, however, there was no such prohibition during the 1990 election cycle. Senators could even supplement the salaries of their Senate staffers with campaign funds.

Therefore, when Jonathan Winer, legal counsel to Senator Kerry, complained to his boss that he could no longer make ends meet on his $53,000-a-year government salary, Kerry was able to pay Winer an extra $1,667 a month from campaign funds. During the cycle, he received $33,341 from the campaign. Such arrangements would be outlawed under legislation that was due to take effect some time in 1992.

Whether congressional employees were getting paid from campaign funds for campaign work or for official work, the system created unfortunate confusion between the two functions.

Confusion between politics and official business was at the heart of the Keating Five scandal, in which five prominent senators were accused of improperly intervening with federal regulators on behalf of a big campaign contributor, Lincoln Savings & Loan owner Charles H. Keating, Jr. One of them, Sen. Alan Cranston, D-Calif., was harshly reprimanded by the Senate Select Ethics Committee in 1991 for improperly offering official assistance to Keating while at the same time soliciting campaign contributions from him.

Although Cranston's case is the most blatant example, lax enforcement of the rules separating politics and official work is pushing the entire Congress to the brink of impropriety.

STROKING SUPPORTERS

Lacking a strong rank-and-file local party membership, an overriding issue, or high name recognition in their home state, members of Congress need to build and maintain an extensive network of supporters who can be mobilized in the event of any serious electoral challenge.

If a member of Congress has a strong support network back home, it is often, at least in part, the result of hundreds of thousands of dollars spent on these people over many years—not just a few greeting cards, small mementos, or an occasional cocktail reception, but expensive gifts such as crystal vases, silver engraved baby cups, and large flower arrangements, as well as lavish parties with live entertainment and plenty of catered food.

In the 1990 election cycle, members of Congress spent nearly $3.7 million to stroke their constituents with gifts and other favors. This included $334,320 for flowers (see box, page 43), $736,762 for holiday cards, $571,308 for gifts, and $12,433 for liquor.

Gift giving and entertainment are no doubt an essential part of politics. But when expenditures for these items grow into the millions of dollars, there is reason to wonder who is benefiting. The incentives that some congressional incumbents offered to their supporters in the 1990 election were sometimes so expensive or so lavish that they could

The Top Fifteen Spenders in the 1990 House Races: Flowers for Constitutents

Rank	Candidate	Expenditures
1	John P. Murtha, D-Pa.	$8,306
2	Barbara B. Kennelly, D-Conn.	7,287
3	Joseph P. Kennedy II, D-Mass.	6,932
4	Gary Condit, D-Calif.	5,918
5	Robert A. Roe, D-N.J.	5,266
6	Joseph D. Early, D-Mass.	5,108
7	Dick Schulze, R-Pa.	5,076
8	Charles B. Rangel, D-N.Y.	4,346
9	Raymond J. McGrath, R-N.Y.	4,296
10	John D. Dingell, D-Mich.	3,958
11	Joe Moakley, D-Mass.	3,906
12	Edward F. Feighan, D-Ohio	3,881
13	Dennis Hastert, R-Ill.	3,659
14	William L. Clay, D-Mo.	3,476
15	Mervyn M. Dymally, D-Calif.	3,438

Note: Totals are for the entire two-year cycle.

almost be considered a form of bribery—the modern day equivalent of "walking around money" distributed by old-time ward heelers. Certainly, the intent of these gifts was the same: to buy the loyalty of their constituents.

Furthermore, it appears that some members are using campaign funds to finance their personal entertaining, as well as to meet their political obligations.

In the Senate, the leading spenders on gifts, entertainment, and constituent stroking were Alan K. Simpson, R-Wyo., who spent $110,255; David L. Boren, D-Okla., $81,252; and Larry Pressler, R-S.D., $67,931. In the House, they were Charles Wilson, D-Texas, $76,121; John P. Murtha, D-Pa., $63,365; John D. Dingell, D-Mich., $57,921; William Lehman, D-Fla., $51,723; and Les Aspin, D-Wis., $51,403 (see Tables 2-6 and 2-7).

Lehman, for example, hosted many invitation-only brunches for residents of the condominiums that dominate his Florida district. He spent more than $31,000 buying meals for constituents at the House dining room and other restaurants. He spent more than $9,000 on gifts, plaques, and other trinkets; $1,939 on flowers to commemorate special occasions or express sympathy in cases of death; and $1,550 on football tickets for the Super Bowl, which he donated to a local non-profit group.

Rep. Ike Skelton, D-Mo., preferred to please constituents with restaurant meals and lavish entertainment. Skelton reported spending $21,136 to take constituents to lunches and dinners, mostly at high-priced restaurants in Washington, D.C. He picked up a $1,734 tab at Maison Blanche, an elegant French restaurant near the White House, and wrote a check for $1,912 to Take Me Home caterers for what he said was a constituent dinner.

In California, Stark spent $3,066 on Oakland A's tickets and $215 on San Francisco Giants tickets, ostensibly to provide entertainment for supporters and campaign volunteers. But few members of Congress were as generous as Rep. Bill Emerson, R-Mo., who insisted that the $700 limousine he rented in January 1989 was to take one of his largest campaign contributors to President Bush's inaugural ball.

Likewise, when it came to selecting extravagant gifts for constituents, some members of Congress spared no expense. Sen. Strom Thurmond, R-S.C., spent more than $29,000 on gifts from Morray Jewelers of Johnston, S.C. Aides said they were wedding gifts purchased in response to the many wedding invitations that Thurmond received.

Some gifts given by members of Congress were less expensive, but decidedly unique—pickle pins from Rep. J. J. Pickle, D-Texas; pine seedlings from David E. Bonior, D-Mich.; and firemen's hats from Rep. Dan Burton, R-Ind. Likewise, Rep. Albert G. Bustamante, D-Texas, reported buying $228 worth of men's and women's briefs at Rivera's Chili Shop for his constituents. Those with less imagination distributed potholders, yardsticks, and refrigerator magnets.

Holiday greeting cards are usually the least expensive way of keeping in touch with constituents, particularly since members of Congress can buy cut-rate stationery and cards at the House and Senate stationery stores. But even Christmas cards can get expensive, if you buy enough of them. Rep. Bill Archer, R-Texas, spent $22,287 to print and mail his cards (see box, page 45).

The Top Fifteen Spenders in the 1990 House Races: Holiday Cards

Rank	Candidate	Expenditures
1	Bill Archer, R-Texas	$22,287
2	Bill Alexander, D-Ark.	20,944
3	Edolphus Towns, D-N.Y.	15,054
4	Don Sundquist, R-Tenn.	13,268
5	Newt Gingrich, R-Ga.	12,713
6	Andy Ireland, R-Fla.	12,704
7	Harold Rogers, R-Ky.	12,070
8	Jerry Huckaby, D-La.	11,691
9	Robert H. Michel, R-Ill.	10,471
10	W. D. "Billy" Tauzin, D-La.	10,346
11	George Miller, D-Calif.	9,551
12	William J. Coyne, D-Pa.	9,485
13	Michael G. Oxley, R-Ohio	8,214
14	Mary Rose Oakar, D-Ohio	8,211
15	Steve Bartlett, R-Texas	7,976

Note: Totals are for the entire two-year cycle.

When it came to entertaining constituents, Rep. Steve Bartlett, R-Texas, was the P. T. Barnum of American politics. While still a member of the House, Bartlett threw an annual Memorial Day picnic that drew thousands of people from his North Dallas congressional district and elsewhere around the city. It was always an extravagant affair, with catered food, beverages, entertainment, balloons, and pony rides. In 1989 and 1990, the picnics cost Bartlett's campaign a total of nearly $200,000, not including the cost of salaries and air fare for his Washington, D.C., staff to attend the events (see box, page 46). Bartlett's well-known picnic proved to be a perfect springboard from which he would eventually launch a successful bid to become mayor of Dallas in 1991.

For most other members of Congress, throwing parties is also a way to strengthen their ties with the most influential people in the

Expenditures for Steve Bartlett's Memorial Day Picnic

	1989 Expenditures	1990 Expenditures
Food	$ 52,334	$36,808
Printing and postage	35,717	25,441
Sound system and stage rental	4,544	3,500
Commemorative T-shirts	4,245	4,793
Shuttle bus rental	3,273	3,633
Tent rental	2,657	3,015
Table/chair rental	1,820	1,856
Decorations	1,402	2,085
Entertainment	1,200	2,300
Restrooms and trash disposal	864	600
Booths for games; prizes	836	530
Photography	730	528
Walkie-talkies	702	729
Pony rides	650	621
City park service	322	482
Supplies	148	492
Security and ambulance service	0	675
Total	**$111,444**	**$88,088**

community. Indeed, these events are the glue that holds their political organizations together.

Solarz, who threw a big fiftieth birthday party for himself in the fall of 1990 and invited all of the important people in his Brooklyn district, said it "generates the kind of good will that can be helpful at election time."

In Texas, Wilson may have hit on an even better method for bringing his supporters together: his annual dominoes tournament for senior citizens at the Lufkin Civic Center in his hometown of Lufkin, Texas. In the 1990 cycle, Wilson spent more than $45,000 to hold his annual tournaments; $28,530 went to buy special sets of dominoes with the double blanks inscribed: "Vote for Charles Wilson." Each participant in the tournament was permitted to take home a set of dominoes. The top players got trophies and the winner got a free trip to the Cherry Blossom Festival in Washington, D.C.—all at the expense of Wilson's campaign fund.

Wilson, who won narrowly in 1990, viewed the dominoes tournament as one of his biggest strengths in the district. "It's a major cultural event in my district," he said. "All over my district, nobody plays [dominoes] with anything else. They say, 'I'm going to play old Wilson [the double blank].' "

While many members of Congress used campaign funds to sponsor amateur sports teams or even entire leagues, few ran as full-blown a program of activities for the community as Rep. Charles A. Hayes, D-Ill., whose South Side Chicago political organization was centered around the Charles Hayes Labor Cultural and Community Center. Housed in a building donated by the Amalgamated Meatcutters, the center provided a variety of programs for local teenagers.

Members of Congress often will organize their network of supporters into a "congressional club." Members of these congressional clubs are entitled to special privileges—usually a regular newsletter, an occasional briefing by a top government official, and at least one annual party.

In Georgia, Democratic Rep. Lindsay Thomas's congressional club, known as "Forum for the First," was made up of more than 5,000 district residents who had either contributed to his campaign or had expressed support for him. Each month, they received a newsletter. Each year, they were invited to a special barbecue and were given a gift, such as a calendar. Robert Hurt, Thomas's administrative assistant, said the "Forum for the First" included many members who had not previously been involved in Democratic politics. While the organization succeeded in recruiting new blood, it also provided Thomas with an organization entirely separate from the Democratic party roster.

"Our list has been developed with blood, sweat, and tears by Lindsay," said Hurt.

Some members of Congress gave their congressional clubs unusual names. Rep. Marty Russo, D-Ill., called his group "Marty's Magnificent Multitude"; Rep. W. J. "Billy" Tauzin, D-La., called his the "Billy Club Society."

Paying to bring influential citizens to Washington, D.C., for the presidential inaugural or for briefings on policy issues is another way for members to curry favor with important constituents, particularly municipal leaders.

Rep. Peter J. Visclosky, D-Ind., spent about $7,400 in 1989 to provide entertainment and a program for some fifty local officials who visited Washington, D.C., from his home district. Reps. William D. Ford, D-Mich., and Dingell combined each year to sponsor a conference in Washington for municipal and school officials from the Detroit area. Rep. John Lewis, D-Ga., sponsored an annual "Minister Fly-In," which brought influential Atlanta church leaders to Washington.

In some urban areas, members of Congress still adhered to the traditions of old-fashioned, big-city machine politics by paying campaign workers and poll watchers on election day. Rep. William O. Lipinski, D-Ill., spent $10,150 to hire election workers and also paid for breakfast at the Yugoslav Hall for all precinct captains in his Chicago district.

DONATIONS

Three California Democrats—Reps. Waxman, Howard L. Berman, and Mel Levine—met regularly during the 1990 cycle to engage in a modern political ritual that would have been impossible without huge sums of special-interest money. Together they decided on a common list of candidates and political organizations that they would support with donations from their campaign accounts. Once their decisions were made, the three men notified Mary Ellen Padilla, who kept the books for all three congressional campaigns. She then issued three separate checks—one from each of their campaign funds—and mailed them to the designated recipients. By election day, the three representatives had given away nearly $500,000.

The unparalleled generosity of this trio has created what is commonly known in Los Angeles political circles as the "Waxman-Berman machine"—a powerful political apparatus that provides valuable assistance to liberal Democratic candidates in California and throughout the nation. It almost goes without saying that campaign contributions from the Waxman-Berman machine have earned the three representatives more influence in Congress than they would otherwise have. In 1979, in fact, Waxman's contributions to other House members helped him to rise to the chairmanship of the powerful Health and the Environment Subcommittee, stepping over many other members with more seniority.

Like some other members of Congress, Waxman also has his own "leadership PAC," which allows him to give an additional $5,000 to candidates he especially likes.

While the Waxman-Berman machine is unique in some ways, it has become a model for other members seeking to expand their influence, both in their home states and inside the halls of Congress. Donations to other candidates, political organizations, and civic groups are at the heart of the empire-building process, which has caused campaign costs to rise in recent years (see Table 2-8).

Just a decade ago, member-to-member giving was considered highly unusual. Now, it is considered absolutely necessary for anyone who hopes to get ahead in party politics. In a sense, contributions to congressional colleagues and other party candidates have come to represent a pledge of fealty to the party. They also are a declaration that the giver is striving to be a genuine player in the game of national politics.

"It clearly builds relationships with colleagues to help them with their elections, just as it builds relationships with colleagues to help them with their legislative activities," Waxman said. "And those relationships are important because, ultimately to do anything around here, you have to have coalitions and support."

In the 1990 elections, members of Congress made contributions totaling more than $4 million from their own campaign war chests to other candidates.

Californians were particularly generous with their campaign funds. In all, members of the California delegation gave away nearly $2.5 million to candidates, political organizations, and charities. IMPAC 2000, an organization formed to assist Democrats involved in reapportionment battles, received nearly $589,000 from Democratic members of Congress from California (see box, page 50).

But donations such as these were also typical in a number of other states, particularly Illinois, Michigan, and New Jersey. In Michigan, where the state House and Senate majorities were slim, there were numerous fund-raising committees set up to collect money for House

Donations by California Democrats
to IMPAC 2000

Representative	Donation
Howard L. Berman	$ 60,000
Nancy Pelosi	52,750
Vic Fazio	50,000
George Miller	47,500
Don Edwards	46,000
Mel Levine	35,000
Robert T. Matsui	35,500
Norman Y. Mineta	35,000
Richard H. Lehman	30,000
Esteban E. Torres	30,000
Henry A. Waxman	30,000
Matthew G. Martinez	28,500
Julian C. Dixon	25,000
Glenn M. Anderson	21,000
Edward R. Roybal	14,500
Ronald V. Dellums	12,500
Pete Stark	11,575
Leon E. Panetta	9,000
Douglas H. Bosco	5,000
Anthony C. Beilenson	5,000
Mervyn M. Dymally	5,000
Total	**$588,825**

and Senate candidates—and members of Congress were clearly expected to support them.

In Illinois, members of Congress in both parties were expected to contribute liberally to the dinners, banquets, and golf outings held to support various party organizations. "We are picnicked and dinnered to death," complained Michel campaign aide Erickson. "We've got it backwards in Illinois. Instead of the office-holders looking to the party for contributions, the party looks to the office-holders."

Indeed, the relationship between party and office-holder seems backwards in most places, not just in Illinois. Candidates not only are expected to support the state and local party, but they usually have to pay extra for the few services that the party organization provides, such as get-out-the-vote efforts and sample ballots. The party organizations turn to the candidates for support because they often lack a cadre of contributors of their own.

Even in states where the party influence is stronger, it is the candidates who carry the primary burden in elections. In Michigan, William Ford allowed other Democratic office seekers in his district to use space in his campaign headquarters; in exchange, he asked them to provide volunteers to help mail thousands of campaign leaflets. His campaign headquarters was decorated with the signs of so many Democrats that it would have been impossible to determine who was paying the rent. Ford's political rallies featured other candidates as well.

Frequently, members of Congress said they felt compelled to spend more money than necessary on their own races in order to raise the profile of the party and help other candidates. In Delaware, Democratic Rep. Thomas R. Carper demonstrated how some office-holders assume functions that once fell to the party and, as a result, raise their own stature among politicians in the state. Although Carper faced aggressive challengers in both the primary and general elections, his aides said he was deeply involved in helping to elect other Democrats. In fact, according to Jeffrey Bullock, Carper employed a larger staff than necessary in order to assist others in his party. This was yet another step in Carper's efforts to rise to the top of the Democratic party leadership in Delaware—an effort that began in 1989 when he unseated party boss Eugene T. Reed. Ultimately, Carper's goal was to be elected governor in 1992.

"The real fund-raising power is with the headliners, not with the party," remarked Bullock.

While most members of Congress use donations to enhance their political influence within the parties, Dannemeyer used his funds to further his opposition to confidentiality in AIDS testing. In the 1990 cycle, Dannemeyer used campaign funds to pay off debts from a 1988 California ballot initiative, Proposition 102, which he coauthored with Paul Gann, the antitax crusader who died of complications from AIDS. The unsuccessful initiative would have ended the confidentiality in AIDS testing and rescinded a California law barring discrimination in employment and insurance for those found to be HIV-positive. He also spent $80,736 to retire the debts of the organization known as Paul Gann Stop AIDS Campaign: Yes on 102. Later in the year, he forgave a $20,000 loan to California Physicians for a Logical AIDS Response, another organization established to support Proposition 102.

It is not surprising that candidates dip into their campaign funds to satisfy the many pleas for donations that they receive from charities as well as from political candidates and party organizations. Many members of Congress do not have the personal wealth necessary to make large contributions to charity. But contributions to local charities are a way for members of Congress to demonstrate their interest in community activities and raise their visibility.

"A $100 contribution to a big church is worth 10,000 leaflets," said Rep. Major R. Owens, D-N.Y., who gave generously to his local churches.

Rep. Beryl Anthony, Jr., D-Ark., was a leader in giving to civic and charitable groups such as the American Heart Association, the Arabian Charity Horse Show Association for Retarded Citizens, the Arkansas Municipal Police Association, and the Little Rock Jaycees. His campaign also bought $300 in tickets to the Miss Arkansas Pageant in both 1989 and 1990.

When candidates raise money for their own election, their contributors have a right to expect it will be spent on the campaign, not given away. Yet we found few members of Congress who saw it as an ethical dilemma. One of the few was Rep. David Dreier, R-Calif., who made contributions only from the interest on his contributions, not from the principle.

"If someone gives him money," said Drier's staff director, Brad Smith, "he doesn't want to take it and then turn around and give it away to someone else."

SEEKING HIGHER OFFICE

With all the money, ambition, and entrepreneurial skills that today's members of Congress possess, it is little wonder that many choose to run for higher office. In most cases, the personal political machines they have built for themselves can be easily retooled to respond to new political opportunities.

At least two Democratic senators who stood for reelection in 1990—Joe Biden of Delaware and Al Gore of Tennessee—used their Senate campaign committees as a springboard for unsuccessful presidential bids in 1988. A number of House members spent money from their existing campaign committees to launch—or at least explore—a race for the Senate. Some House members also used their campaign funds to prepare for gubernatorial bids.

As the examples of Gore and Biden clearly prove, there is no guarantee of success for members of Congress who have an existing campaign treasury to assist them. But it certainly gives them an advantage over candidates who must start from scratch.

Several of the consultants that Biden hired for his presidential bid—including John Marttila and Thomas Kiley of Boston, Patrick Caddell of Cambridge, Mass., and Tom Donilan of Washington, D.C.—received travel expenses from Biden's Senate campaign committee. In addition, the committee paid more than $40,000 for thirteen meetings and meals in New York and Los Angeles, all obviously related to his presidential campaign.

After Biden established his presidential campaign committee, that organization bought furniture and equipment from his Senate campaign. When the presidential campaign ended in failure amid charges that he had plagiarized speeches of British Labour party leader Neil Kinnock, Biden sold the furniture and equipment back to the Senate campaign. Finally, in 1989, Biden's Senate campaign paid out $50,000 to retire debts from the presidential campaign.

While members of Congress are permitted to use their campaign funds to pay off debts arising from campaigns for other offices or to explore the possibility of running for other offices, they cannot necessarily raise money for one campaign and simply transfer it to another without restrictions. It must first be established that no single contributor gave more than the legal limit of $2,000 to the two campaigns.

In December 1987, Gore transferred $24,000 from his Senate campaign to his presidential war chest. The transfer was not questioned by FEC auditors until after Gore had dropped out of the 1988 presidential race. Marla Romash, Gore's press secretary, said the senator later transferred the money back into the Senate campaign in response to the FEC inquiry, even though he contended that the original transfer was consistent with the "letter and the spirit of the law."

Three Democratic House members from California—Boxer, Levine, and Robert T. Matsui—used their House campaign funds to begin raising money to run for the Senate in 1992. Matsui dropped out of the race six months later. Tom Keanery, Matsui's legislative assistant, acknowledged that the representative held a number of fund-raisers in 1990—all sponsored by his House campaign committee—that he would not have held had he not been planning to run for the Senate. Likewise, Levine made numerous fund-raising trips to cities around the country and held a fund-raiser in New York City in preparation for his Senate bid. Those trips were financed by his House campaign committee. Boxer not only opened an office in Los Angeles, but she also hired a Los Angeles public relations firm at a cost of $10,300 to introduce her around Southern California.

Rep. Bill Richardson, D-N.M., used House campaign funds to briefly explore a possible bid to become governor of New Mexico. He later decided to remain in his House seat. In May 1989, Richardson paid pollster Peter D. Hart of Washington, D.C., $23,000 to conduct a statewide poll to test his popularity and name recognition. He also paid $1,000 to his Santa Fe media adviser, Chris Brown of Brown Inc., for travel and consultations on the possible gubernatorial race and $1,000 to Albuquerque-based Modern Analytical Political Strategies for a targeting study to identify potential strengths with voters in New Mexico.

Likewise, Rep. Dan Glickman, D-Kan., opened a $500-a-month fund-raising office for himself in downtown Washington, D.C., in early 1989 and paid fund-raiser Nancy Jacobson $979 a month from his House campaign funds to explore his fund-raising potential for a possible Senate bid against Sen. Nancy Kassebaum, a Republican. He eventually decided to abandon the effort, but not before he had raised $225,000 for his House campaign in the first seven months of 1989.

While Boxer, Levine, Matsui, Richardson, and Glickman were looking to new challenges, Tauzin was raising House funds to pay off a debt left over from his highly unsuccessful 1987 bid for governor of Louisiana. In 1990, he transferred $275,600 from his House funds to cover those debts.

Tauzin said both the FEC and state elections officials, acting on a complaint filed by one of his opponents, approved his decision to use House money to pay off his gubernatorial debt. State law was changed in 1988 to limit the amount that could be transferred from a federal to a state account, but the new law made an exception for his old debts.

Even those candidates who lose or drop out of the race for higher office usually come away from the experience with an enhanced political organization. That was the case with Reps. Patricia Schroeder, D-Colo., and Philip M. Crane, R-Ill., who still raise money primarily from the direct-mail fund-raising list they developed during unsuccessful presidential bids.

Table 2-1 The Top Twenty-Five Spenders in the 1990 Congressional Races: Total Overhead

Rank	House Candidate	Expenditures	Senate Candidate	Expenditures
1	Richard A. Gephardt, D-Mo.	$557,746	Bill Bradley, D-N.J.	$3,878,383
2	Joseph P. Kennedy II, D-Mass.	450,283	Rudy Boschwitz, R-Minn.	2,808,253
3	Newt Gingrich, R-Ga.	436,109	Phil Gramm, R-Texas	2,710,962
4	Marguerite Chandler, D-N.J.	379,419	Tom Tauke, R-Iowa	1,968,225
5	Helen Delich Bentley, R-Md.	369,910	John Kerry, D-Mass.	1,838,159
6	Jolene Unsoeld, D-Wash.	356,524	Tom Harkin, D-Iowa	1,738,534
7	Rosa DeLauro, D-Conn.	338,642	Paul Simon, D-Ill.	1,481,366
8	William H. Gray III, D-Pa.	331,576	Carl Levin, D-Mich.	1,359,127
9	Dick Zimmer, R-N.J.	328,038	Harvey B. Gantt, D-N.C.	1,232,307
10	Howard Wolpe, D-Mich.	326,778	Lynn Martin, R-Ill.	1,185,156
11	Vin Weber, R-Minn.	313,142	Jim Rappaport, R-Mass.	1,020,393
12	Hugh D. Shine, R-Texas	311,490	Mark O. Hatfield, R-Ore.	1,005,078
13	Martin Frost, D-Texas	311,479	Jesse Helms, R-N.C.	998,319
14	Chet Edwards, D-Texas	309,684	John D. Rockefeller IV, D-W.Va.	995,585
15	Steve Bartlett, R-Texas	293,100	Daniel R. Coats, R-Ind.	969,025
16	Sam M. Gibbons, D-Fla.	282,907	Mitch McConnell, R-Ky.	933,955
17	Don Young, R-Alaska	282,493	Max Baucus, D-Mont.	825,795
18	Barney Frank, D-Mass.	280,392	Joseph R. Biden, Jr., D-Del.	803,263
19	Mike Kopetski, D-Ore.	280,191	Sam Nunn, D-Ga.	767,263
20	Thomas J. Downey, D-N.Y.	279,908	Pete V. Domenici, R-N.M.	759,520
21	Maxine Waters, D-Calif.	279,372	Larry Pressler, R-S.D.	752,279
22	James P. Moran, Jr., D-Va.	270,689	J. Bennett Johnston, D-La.	751,193
23	Thomas J. Bliley, Jr., R-Va.	264,050	Bill Schuette, R-Mich.	741,455
24	Ron Wyden, D-Ore.	263,714	Al Gore, D-Tenn.	739,714
25	John P. Murtha, D-Pa.	263,601	Hank Brown, R-Colo.	706,237

Note: Totals for the House are for the entire two-year cycle, including special elections; totals for the Senate are for the entire six-year cycle.

Table 2-2 The Top Twenty-Five Spenders in the 1990 Congressional Races: Salaries

Rank	House		Senate	
	Candidate	Expenditures	Candidate	Expenditures
1	Richard A. Gephardt, D-Mo.	$196,191	Bill Bradley, D-N.J.	$1,295,006
2	John Bryant, D-Texas	186,519	Rudy Boschwitz, R-Minn.	1,190,050
3	Chet Edwards, D-Texas	179,155	Tom Tauke, R-Iowa	880,055
4	Hugh D. Shine, R-Texas	177,449	Phil Gramm, R-Texas	756,790
5	Jolene Unsoeld, D-Wash.	176,929	Carl Levin, D-Mich.	732,749
6	Rosa DeLauro, D-Conn.	173,712	Tom Harkin, D-Iowa	723,171
7	Joseph P. Kennedy II, D-Mass.	173,621	John Kerry, D-Mass.	630,012
8	Maxine Waters, D-Calif.	173,503	Jim Rappaport, R-Mass.	628,947
9	Marguerite Chandler, D-N.J.	167,807	Harvey B. Gantt, D-N.C.	556,807
10	Dick Zimmer, R-N.J.	157,172	Paul Simon, D-Ill.	532,262
11	Thomas H. Andrews, D-Maine	150,683	Lynn Martin, R-Ill.	428,283
12	James P. Moran, Jr., D-Va.	145,634	John D. Rockefeller IV, D-W.Va.	322,384
13	Les Aspin, D-Wis.	143,688	Jesse Helms, R-N.C.	320,281
14	Bob Williams, R-Wash.	142,701	Dan Coats, R-Ind.	312,275
15	Howard Wolpe, D-Mich.	139,480	Max Baucus, D-Mont.	301,710
16	Martin Frost, D-Texas	138,125	Hank Brown, R-Colo.	300,934
17	Bill McCollum, R-Fla.	130,068	Neil Rolde, D-Maine	291,318
18	Wally Herger, R-Calif.	129,468	Hal Daub, R-Neb.	268,728
19	Helen Delich Bentley, R-Md.	129,260	Hugh Parmer, D-Texas	263,210
20	Mike Kopetski, D-Ore.	129,133	Bill Schuette, R-Mich.	260,397
21	Jim Ramstad, R-Minn.	128,663	Harvey I. Sloane, D-Ky.	252,480
22	C. Christopher Cox, R-Calif.	128,589	Josie Heath, D-Colo.	250,714
23	Manny Hoffman, R-Ill.	127,253	Mark O. Hatfield, R-Ore.	248,591
24	Thomas J. Biley, Jr., R-Va.	124,110	Mitch McConnell, R-Ky.	246,160
25	John Linder, R-Ga.	121,599	Al Gore, D-Tenn.	242,410

Note: Totals for the House are for the entire two-year cycle, including special elections; totals for the Senate are for the entire six-year cycle.

Table 2-3 The Top Twenty-Five Spenders in the 1990 Congressional Races: Travel

Rank	House Candidate	Expenditures	Senate Candidate	Expenditures
1	Robert W. Davis, R-Mich.	$110,962	Rudy Boschwitz, R-Minn.	$385,636
2	Bill Dickinson, R-Ala.	93,910	Larry Pressler, R-S.D.	368,725
3	Vin Weber, R-Minn.	84,755	Tom Tauke, R-Iowa	337,057
4	Richard A. Gephardt, D-Mo.	82,631	Phil Gramm, R-Texas	329,131
5	Bill Alexander, D-Ark.	82,258	Alan K. Simpson, R-Wyo.	304,574
6	Carl C. Perkins, D-Ky.	79,723	Tom Harkin, D-Iowa	288,974
7	Bud Shuster, R-Pa.	71,638	Bill Bradley, D-N.J.	264,074
8	John P. Murtha, D-Pa.	64,513	Paul Simon, D-Ill.	250,002
9	William H. Gray III, D-Pa.	63,940	Jesse Helms, R-N.C.	243,615
10	Mel Levine, D-Calif.	62,895	Lynn Martin, R-Ill.	211,249
11	Newt Gingrich, R-Ga.	60,410	Daniel R. Coats, R-Ind.	204,239
12	Howard L. Berman, D-Calif.	60,032	Max Baucus, D-Mont.	198,873
13	Carroll Hubbard, Jr., D-Ky.	59,509	Joseph R. Biden, Jr., D-Del.	198,264
14	Joseph P. Kennedy II, D-Mass.	59,366	J. Bennett Johnston, D-La.	198,240
15	Bill Emerson, R-Mo.	58,777	John D. Rockefeller IV, D-W.Va.	193,536
16	Ron Marlenee, R-Mont.	58,754	John Kerry, D-Mass.	191,532
17	Ronald V. Dellums, D-Calif.	58,271	Mark O. Hatfield, R-Ore.	184,908
18	Robert T. Matsui, D-Calif.	55,409	Ted Stevens, R-Alaska	168,609
19	Jack Brooks, D-Texas	55,362	Harvey I. Sloane, D-Ky.	161,697
20	Mike Espy, D-Miss.	52,258	Harvey B. Gantt, D-N.C.	147,883
21	Steve Bartlett, R-Texas	49,066	Bill Schuette, R-Mich.	137,347
22	Albert G. Bustamante, D-Texas	48,449	Al Gore, D-Tenn.	131,560
23	Don Young, R-Alaska	46,910	Howell Heflin, D-Ala.	124,711
24	Don Sundquist, R-Tenn.	46,330	David Pryor, D-Ark.	123,713
25	Norm Dicks, D-Wash.	45,979	Pete V. Domenici, R-N.M.	119,350

Note: Totals for the House are for the entire two-year cycle, including special elections; totals for the Senate are for the entire six-year cycle.

Table 2-4 The Top Twenty-Five Spenders in the 1990 Congressional Races: Lawyers and Accountants

	House		Senate	
Rank	Candidate	Expenditures	Candidate	Expenditures
1	William H. Gray III, D-Pa.	$208,432	Phil Gramm, R-Texas	$579,523
2	Harold E. Ford, D-Tenn.	183,000	Jesse Helms, R-N.C.	127,574
3	Joseph M. McDade, R-Pa.	158,346	John D. Rockefeller IV, D-W.Va.	98,624
4	Newt Gingrich, R-Ga.	147,490	David Duke, R-La.	87,102
5	Barney Frank, D-Mass.	143,122	Paul Simon, D-Ill.	79,357
6	Don Young, R-Alaska	106,313	Pete Domenici, R-N.M.	75,989
7	Frank Annunzio, D-Ill.	80,418	Ted Stevens, R-Alaska	65,834
8	Hamilton Fish, Jr., R-N.Y.	78,216	Bill Bradley, D-N.J.	62,499
9	Richard A. Gephardt, D-Mo.	73,802	Hank Brown, R-Colo.	43,500
10	James M. Inhofe, R-Okla.	72,582	Claiborne Pell, D-R.I.	40,271
11	Bill Lowery, R-Calif.	66,528	Howell Heflin, D-Ala.	40,099
12	Robert J. Lagomarsino, R-Calif.	61,822	Sam Nunn, D-Ga.	35,195
13	David E. Price, D-N.C.	48,190	Rudy Boschwitz, R-Minn.	33,948
14	Nicholas Mavroules, D-Mass.	40,966	Jim Rappaport, R-Mass.	29,842
15	John D. Dingell, D-Mich.	40,802	John Kerry, D-Mass.	27,807
16	Maxine Waters, D-Calif.	40,292	John W. Warner, R-Va.	23,471
17	John Porter, R-Ill.	38,872	Bill Schuette, R-Mich.	23,350
18	Bill Alexander, D-Ark.	38,265	Tom Harkin, D-Iowa	23,299
19	Dan Schaefer, R-Colo.	37,147	David L. Boren, D-Okla.	20,131
20	Roy Dyson, D-Md.	34,457	Hugh Parmer, D-Texas	19,824
21	Gary Condit, D-Calif.	31,393	Patricia Saiki, R-Hawaii	16,408
22	Lewis F. Payne, D-Va.	29,676	Christine Todd Whitman, R-N.J.	15,693
23	Don Ritter, R-Pa.	29,050	Larry E. Craig, R-Idaho	14,005
24	Edward Madigan, R-Ill.	28,364	Strom Thurmond, R-S.C.	13,750
25	Marty Russo, D-Ill.	28,091	Larry Pressler, R-S.D.	13,041

Note: Totals for the House are for the entire two-year cycle, including special elections; totals for the Senate are for the entire six-year cycle.

Table 2-5 The Top Twenty-Five Spenders in the 1990 Congressional Races: Rent

Rank	House Candidate	Expenditures	Senate Candidate	Expenditures
1	Stephen L. Neal, D-N.C.	$54,100	Bill Bradley, D-N.J.	$263,601
2	Helen Delich Bentley, R-Md.	48,037	Rudy Boschwitz, R-Minn.	141,727
3	Richard A. Gephardt, D-Mo.	40,480	Phil Gramm, R-Texas	131,697
4	Thomas J. Downey, D-N.Y.	40,030	John Kerry, D-Mass.	129,192
5	Constance A. Morella, R-Md.	33,565	Mark O. Hatfield, R-Ore.	124,316
6	Ray Thornton, D-Ark.	33,402	Daniel K. Akaka, D-Hawaii	97,091
7	Steve Bartlett, R-Texas	32,579	Tom Harkin, D-Iowa	84,247
8	Sam M. Gibbons, D-Fla.	29,348	Paul Simon, D-Ill.	71,961
9	Susan Molinari, R-N.Y.	28,263	Harvey B. Gantt, D-N.C.	70,979
10	Eleanor Holmes Norton, D-D.C.	28,231	Sam Nunn, D-Ga.	67,336
11	Thomas R. Carper, D-Del.	28,020	Joseph R. Biden, Jr., D-Del.	67,321
12	Joseph P. Kennedy II, D-Mass.	25,730	Tom Tauke, R-Iowa	55,447
13	Barbara Boxer, D-Calif.	25,300	Bill Schuette, R-Mich.	55,387
14	Mickey Edwards, R-Okla.	25,118	John D. Rockefeller IV, D-W.Va.	54,130
15	Jim Bunning, R-Ky.	24,534	Mitch McConnell, R-Ky.	53,997
16	Sander M. Levin, D-Mich.	23,847	Carl Levin, D-Mich.	45,672
17	Don Young, R-Alaska	23,578	David Duke, R-La.	38,276
18	Howard Coble, R-N.C.	23,168	Daniel R. Coats, R-Ind.	37,480
19	Stan Parris, R-Va.	22,893	Patricia Saiki, R-Hawaii	33,997
20	Michael Bilirakis, R-Fla.	21,890	Hal Daub, R-Neb.	33,915
21	Thomas J. Bliley, Jr., R-Va.	21,879	Lynn Martin, R-Ill.	32,118
22	Dan Rostenkowski, D-Ill.	21,600	Hank Brown, R-Colo.	31,100
23	Sidney R. Yates, D-Ill.	21,305	Neil Rolde, D-Maine	30,021
24	Richard H. Baker, R-La.	20,884	Jim Rappaport, R-Mass.	29,730
25	William W. Koeppel, R-N.Y.	20,727	Jim Exon, D-Neb.	29,593

Note: Totals for the House are for the entire two-year cycle, including special elections; totals for the Senate are for the entire six-year cycle.

Table 2-6 The Top Twenty-Five Spenders in the 1990 Congressional Races: Constituent Entertainment and Gifts

Rank	House Candidate	Expenditures	Senate Candidate	Expenditures
1	Charles Wilson, D-Texas	$76,121	Alan K. Simpson, R-Wyo.	$110,255
2	John P. Murtha, D-Pa.	63,365	David L. Boren, D-Okla.	81,252
3	John D. Dingell, D-Mich.	57,921	Larry Pressler, R-S.D.	67,931
4	William Lehman, D-Fla.	51,723	David Pryor, D-Ark.	61,926
5	Les Aspin, D-Wis.	51,403	Ted Stevens, R-Alaska	57,850
6	Dick Schulze, R-Pa.	43,643	J. Bennett Johnston, D-La.	57,275
7	Curt Weldon, R-Pa.	42,207	Paul Simon, D-Ill.	48,379
8	Joseph D. Early, D-Mass.	40,880	Strom Thurmond, R-S.C.	47,936
9	Edolphus Towns, D-N.Y.	38,206	Max Baucus, D-Mont.	44,288
10	John J. "Jimmy" Duncan, Jr., R-Tenn.	34,919	Rudy Boschwitz, R-Minn.	33,677
11	Don Young, R-Alaska	31,126	Howell Heflin, D-Ala.	31,874
12	Cardiss Collins, D-Ill.	29,907	Jim Exon, D-Neb.	29,733
13	Ike Skelton, D-Mo.	29,351	Sam Nunn, D-Ga.	28,450
14	Lawrence J. Smith, D-Fla.	28,770	Phil Gramm, R-Texas	27,501
15	Duncan Hunter, R-Calif.	28,690	John Kerry, D-Mass.	27,362
16	Michael Bilirakis, R-Fla.	28,085	Mark O. Hatfield, R-Ore.	26,350
17	Bill Alexander, D-Ark.	26,956	Al Gore, D-Tenn.	24,580
18	Hamilton Fish, Jr., R-N.Y.	26,723	Thad Cochran, R-Miss.	21,180
19	W. J. "Billy" Tauzin, D-La.	26,299	Pete V. Domenici, R-N.M.	21,102
20	G. V. "Sonny" Montgomery, D-Miss.	26,272	Joseph R. Biden, Jr., D-Del.	19,333
21	William O. Lipinski, D-Ill.	25,902	Bill Bradley, D-N.J.	17,938
22	Robert A. Roe, D-N.J.	25,181	Jesse Helms, R-N.C.	16,574
23	Bill Archer, R-Texas	24,692	Daniel K. Akaka, D-Hawaii	15,358
24	Thomas J. Manton, D-N.Y.	24,591	Nancy Landon Kassebaum, R-Kan.	14,382
25	Major R. Owens, D-N.Y.	24,372	Tom Harkin, D-Iowa	14,274

Note: Totals for the House are for the entire two-year cycle, including special elections; totals for the Senate are for the entire six-year cycle.

Table 2-7 The Top Twenty-Five Spenders in the 1990 Congressional Races: Meals

Rank	House		Senate	
	Candidate	Expenditures	Candidate	Expenditures
1	Bud Shuster, R-Pa.	$106,986	Ted Stevens, R-Alaska	$46,095
2	Matthew J. Rinaldo, R-N.J.	25,360	John Kerry, D-Mass.	38,651
3	Dennis M. Hertel, D-Mich.	24,675	Paul Simon, D-Ill.	32,170
4	Bill Lowery, R-Calif.	23,214	Lynn Martin, R-Ill.	30,939
5	Richard H. Lehman, D-Calif.	19,002	Bill Bradley, D-N.J.	23,699
6	Dan Burton, R-Ind.	18,865	Daniel K. Akaka, D-Hawaii	19,595
7	John P. Murtha, D-Pa.	18,219	J. Bennett Johnston, D-La.	19,399
8	Guy Vander Jagt, R-Mich.	17,567	Sam Nunn, D-Ga.	18,008
9	William Lehman, D-Fla.	17,464	Alan K. Simpson, R-Wyo.	16,663
10	Dale E. Kildee, D-Mich.	16,840	Larry E. Craig, R-Idaho	14,649
11	Charles Hatcher, D-Ga.	16,499	Max Baucus, D-Mont.	14,289
12	Charles Wilson, D-Texas	15,452	Rudy Boschwitz, R-Minn.	13,979
13	Bill Archer, R-Texas	15,404	David Pryor, D-Ark.	11,816
14	Jerry Huckaby, D-La.	14,149	Joseph R. Biden, Jr., D-Del.	11,812
15	Norman F. Lent, R-N.Y.	13,177	Thad Cochran, R-Miss.	11,769
16	Dick Schulze, R-Pa.	13,028	Howell Heflin, D-Ala.	11,521
17	Robert T. Matsui, D-Calif.	12,412	Larry Pressler, R-S.D.	11,260
18	Bob Traxler, D-Mich.	12,310	Jim Exon, D-Neb.	10,945
19	Thomas J. Bliley, Jr., R-Va.	12,165	Mark O. Hatfield, R-Ore.	10,808
20	Bill Richardson, D-N.M.	12,141	Tom Tauke, R-Iowa	10,116
21	William H. Gray III, D-Pa.	12,112	Hank Brown, R-Colo.	9,893
22	Albert G. Bustamante, D-Texas	12,069	Bill Cabaniss, R-Ala.	9,887
23	Denny Smith, R-Ore.	11,669	Jesse Helms, R-N.C.	9,787
24	Barbara B. Kennelly, D-Conn.	11,212	Mitch McConnell, R-Ky.	8,722
25	Julian C. Dixon, D-Calif.	11,203	Daniel R. Coats, R-Ind.	8,498

Note: Totals for the House are for the entire two-year cycle, including special elections; totals for the Senate are for the entire six-year cycle.

Table 2-8 The Top Twenty-Five Spenders in the 1990 Congressional Races: Total Donations

Rank	House		Senate	
	Candidate	Expenditures	Candidate	Expenditures
1	Howard L. Berman, D-Calif.	$211,372	Strom Thurmond, R-S.C.	$734,766
2	Nandy Pelosi, D-Calif.	191,984	J. Bennett Johnston, D-La.	251,948
3	Charles B. Rangel, D-N.Y.	174,010	Alan K. Simpson, R-Wyo.	144,937
4	Vic Fazio, D-Calif.	157,286	Thad Cochran, R-Miss.	97,785
5	Mel Levine, D-Calif.	157,061	Nancy Landon Kassebaum, R-Kan.	75,223
6	Beryl Anthony, Jr., D-Ark.	134,871	Al Gore, D-Tenn.	57,130
7	Edward R. Roybal, D-Calif.	133,946	Jim Exon, D-Neb.	53,326
8	Frank J. Guarini, D-N.J.	130,866	John D. Rockefeller IV, D-W.Va.	48,467
9	Steny H. Hoyer, D-Md.	129,167	Bill Bradley, D-N.J.	45,224
10	George Miller, D-Calif.	128,353	John W. Warner, R-Va.	38,623
11	Henry A. Waxman, D-Calif.	123,492	David Pryor, D-Ark.	36,464
12	William E. Dannemeyer, R-Calif.	121,478	Rudy Boschwitz, R-Minn.	35,814
13	Bill Thomas, R-Calif.	116,028	Howell Heflin, D-Ala.	35,117
14	James H. Scheur, D-N.Y.	114,680	David L. Boren, D-Okla.	34,502
15	Thomas J. Manton, D-N.Y.	109,794	Jesse Helms, R-N.C.	34,138
16	John P. Murtha, D-Pa.	105,615	Ted Stevens, R-Alaska	32,199
17	Robert T. Matsui, D-Calif.	97,795	Carl Levin, D-Mich.	28,224
18	Robert A. Roe, D-N.J.	95,019	Phil Gramm, R-Texas	22,902
19	Richard H. Lehman, D-Calif.	90,271	Sam Nunn, D-Ga.	19,560
20	Don Edwards, D-Calif.	84,969	Max Baucus, D-Mont.	19,255
21	John D. Dingell, D-Mich.	84,402	William S. Cohen, R-Maine	18,965
22	Raymond J. McGrath, R-N.Y.	83,918	Claiborne Pell, D-R.I.	17,500
23	Marty Russo, D-Ill.	80,721	Pete Domenici, R-N.M.	15,287
24	William H. Gray III, D-Pa.	80,639	Larry Pressler, R-S.D.	13,569
25	Guy Vander Jagt, R-Mich.	75,428	Tom Harkin, D-Iowa	13,067

Note: Totals for the House are for the entire two-year cycle, including special elections; totals for the Senate are for the entire six-year cycle.

CHAPTER 3

Political Expenditures
A Personal Slush Fund

I n the spring of 1990, Rep. Dennis M. Hertel, D-Mich., and his wife Cynthia enjoyed a leisurely, eight-day stay at South Seas Plantation in Captiva, Fla. Their accommodations during the first three days of the visit were courtesy of the Electronics Industry Association (EIA); the next five days were paid for by Hertel's campaign.

Under House and Senate ethics rules, members of Congress must use campaign funds for political—not personal—purposes. Yet the commonly accepted definition of a political expenditure has grown so broad and enforcement of the rules has been so lax that congressional campaigns now routinely make purchases that on their face appear to be personal, such as resort vacations, luxury automobiles, expensive meals, apartments, country club memberships, tuxedos, home improvements, baby sitting, and car phones.

EXTRAVAGANCE AT CAMPAIGN EXPENSE

Indeed, some members of Congress appear to use their campaign treasuries as little more than giant slush funds for purchasing whatever items they cannot buy with the stipend they receive from the federal government to run their congressional offices or with their own money.

Ready access to large sums of campaign cash also has fostered an almost routine extravagance in every task undertaken by members of

Congress, from buying dinner for constituents to hiring a lawyer. Special-interest money has effectively raised the standard of living for many members of Congress, permitting them to enjoy a lifestyle that could not be sustained on their own income. In many cases, in fact, it has transformed middle-class politicians into members of the country-club set, isolating them from their own constituency.

In the 1990 cycle, Reps. Bill Dickinson, R-Ala., C. W. Bill Young, D-Fla., Charles Hatcher, D-Ga., Marvin Leath, D-Texas, and Edward Madigan, R-Ill., were among those who bought themselves expensive, new cars with their campaign funds. Majority Leader Richard A. Gephardt, D-Mo., Sen. Larry Pressler, R-S.D., and Rep. Robert W. Davis, D-Mich., frequently chartered airplanes for themselves. Sens. David Pryor, D-Ark., and Sam Nunn, D-Ga., rented apartments with campaign funds. Reps. Beryl Anthony, Jr., D-Ark., J. J. Pickle, D-Texas, Ronald V. Dellums, D-Calif., and many others used campaign money to pay for country club memberships. Reps. William L. Clay, D-Mo., Jim Slattery, D-Kan., Wayne T. Gilchrest, R-Md., and William J. Coyne, D-Pa., paid for tuxedos with their campaign funds.

At least two elderly members of Congress—Sen. Strom Thurmond, R-S.C., and Rep. Edward R. Roybal, D-Calif.—used campaign money to endow academic chairs in their names during the 1990 election cycle. Rep. Carroll Hubbard, Jr., D-Ky., used campaign money to commission an artist to paint a $3,000 portrait of his father. In addition, Reps. Tom Lantos, D-Calif., Esteban E. Torres, D-Calif., Hubbard, and others paid relatives to work on their campaigns.

Sen. David L. Boren, D-Okla., an outspoken advocate of campaign finance reform, used thousands of dollars from his campaign funds to decorate his Senate office. Prior to the 1990 election, he spent more than $6,000 on furniture and picture framing. Afterwards, he paid $15,480 for Indian art, $4,495 for a jumbo illuminated globe from Hammacher Schlemmer, and $522 on a lamp from Gumps.

Most of these expenditures were not even remotely improper under current congressional ethics rules. While many of them appeared to be personal expenditures, most have a plausible political justification. A campaign car, for example, is usually viewed as the cheapest way for a candidate to travel around the district. Chartered airplanes are sometimes rationalized as the only logical alternative for those incumbents who represent big states or districts. Country club memberships are defended as necessities for incumbents who need to entertain political supporters and throw fund-raisers.

But some expenditures, such as Hertel's resort vacation, are more difficult to justify.

Hertel, a former state legislator and father of four who has no personal assets other than a mortgaged condominium and a small savings account, routinely used his campaign funds to pay for his meals and for occasional vacation expenses. His campaign spending reports to the Federal Election Commission (FEC) listed dozens of meals at Washington, D.C.-area restaurants. The bills ranged from a high of about $60 to as little as $6.50.

In the past, Hertel had often taken advantage of trips offered by special-interest groups to members of Congress who want to visit warm weather resorts in the middle of the winter. In 1987, for example, he took his wife and children on a free trip to Disney World in Orlando, Fla. During such trips, his FEC reports indicated, he sometimes paid for incidental expenses such as meals, car rental, gifts, and film with campaign funds.

Beginning in 1990, members of Congress were no longer permitted to accept any trip from a corporation or lobbying group that exceeded three days. Thus, when Hertel was invited to appear on a panel at the EIA's 1990 winter conference at South Seas Plantation in April 1990, he and his wife could only accept free lodging from the EIA for three nights. So he dipped into his campaign treasury to pay for five additional nights. In all, the campaign paid $1,130 for lodging and purchased at least two meals of $30 and $396.

These expenditures had no apparent political purpose. When we asked him to explain, Hertel justified charging the additional costs to his campaign on the grounds that he held political discussions in Florida after the EIA meeting had ended. But he declined to name any of the people with whom he spoke about politics. Instead, his office provided the following written statement: "Several political advisors, supporters, and contacts also attended the conference and stayed after it ended. Congressman Hertel held political and issue discussions with these and other individuals in the days following the end of the conference. These discussions, held after the conference ended, were for bona fide campaign purposes."

Although eighteen other House members went to the same EIA

conference as Hertel, only one other—Rep. Albert G. Bustamante, D-Texas—charged lodging or meals to a campaign committee. Bustamante charged his campaign $362 for expenses at the South Seas Plantation.

Hertel's vague response about the trip demonstrates the weakness of the current standards governing campaign spending. Because the rules are not clear and enforcement is lax, a member of Congress need only assert that an expenditure by his campaign committee had a political purpose and it is generally considered to be within the realm of reasonable election spending. Neither the FEC nor the House and Senate ethics committees attempt to verify the honesty of spending reports filed by the campaigns. There is no requirement for candidates to submit any receipts. No regular audits are conducted.

Many of the the FEC reports filed by congressional candidates contain items—such as Hertel's Florida trip—that strain any common-sense standard for political spending. When a member of Congress picks up the tab for an expensive dinner in London, Jerusalem, or Timbuktu, what possible relationship could this have to a reelection campaign? When a member of Congress reports buying a $100 "constituent gift" at a gift shop in Florida, it seems likely that the constituent was really a friend or relative. When a member of Congress reports spending about $900 a week on political meetings, any reasonable person might suspect that it may not be the truth.

The rules of Congress are not silent on this matter. Expenditures such as these were addressed most recently by the House ethics committee in a 1986 ruling in a case involving a former representative, James Weaver, D-Ore. In that case, the committee ruled that campaign funds should not be spent for any purpose that is not "exclusively and solely" for the benefit of the campaign. "Moreover," the committee added, "a bona fide campaign purpose is not established merely because the use of campaign money *might* result in a campaign benefit as an incident to benefits personally realized by the recipient of such funds, such as where . . . the individual has the discretion of whether to share benefits he might realize from the use of campaign money." *

The committee's ruling would seem to apply not only to Hertel's

---

* Committee of Official Conduct, House of Representatives, "Investigation of the Financial Transactions of Representative James Weaver with his Campaign Organization," H. Report 99-933, 99th Congress, 2nd Sess., 1986, 13. Emphasis added.

Florida trip, but also to many other expenditures reported by congressional candidates during the 1990 cycle: the $7,000 that Rep. Barbara-Rose Collins, D-Mich., spent on an "image consultation" and a new wardrobe; the $325 that Rep. Larry J. Hopkins, R-Ky., spent at Uthai's Gems in Bangkok; the $244 that Senator Pryor spent on Cotton Bowl tickets that were given to his brother; the $1,095 that Representative Anthony paid for "hunting and resort fees" in Buchner, Ark.; and the $327 that Rep. Robert A. Roe, D-N.J., spent at a restaurant in Paris.

It is hard to escape the obvious conclusion that in many instances campaign funds are being used by members of Congress for purposes that are primarily personal under the definition laid down by the House ethics committee.

Similarly, when members of Congress report thousands of dollars of unitemized expenses, they leave the impression that they are dipping into their campaign treasuries for pocket money. Under the rules, members are not required to itemize expenditures of less than $200. Using that loophole, Rep. Doug Walgren, D-Pa., failed to itemize $89,202 of his spending in reports to the FEC during the 1990 cycle. Reps. Charles B. Rangel, D-N.Y., failed to itemize $84,741, and Austin J. Murphy, D-Pa., failed to itemize $78,250.

In addition, many members submitted reports that masked the true nature of their expenditures by using vaguely worded descriptions.

Of course, not all members of Congress are as blatant about spending campaign money on purchases that seem to bring them personal benefit. Some actually try to stay well within the rules, even as vague as the rules may be. In fact, a few are downright stingy with their campaign funds.

Newcomers to Congress are particularly frugal with their campaign treasuries. Seldom do first-term lawmakers buy fancy cars, expensive meals, or other luxuries. But the longer they serve in Congress, the higher they rise in the hierarchy, the less opposition they face, and the more special-interest money they have available to them, the more likely they become to devote their campaign funds to seemingly frivolous or extravagant expenditures.

Indeed, it is a mark of seniority and status to be able to spend campaign funds freely. Senior lawmakers such as House Ways and Means Chairman Dan Rostenkowski, D-Ill., are clearly admired by their colleagues for their ability to maintain a campaign war chest in excess of $1 million.

There is also a distinct difference between campaign spending patterns in the Senate and in the House, especially when it comes to buying luxuries. Because contested Senate races cost so much more than House races, fewer senators appear to spend their campaign funds on unnecessary purchases. Then, too, the Senate has a higher percentage of millionaires than the House, so senators often can afford to buy some of these items with their own resources. The reelection campaigns of incumbent senators also receive more press scrutiny than those of entrenched House members, thereby forcing most senators to be more cautious than their counterparts in the House.

Senators also are strictly prohibited from pocketing their campaign money when they retire. Senior House members could take advantage of the so-called grandfather clause until 1993 to convert excess campaign funds to personal use upon their retirement. In the case of a member's death, campaign funds become the property of the member's estate. When Rep. Silvio O. Conte, R-Mass., died in 1991, his campaign funds were used to pay for the funeral, burial, and a $35,000 tombstone.

Campaign spending by members of Congress is a highly individual matter, reflecting a candidate's personality and approach to the job. A frugal, serious legislator such as Rep. Anthony C. Beilenson, D-Calif., would be expected to watch his expenditures closely, as he does. A free-wheeling, aggressive politician such as House Minority Whip Newt Gingrich, R-Ga., would be expected to spend campaign funds more loosely. Indeed, the personal habits and attitudes of members of Congress are revealed in the way they raise and spend their campaign funds.

Whenever a member of Congress spends $500 from campaign funds for dinner at a fancy restaurant or $3,000 for a painting, contributors are unknowingly footing the bill. It takes many small contributions from loyal supporters back home to pay for such extravagances. If small contributors were aware that their money was being spent on unnecessary purchases, perhaps they would be less likely to contribute in the future.

Alice S. Hamburg, a retiree in Berkeley, Calif., who wrote a check for $250 to Dellums in May 1990, told us: "I'm not happy about the

The Top Fifteen Spenders in the 1990 House Races: Cellular Phone Expenses

Rank	Candidate	Expenditures
1	Joseph P. Kennedy II, D-Mass.	$16,831
2	George J. Hochbrueckner, D-N.Y.	12,367
3	Bill Dickinson, R-Ala.	12,122
4	Dick Zimmer, R-N.J.	12,011
5	John Hiler, R-Ind.	9,441
6	C. Christopher Cox, R-Calif.	8,914
7	Jim Bacchus, D-Fla.	8,759
8	Jolene Unsoeld, D-Wash.	8,188
9	Norm Dicks, D-Wash.	8,028
10	Mike Pence, R-Ind.	7,593
11	Dave Camp, R-Mich.	7,566
12	Chet Edwards, D-Texas	7,505
13	Marty Russo, D-Ill.	7,246
14	Robert G. Torricelli, D-N.J.	6,871
15	Tom Lewis, R-Fla.	6,651

Note: Totals are for the entire two-year cycle.

amount of money that Dellums feels he has to raise when he has no opposition, but unfortunately that is the way the system works."

AUTOMOBILES AND APARTMENTS

Luxury automobiles, often equipped with cellular phones, have become a common campaign expenditure for many incumbents, who either leased cars or purchased them outright (see box, above). House members usually buy no more than one campaign car, but senators often buy several vehicles with their campaign funds.

A car is a political necessity whenever incumbents return to their districts on campaign business. But some members of Congress bend the rules by keeping their campaign cars in Washington, D.C., where it is harder to justify them as a campaign-related expense. Outside of a few fund-raisers and party meetings, most of the driving that incumbents do in the nation's capital is for either personal or official business, not for campaign purposes.

During the six years leading up to his 1990 reelection, Sen. Ted Stevens, R-Alaska, spent $71,782—more than any other member of Congress—on automobiles and maintenance, much of it at Washington, D.C., area auto dealerships (see Table 3-1). When asked to explain these expenses, an aide responded: "All the information required by the FEC is in the reports."

Later, a source said that Stevens kept one campaign car in Alaska and two other cars in the Washington, D.C., area for the personal use of the senator and his wife. Thus, the campaign would appear to have owned or maintained the Stevens's personal cars. Stevens has long been an antagonist in the debate over stricter controls on campaign funds and once even sponsored a motion to cut off funding for the FEC.

Senator Nunn spent $56,782 on campaign cars over the six-year period, including the costs of insurance, license plates, registration, and maintenance. In October 1985, Nunn's campaign purchased a $14,195 automobile from Jay Pontiac in Columbus, Ga., to be used exclusively by the campaign in Georgia. In May 1986, the campaign began paying for half the lease on a campaign car, which served as both Nunn's personal car as well as his campaign car in Washington, D.C. Then in March 1989, the campaign sold the Pontiac in Georgia and replaced it with a Jeep for $23,661.

In the House, Dickinson exceeded all others by maintaining two cars and a van at a total cost of $66,811. Madigan's campaign paid more than $26,000 during the two years to lease two new cars, one of them a convertible that he described as a "parade car." He later returned the "parade car" to the leasing company when he became President George Bush's secretary of agriculture.

While most House members reported having only one campaign car, it was often an expensive, late model automobile. Clay used his campaign funds to lease a $799-a-month automobile for his use in the Washington, D.C., area. Clay's campaign aides refused to discuss it or even identify what type of car the St. Louis representative was driving. Young paid $30,000 for his powder blue Lincoln Continental; Hatcher bought an $18,000 Ford LTD; Leath purchased a $23,000 Lincoln Town Car that he kept when he retired.

Of all those who maintained campaign vehicles, Rep. Ralph M. Hall, D-Texas, seemed to have the worst luck. During the 1990 cycle, he paid nearly $30,000 to purchase a new 1990 Ford LTD and maintain a previously purchased 1985 Ford Econoline van. Months after the campaign, the van was destroyed when it burst into flames and had to be replaced.

While members of Congress found it easy to defend their decisions to purchase campaign cars with political funds, they sometimes had difficulty explaining to hometown journalists why they needed such luxurious automobiles. When Young was asked by David Dahl of the *St. Petersburg Times* to justify his new Lincoln, he replied that he chose it because "it's big" and could haul several passengers.

"There is a very legitimate need for transportation," Young added. "I don't think this is the kind of campaign expenditure that people are concerned about. This is all up front. It's a pure provision of transportation for political purposes. There's nothing hidden here. There's nothing improper about it at all." *

It is much more unusual for a member of Congress to rent an apartment with campaign funds, as Nunn and Pryor did during the 1990 cycle. Both senators apparently received approval from the Senate ethics committee before renting their apartments.

Pryor's campaign rented a $900-a-month apartment in Little Rock, Ark., about forty miles from his permanent home in the nearby resort town of Hot Springs. Pryor's press secretary, Damon Thompson, said that his boss reasoned that even though he did not go back to Arkansas every weekend, the rent was "less than the cost of a hotel room" and that the apartment could be used by the staff and guests when not occupied by the senator himself.

Nunn's $500-a-month apartment in Atlanta served as both an office for the staff and a place for Nunn to sleep when he was in the city.

TRAVEL AND ENTERTAINMENT

Travel is one of the necessities of life for members of Congress and no one could blame them for wanting to go in comfort. But the avail-

---

* David Dahl, "Campaigning in a Luxury Car," *St. Petersburg Times,* September 27, 1990, 1A.

ability of millions of dollars of campaign contributions from special-interest groups has allowed many incumbents to adopt a style of travel normally reserved only for top corporate executives and the very rich. Reports submitted to the FEC by members of Congress contain page upon page of expenditures for such things as chartered airplanes, expensive restaurant meals, and luxury hotels—and many of them appear to be for purposes that are more personal than political.

Flying aboard corporate jets was a good deal for members of Congress. In the 1990 cycle, they were required by the FEC to reimburse the corporations for no more than the equivalent of first-class commercial air fare, usually much lower than the standard charter rate. Under FEC rules, they had to pay charter rates only if there was no regular, commercial air service to their destination.

It was technically illegal for members of Congress to solicit charter flights or "anything of value" from corporations or lobbying groups, but it was perfectly legal for their campaign committees to solicit corporate flights, and so they did it that way. Essentially, this loophole permitted corporations to make a back-door campaign contribution to members of Congress by subsidizing their travel. The FEC, under pressure from Common Cause, promised to reconsider this regulation prior to the 1992 election.

During the 1990 cycle, Majority Leader Gephardt spent $25,596 to charter airplanes, most of them belonging to American corporations with interest in legislation that comes before the House: Pet Inc., Mercantile Bancorporation, REM Corp., Chandler's Development Co., and Circus Circus Enterprises Inc. Deborah Johns, Gephardt's press secretary, said that her boss chose to fly on corporate aircraft because he had to travel often. "He frequently travels on behalf of other candidates," she noted. "Sometimes they pay for him to fly in, sometimes he pays for the trip."

Gephardt was not the only top party leader to travel on corporate jets. Both the Republican and Democratic campaign committees were said to keep lists of available corporate aircraft that could be called upon frequently to ferry members of Congress to big party fund-raisers. As Laura Nichols, spokeswoman for the Democratic Congressional Campaign Committee, put it: "We know where to go if we need to procure a plane."

The political trips that members of Congress make aboard corporate jets are different from junkets that corporations and lobbying groups provide outright to members, such as Hertel's trip to Florida. Whenever members of Congress agree to make a speech, their travel expenses are paid entirely by the sponsoring organization.

While Representative Davis also favored chartered air travel, he did not have access to cut-rate corporate jets, apparently because he was not a part of the congressional leadership. As a result, Davis's preference for charter airplanes boosted his campaign travel expenses to $110,962—the highest travel budget of any House member. Davis said he needed to charter planes because his district covered 40 percent of the land mass of the state of Michigan, making travel by automobile very time-consuming.

Under a little-known provision of the Federal Aviation Administration regulations, pilots may be paid less than the going charter rate for transporting congressional candidates without being credited with an in-kind contribution. Rep. Richard H. Lehman, D-Calif., took advantage of that regulation to pay his pilot, Paul Broussard, a supporter, just $300 per flight—a fraction of the going rate. Like Davis, Lehman said his district was too big to be traveled easily by car.

Predictably, most members of Congress who spent large sums on travel either came from big districts, played a big role in national party activities, represented West Coast districts, or sought a higher office in the 1990 cycle.

The federal government provides members of Congress with a liberal budget for travel between their hometowns and Washington, D.C., but most incumbents used campaign funds to finance trips that were intended for purely political purposes. That included trips back home for political functions; trips to party conferences, such as the national nominating conventions; travel for staff employed by the campaign; and trips to assist other members of Congress in fund-raising.

Many members of Congress also reported spending large sums to ferry their spouses between their hometowns and Washington, D.C. Rep. Jerry Huckaby, D-La., set the pace for family travel at campaign expense. Over two years, he spent nearly $13,000 to fly his family round-trip for holidays and to attend fund-raising events. Huckaby's wife made thirteen such trips, his son made six trips and his daughter made two. More than half of all the trips coincided with holidays.

Sen. Alan K. Simpson, R-Wyo., used $4,686 from his campaign funds to pay for air fare so his wife, Ann, could accompany him on an official trade mission to Australia. Simpson's expenses were paid for by the Senate, but his wife's were not. Donald L. Hardy, Simpson's administrative assistant, who accompanied the senator at Senate expense, said that Ann Simpson's expenses were deemed to be a legitimate campaign expense because she talked to Australians about buying products from Wyoming.

Whenever members of Congress were traveling, they frequently charged some of their meals to the campaign, whether or not the trip had an explicit campaign purpose. Simpson's campaign, for example, picked up at least one $333 dinner tab at Stephane's Restaurant in East Hawthorn, Australia. Rep. Henry A. Waxman, D-Calif., used campaign funds to pay for a $788 hotel bill at the King David Hotel in Jerusalem. Rep. Robert G. Torricelli, D-N.J., spent $7,400 on 130 meals in Washington, D.C., New Jersey, New York, Florida, Thailand, Taiwan, and Italy.

Many members of Congress said that their travel-related expenses were entirely for campaign business. Yet when Rep. Bud Shuster, R-Pa., and his staff spent nearly $107,000—or about four times more than any other campaign—for political meals, that explanation seemed implausible.

Country club memberships were often purchased with campaign funds. Representative Pickle said he used his two campaign-funded country club memberships to entertain constituents. An aide to Rep. Harold L. Volkmer, D-Mo., said he saw Volkmer's country club dues as a legitimate expense because "it's a matter of keeping in touch with old friends, and, of course, he does take visitors to the country club." H. Lee Halterman, legal counsel to Dellums, said the campaign paid for a membership in the Lakeview Club in Berkeley, Calif., because "it's a gathering place for political leaders."

To improve his appearance at political events, Clay of Missouri spent $333 on a new tuxedo. For similar reasons, Sen. Paul Simon, D-Ill., paid a tuxedo shop $299 for bow ties.

Members of Congress cited political reasons to justify an array of other travel and entertainment expenses that were not entirely political. Seven House members dipped into campaign funds to pay for their dues at the House gym. To boost office morale, Simpson's campaign funded beer parties for his Senate staff and also bought Washington Redskins tickets, which were given to the winner of a weekly office drawing.

RELATIVES ON THE PAYROLL

Carol Hubbard, wife of Kentucky Democrat Carroll Hubbard, received an unusual birthday gift from her husband's campaign committee: a fancy fund-raising party held on her birthday and payments totaling $5,659 for organizing the event herself.

When relatives' names show up on the campaign payroll, it is bound to raise some suspicions that the job may be a sinecure. Before the days of multimillion-dollar congressional campaigns, relatives more often were expected to work as unpaid volunteers in political campaigns.

Of course, some relatives still help out without demanding payment. A number of wives serve without pay as treasurers or even managers of their husbands' campaigns. One such volunteer wife was Katherine James, who by her own account helped to run the successful reelection campaign of her husband, Rep. Craig T. James, R-Fla. Likewise, Becky Browder, wife of Rep. Glen Browder, D-Ala., served without pay as her husband's campaign treasurer.

But increasingly, there was a tendency among congressional candidates, particularly well-entrenched incumbents, to put their relatives on the payroll. In California, Lantos's campaign employed both his daughter, Katrina Lantos-Swett, and his son-in-law, Timber Dick, even though neither of them lived in his district. He also invested his campaign funds in the winning campaign of his other son-in-law, Rep. Dick Swett, D-N.H., Katrina's husband. This led to charges of improper conduct filed with the FEC by Lantos's opponent, Republican Bill Quraishi. Lantos insisted that these allegations had "no merit."

Katrina Lantos-Swett, who lived in New Hampshire, received more than $25,000 in consulting fees and expense reimbursements from her father's 1990 campaign in California. According to Quraishi's FEC complaint, Lantos's daughter was never paid a consulting fee for her work until she received a lump-sum payment on April 27, 1987—one month before she and her husband bought a house in Bow, N.H. But Robert R. King, Lantos's administrative assistant, insisted that payments to Katrina had been "traditional over the years." Katrina also served as treasurer of her husband's campaign, but she received no salary for that job.

King said that Timber Dick, Lantos's other son-in-law, who lives in Colorado, was paid $16,800 from the representative's campaign treasury for his help on fund raising and developing campaign materials. He said Dick had been more active in the campaign in previous years.

Spouses often received expenses—but no salary—from the campaigns. Janice Gallegly, wife of Rep. Elton Gallegly, R-Calif., took nearly $22,000 for what was reported to the FEC as "office/travel/mileage" and unspecified other "reimbursements." At the end of the 1990 cycle, the campaign still owed her $705 for mileage. Joan Rose, wife of Rep. Charlie Rose, D-N.C., received $15,655 for her campaign-related expenses.

Lee Anderson, wife of Rep. Glenn M. Anderson, D-Calif., ran her husband's campaign while also overseeing the family business back in Hawthorne, Calif. However, she charged her husband's campaign $2,860 to purchase and maintain a car phone and $30,979 for travel, even though she earned no salary. She and her husband, who were the only members of his "fund-raising committee," also charged the campaign for a number of restaurant dinners eaten by the fund-raising committee.

Rep. Robert K. Dornan, R-Calif., relied on a firm owned by his daughter, Robin, a former fund-raiser for the conservative Heritage Foundation, to give him advice. Her fees in the 1990 election cycle came to nearly $60,000. At the same time, another Dornan daughter, Terry, received more than $14,000 for answering contributors' mail.

Likewise, Torres of California employed Carmen Garcia, his daughter, as his primary consultant. Ever since her father first ran for Congress in 1982, Garcia has been deeply involved in his reelection efforts. Her principal function was fund raising, a service she also provides for nonprofit groups in the Los Angeles area. For her fund-raising expertise, Garcia received $53,242 from the Torres campaign during the 1989-1990 cycle. She also took overall responsibility for running her father's campaign and maintained the campaign database on a computer in her office. In addition, she personally produced all his television ads.

Rep. Dennis E. Eckart, D-Ohio, paid his father $250 for each speech he made on behalf of his son, for a total of $6,250.

In the modern age, no one would demand that any relative work on a campaign without pay. Still, it is clear that the availability of special-interest money has encouraged incumbents to pay relatives for work they otherwise might do on a volunteer basis, further driving up the costs of campaigning.

LEGAL BILLS

When members of Congress get into trouble with the law, they turn to their campaign contributors for help. Some establish separate legal defense funds, but most simply use money from their campaign treasury to pay their lawyers. Even when an incumbent's legal problem has nothing to do with his campaign, campaign funds are often used to pay the bills.

Ethics investigations were responsible for many legal bills in the 1990 cycle. Beginning with the ouster of House Speaker Jim Wright, D-Texas, in 1989, there was a flurry of cases of alleged impropriety that ensnared a number of members of Congress. All led to lengthy—and costly—investigations by the House and Senate ethics committees and big legal bills.

House Minority Whip Gingrich spent $147,490 on lawyers and accountants during the 1990 cycle, most of it to battle an ethics complaint against him. Among other things, Gingrich was accused of impropriety in forming a partnership financed by his political supporters to promote a book that he coauthored in 1984 entitled *Window of Opportunity*. The complaint against Gingrich, filed by Rep. Bill Alexander, D-Ark., portrayed the book deal as a clever scheme on Gingrich's part to use political donations to generate personal income for himself. After a lengthy investigation, the House ethics committee dismissed the complaint, which appeared to have been filed primarily in retaliation for Gingrich's leading role in Wright's downfall.

Rep. Barney Frank, D-Mass., spent $143,122 battling allegations relating to his relationship with a male prostitute, Steve Gobie, who claimed he had operated a sex-for-hire business out of Frank's apartment. In July 1990, the House voted 408-18 to reprimand Frank for misusing his office by, among other things, intervening to quash Gobie's parking tickets.

In Memphis, meanwhile, Rep. Harold E. Ford, D-Tenn., continued to battle longstanding charges of bank, mail, and tax fraud stemming from an alleged influence-buying scheme. In addition to spending $183,000 from his campaign coffers on legal and accounting fees, Ford also collected donations for a separate legal defense fund that has raised more than $350,000 since the charges were first brought against him in 1987.

One of the largest legal bills reported in the 1990 election cycle was the more than $100,000 Rep. Don Young, R-Alaska, paid to settle a libel suit filed against him by his 1988 opponent, Peter Gruenstein. Young had accused Gruenstein of laundering campaign contributions. Gruenstein charged that Young's accusations made people believe he was in the illegal drug trade. After a long period of litigation, Gruenstein received an undisclosed settlement. Young's payment to his lawyer from campaign funds presumably included the money that Gruenstein received as part of the settlement, but the terms of the settlement apparently prevented Young from talking about it.

The story of Rep. William H. Gray III's legal bills was particularly intriguing. Before resigning in 1991, Gray, D-Pa., the majority whip, piled up thousands of dollars of legal bills, even though he consistently denied recurring rumors that he was under investigation by the Justice Department. Aides insisted the payments to Washington lawyer Abbe Lowell were to pay for an audit of Gray's finances. Gray's former accountant, Neil Godick, had been charged with fraud for activities unrelated to his work for Gray. Lowell indicated that Gray decided to audit his finances after Godick got into trouble. In the 1990 cycle, Gray spent $208,432 from his campaign coffers on lawyers and accountants.

Another big spender on attorney's fees was Gephardt, who amassed $73,802 in legal bills—including $40,000 in pro bono legal services contributed by Robert F. Bauer of the law firm of Perkins Coie in Washington, D.C. Gephardt was not the subject of either an ethics investigation or a criminal probe, but Bauer explained that the expenses stemmed from an FEC audit of Gephardt's failed 1988 presidential campaign. Under federal law, according to Bauer, a lawyer is permitted to contribute in-kind legal work in excess of the $2,000 limit on contributions.

In 1990, Sen. Tom Harkin, D-Iowa, who has established a legal defense fund, was still struggling to pay off a legal debt arising from a controversial press release that his campaign issued in the final weeks of his 1984 victory over Sen. Roger Jepsen, R-Iowa. The release charged that a Defense Department official detailed to Jepsen's office was actually working for the Republican's campaign. The official sued Harkin unsuccessfully, but took it all the way to the Supreme Court. Harkin was left with a debt of $160,000 to Akin, Gump, Strauss, Hauer, and Feld, where his wife is a law partner.

Having a big campaign fund certainly helps to protect members of Congress from incurring any personal legal liability in office. Even fines for violating FEC regulations are normally paid out of campaign funds. Rep. Dave Nagle, D-Iowa, wrote a $4,000 check from his campaign treasury to pay a fine levied by the FEC. The penalty stemmed from a $20,000 loan that Nagle's campaign received in December 1988 that was cosigned by two Iowa lawyers, H. Daniel Holm, Jr. and Edward Gallagher, Jr. The FEC ruled that their willingness to back the loan constituted an illegal donation in excess of the $2,000 limit.

PLANNING FOR THE FUTURE

Older members of Congress looked to their campaign funds as a way of preparing for retirement or posterity. During the 1990 cycle, senior House members were still eligible to convert their campaign funds to personal use upon retirement, and all members of Congress were free to make large charitable donations to insure they would be remembered fondly after death.

For at least five members of Congress who retired or died during the 1990 cycle, their campaign funds were either converted immediately to personal use or turned over to their estates. Senator Thurmond and Representative Roybal—neither of them interested in retirement—chose to forge lasting marks in their home states by making large charitable contributions.

Thurmond, who was approaching ninety, spent $100,000 to endow a chair in political science in his name at the University of South Carolina, $100,000 to create a political science professorship at Clemson University, and $398,091 for educational scholarships to be distributed by the state-supported Strom Thurmond Foundation. He also gave $5,000 for scholarships to virtually every institution of higher learning in South Carolina, bringing his total commitment to $733,091 (see box, page 82).

Likewise, Roybal used $100,000 from his campaign treasury to endow a chair in the study of gerontology in his own name at California State University in Los Angeles. Born in 1916, Roybal, chairman of the House Select Committee on Aging, said he got the idea of an endowed chair from several of his elderly constituents and eventually

Strom Thurmond's Contributions to Colleges and Universities

Recipient	Type of Donation	Amount
Strom Thurmond Foundation	educational scholarships	$398,091
University of South Carolina, Aiken	political science chair	100,000
Clemson University Foundation	political science chair	100,000
Aiken Tech	scholarship	10,000
Central Wesleyen College	scholarship	5,000
Chesterfield-Marlboro Tech	scholarship	5,000
Claflin College	scholarship	5,000
Coker College	scholarship	5,000
Columbia Bible College	scholarship	5,000
Columbia College	scholarship	5,000
Denmark Tech	scholarship	5,000
Florence-Darlington Tech	scholarship	5,000
Greenville Tech	scholarship	5,000
Horry-Georgetown Tech	scholarship	5,000
Lutheran Theological Seminary	scholarship	5,000
Midlands Tech	scholarship	5,000
Newberry College	scholarship	5,000
Orangeburg-Calhoun Tech	scholarship	5,000
Piedmont Tech	scholarship	5,000
Southern Methodist College	scholarship	5,000
Spartanburg Tech	scholarship	5,000
Sumter Area Tech	scholarship	5,000
Tech College of the Low Country	scholarship	5,000
Tri-County Tech	scholarship	5,000
Triden Tech	scholarship	5,000
Winthrop College	scholarship	5,000
Williamsburg Tech	scholarship	5,000
Wofford College	scholarship	5,000
York Tech	scholarship	5,000
Total		**$733,091**

agreed to help them raise the necessary $350,000. He contributed $100,000 and persuaded other contributors to provide the rest.

Such generosity by senior members of Congress was almost unheard of before they began generating large amounts of extra cash in their campaign treasuries. Even though the contributions by Thurmond and Roybal were unusually large, they were a natural extension of the philanthropy with campaign funds that has become common among most members of Congress.

It was not until recent years that members of Congress were restricted from using their campaign funds for personal use. When campaign funds were smaller, it was perfectly legal for every member of Congress to do whatever he or she wanted with the money. But as the size of these funds grew, Congress gradually came under pressure to put restrictions on them.

In 1979, Congress amended federal election laws to prohibit the conversion of campaign funds for personal use. In doing so, House members of the 96th Congress exempted—or grandfathered—themselves. Today, the "grandfather clause" still permits House members who began serving prior to January 8, 1980 to use their campaign funds in retirement. But under a new law enacted in late 1989—following a big pay raise and the embarrassing ethics investigation of former House Speaker Jim Wright—those members who retire after January 1993 cannot exercise their rights under the grandfather clause. Furthermore, they have no incentive to raise additional money prior to 1993, because they cannot take any more money with them than they already had in their accounts when the new law passed in 1989.

Wright himself was one of the beneficiaries of the grandfather clause. After retiring, he spent about $381,000 out of his campaign treasury on legal fees and personal expenses.

In fact, during the 1990 cycle, the grandfather clause was more of a legal defense fund than a retirement provision. Among those who used their excess campaign funds for legal expenses were Rep. Tony Coelho, D-Calif., who resigned after being accused of accepting improper investment help from a savings and loan executive, and Rep. Robert A. Garcia, D-N.Y., who used his campaign funds to defend himself in a criminal trial.

Even death could not legally separate veteran House members from their campaign funds. In 1989, a year after the death of Rep. John J. Duncan, Sr., R-Tenn., his son, John Jr., not only inherited his father's House seat but also got a $99,000 share of the leftover campaign funds. FEC records showed that Duncan's widow and four children divided the $605,000 campaign treasury. Likewise, the estates of two House members who died during the 1990 cycle received their campaign funds. The heirs of Rep. William F. Nichols, D-Ala., got $438,561; the heirs of Rep. Claude Pepper, D-Fla., got $37,353.

Other "grandfathered" House members who retired from Congress after the 1990 election included George W. Crockett, Jr., D-Mich., who had $43,717 in his fund; Bill Frenzel, R-Minn., $117,447; Augustus F. Hawkins, D-Calif., $141,684; Leath, $447,030; Madigan, $542,570; Virginia Smith, R-Neb., $27,070; and Bob Whittaker, R-Kan., $536,257.

Retiring House members often view their campaign money as an end-of-career reward for the sacrifices of public life. When Leath was asked what he intended to do with his campaign contributions, he told the *Waco Herald Tribune:* "I may go back and figure up what it cost in the three years that I spent running for Congress and resigning every job that I had during that period of time. Everything it took for my family to live came out of my pocket. I put several large campaign contributions into my campaign at that time and wasn't smart enough to do it in the form of notes where I could come back at a point in time and have the campaign pay me the notes. I might reconstruct that and pay that money out, which I think is perfectly legitimate for me to do. I will cross that bridge when I come to it." * Leath, who had dreams of becoming a country and western singer after retiring from Congress, became a lobbyist instead.

As the 1993 deadline for converting campaign funds into a retirement nest egg approached, many "grandfathered" members of Congress were clearly ready to retire with the money. But some members of Congress with the fattest campaign funds declined this once-in-a-lifetime opportunity. Among them was House Ways and Means Chairman Dan Rostenkowski, D-Ill., who would have been eligible to pocket more than $1 million. After serious consideration, he decided against retirement.

---

* Drew Parma, "Lawmaker Hangs Up His Spurs," *Waco Herald Tribune,* August 12, 1990, 1A.

Table 3-1 The Top Twenty-Five Spenders in the 1990 House Races: Campaign Automobile Expenses

	House		Senate	
Rank	Candidate	Expenditures	Candidate	Expenditures
1	Bill Dickinson, R-Ala.	$66,811	Ted Stevens, R-Alaska	$71,782
2	C.W. Bill Young, R-Fla.	48,785	Sam Nunn, D-Ga.	56,782
3	Richard T. Schulze, R-Pa.	36,103	John Kerry, D-Mass.	44,296
4	Ralph M. Hall, D-Texas	29,923	Mark O. Hatfield, R-Ore.	43,231
5	Raymond J. McGrath, R-N.Y.	28,646	J. Bennett Johnston, D-La.	36,776
6	Terry L. Bruce, D-Ill.	28,518	Daniel K. Akaka, D-Hawaii	36,589
7	Bill Grant, R-Fla.	27,110	Tom Tauke, R-Iowa	32,619
8	Robert A. Roe, D-N.J.	26,959	Bill Bradley, D-N.J.	27,316
9	Edward Madigan, R-Ill.	26,460	Claiborne Pell, D-R.I.	17,879
10	John T. Myers, R-Ind.	26,016	William S. Cohen, R-Maine	17,752
11	John P. Murtha, D-Pa.	25,836	Rudy Boschwitz, R-Minn.	16,638
12	Joseph D. Early, D-Mass.	25,234	Nancy B. Spannaus, I-Va.	13,794
13	Denny Smith, R-Ore.	24,685	Lynn Martin, R-Ill.	12,879
14	Austin J. Murphy, D-Pa.	24,637	Hal Daub, R-Neb.	10,697
15	Marguerite Chandler, D-N.J.	23,447	David L. Boren, D-Okla.	9,497
16	Richard E. Neal, D-Mass.	22,885	John A. Durkin, D-N.H.	9,250
17	Dan Rostenkowski, D-Ill.	22,394	Mitch McConnell, R-Ky.	8,809
18	Robert G. Torricelli, D-N.J.	22,136	Harvey I. Sloane, D-Ky.	8,352
19	Gary L. Ackerman, D-N.Y.	21,361	Carl Levin, D-Mich.	7,743
20	Floyd H. Flake, D-N.Y.	21,186	Alan K. Simpson, R-Wyo.	6,000
21	Pete Stark, D-Calif.	20,975	Neil Rolde, D-Maine	5,581
22	Charles Hatcher, D-Ga.	19,804	Bill Schuette, R-Mich.	4,882
23	Douglas H. Bosco, D-Calif.	19,037	Joseph R. Biden, Jr., D-Del.	4,760
24	William L. Clay, D-Mo.	18,126	Robert C. Smith, R-N.H.	4,480
25	Robin Tallon, D-S.C.	17,832	Max Baucus, D-Mont.	3,832

Note: Totals for the House are for the entire two-year cycle, including special elections; totals for the Senate are for the entire six-year cycle.

CHAPTER 4

Challengers and Others
Bucking the System

Politics has got so expensive that it takes lots of money to even get beat with.

Will Rogers, 1931

N o one knows better than Christine Todd Whitman the frustration an underfunded political challenger feels when running against an incumbent with limitless amounts of money. Prior to the 1990 election, Whitman did everything she could simply to get herself recognized as the GOP opponent of Sen. Bill Bradley, D-N.J. She went door to door with local candidates. She begged newspaper and television reporters to press Bradley for his position on the controversial state tax increase, which he declined to discuss.

Unable to afford ads in the expensive New York City and Philadelphia media markets that broadcast into New Jersey, Whitman passed out audiocassettes at commuter train stations and asked voters to listen to her commercials as they drove home.

When her fund raising failed to produce more than $600,000, she borrowed $125,000 from the Bank of New York and eventually paid off the loan with her own money after election day. The National Republican Senatorial Committee pledged to give Whitman money, but it took back $190,000 three weeks before the election in order to devote more money to another race.

Bradley, meanwhile, had so much money—nearly $12.9 million, to be precise—that he could afford such extravagances as a $10,000-a-month office. He filled the New Jersey air waves with more than $3.3 million worth of radio and television ads. He invested nearly $2.5 million in fund-raising parties, $1.2 million in polls, and about $1.3 million in salaries.

When the election returns were in, Bradley had won with only a bare 50 percent of the vote, compared with Whitman's 47 percent—an embarrassingly narrow victory for an incumbent senator whose popularity was previously thought to be so high that some Democrats touted him as a presidential contender.

Afterwards, there was little doubt in Whitman's mind that she could have defeated Bradley if she had a little more money to spend in the high-priced media markets reaching northern New Jersey. She had been in a perfect position to capitalize upon the antitax sentiment that swept New Jersey in 1990 in reaction to Democratic governor Jim Florio's tax hikes, but she simply did not have enough money to take advantage of the political luck that had come her way.

"We did very well with very little," she said philosophically. "But we've got to stop the huge imbalance of spending in these races. For challengers [who are outspent], it's really a question of people not even knowing who they are."

Whitman's story demonstrates how the big money flows to incumbents, leaving most challengers—even some of the strongest ones—with little hope of winning anything but a vacant congressional seat.

In 1990, the average Senate incumbent spent more than $4.1 million, compared with $1.7 million spent by an average challenger. In hot Senate races where the winner received 60 percent or less of the vote, the disparity was $6.7 million for incumbents, $2.6 million for challengers. In hot House races, the average incumbent spent $577,145—nearly two and one-half times the $224,363 spent by the average challenger. In all House races, of course, the disparity was even greater: $390,387 for incumbents, $133,231 for challengers.

But the most important disparities can be seen in expenditures that truly make a difference between winning and losing, such as advertising and voter contact. Even though incumbents squander money on overhead and unnecessary expenditures, they still have an enormous spending advantage on the things that matter.

When spending money for radio and television advertising in hotly contested races, Senate incumbents averaged nearly $2.3 million, compared with about $1 million for challengers. House incumbents in such races spent $148,223, compared with $67,876 for challengers. Likewise, on fund raising in hotly contested races, Senate incumbents spent an average of nearly $2.3 million, compared with $478,585 for challengers; House incumbents spent $83,928, compared with $20,736 for challengers.

More than any other statistics, these figures explain why 96 percent of all incumbents seeking reelection won in 1990 and why incumbency has become a major issue of debate in the United States, prompting reformers to propose outright limits on congressional terms.

Political consultant Peter Fenn, of the Washington, D.C., firm of Fenn & King Communications, said he advises aspiring politicians to not even consider running for the House if they cannot raise at least $200,000. "Unless it's an odd situation, where you have a wounded incumbent and don't need much money, it really takes $200,000 for anyone to be a viable congressional candidate."

In Senate races, the minimum is much higher. That Paul Wellstone, an underfunded college professor, was able to defeat Sen. Rudy Boschwitz, R-Minn., in 1990 was widely considered a political miracle. But Wellstone's campaign actually cost just under $1.5 million—more than some incumbent senators spent on their reelection in other states.

In 1990, there were several challengers who, like Whitman, might have won if they had raised a little more money. Democrat David Worley might have defeated House Minority Whip Newt Gingrich, R-Ga., if he had not been outspent by more than five to one. Gingrich's $1.6 million campaign treasury allowed the Republican incumbent to spend about $240,000 on broadcast ads in the final three weeks of the campaign, a total that was only $50,000 less than what Worley spent on his entire campaign.

Likewise, Democrat Cynthia Sullivan received 48 percent of the vote against Rep. John Miller, R-Wash., even though she spent $364,904 against his $762,233. Democrat Andy H. Fox got 49 percent of the vote against Rep. Herbert H. Bateman, R-Va., despite a spending disadvantage of $101,095 to $548,393.

As in Whitman's case, the national parties often fail to identify the truly close races where a few thousand extra dollars might turn the tide. Worley, for example, got less than $11,000 in direct contributions and independent expenditures from the national Democratic party. The Democrats gave only slightly more than $5,700 to Sullivan in Washington and only $100 to Fox in Virginia.

Whitman was not bitter about her narrow loss. As unfair as her race appeared to be, she recognized that there were hundreds of other challengers in 1990 who never even got close, either in money or votes. Indeed, the system is so clearly rigged against challengers that one wonders why most of these people even bothered running. In most cases, even their own party refused to support them with any money.

Democrat Michael Gordon also ran for Congress from New Jersey in 1990. But Gordon is more representative of the vast majority of challengers whose failure to raise sufficient funds left them with little hope of even narrowing the incumbent's usual margin of victory. He raised and spent slightly more than $100,000 in an effort to unseat Rep. Dean A. Gallo, R-N.J., who spent $688,689. On election day, Gordon received 33 percent of the vote—a mere 3 percent more than Gallo's previous challenger, John C. Shaw, who spent no money at all.

Throughout much of the campaign, Gordon sat in the back room of a dingy storefront in West Orange, N.J., telephoning people he hoped would contribute to his campaign. While Gallo threw splashy parties for community leaders at a nearby racetrack, Gordon was begging checks of $200 or less from friends and business associates. He received no financial help from the Democratic party.

"Fund raising is the most difficult part of the job," Gordon complained prior to the November election. "People have been convinced—probably by the numbers—that this is a very difficult challenge."

Even today, Gordon, an attorney, seems undaunted by the monumental task he faced in trying to oust Gallo and hopes to run again when his children are a little older. He believes that he could have beaten Gallo had it not been for the antitax sentiment that hurt all New Jersey Democrats in 1990. Like so many other challengers, he has been encouraged by what he sees as a growing anti-incumbent sentiment in the country.

"I thought I had a chance," Gordon said. "There is a general sense that professional politicians don't adequately represent this country. You need more citizen-activists, like me. I had a good sense of what issues are important to people. . . . It was difficult, it was a challenge, but it was worth doing."

An even more hapless challenger—typical of hundreds of others around the country—was Republican Burl C. Adkins, who raised $42,511, organized about 100 volunteers, and captured 37 percent of the vote in a futile effort to unseat Rep. William D. Ford, D-Mich., who spent $354,729.

Adkins, who ran his campaign out of the garage of his modest brick home in suburban Detroit, received no money from the GOP. He noted that in order to get help from the Republican or Democratic parties, a candidate has to raise a minimum amount of money himself. For most challengers, that is an impossible task. "The party was looking for me to raise $50,000 to $100,000 in the primary," he said. "I tried everything I possibly could to raise money. I just couldn't do it."

At a national level, the Republican and Democratic parties provide substantial funds to only a few Senate challengers and perhaps no more than a dozen House challengers during each election cycle (see Tables 4-1 and 4-2). Much of the party money is devoted, instead, to protecting vulnerable incumbents or supporting candidates in open seats. Even some well-funded incumbents seem to have priority over challengers when the party money is dispensed. For example, Sen. Phil Gramm, R-Texas, received more than $1 million from the National Republican Senatorial Committee, even though he was well on his way to spending more than $12.2 million against a Democratic challenger who had less than $1.7 million to spend.

But even those challengers who received the maximum possible assistance from their national party usually did not get enough money to alter the balance of the race. In Nebraska, for example, Republican challenger Ally Milder had the benefit of $9,998 in direct contributions and $49,774 in coordinated expenditures from the National Republican Congressional Committee (NRCC). But even such a substantial contribution was of only marginal value in a race where the incumbent, Rep. Peter Hoagland, D-Neb., raised $935,652, or about $300,000 more than Milder was able to raise.

In Illinois, the GOP provided the Senate challenger, Rep. Lynn Martin, with nearly $900,000 in donations and services in her bid against Democratic incumbent Sen. Paul Simon. The Democratic party provided Simon with an almost identical amount of financial assistance, negating whatever advantage Martin might have gotten from her party's assistance.

Perhaps the best assistance the party can provide is big-name help in fund raising. In 1990, for example, the Republican party arranged for President Bush, his wife Barbara, and many top cabinet members to appear at fund-raisers for challengers in targeted races.

One of the most popular speakers on the Republican fund-raising circuit was former Lt. Col. Oliver L. North, the ex-White House aide who played a central role in the Iran-contra affair. About a half-dozen challengers paid North as much as $25,000 for an appearance. At a typical North fund-raiser, guests paid $125 to hear his dinner speech; those who paid $250 got their pictures taken with the conservative Republican hero. North even went campaigning door to door with unsuccessful GOP candidate J. Kenneth Blackwell in Cincinnati.

Reformers have sometimes overstated the extent to which the lack of money shuts nonincumbents out of the process. In 1990, at least nine underfunded challengers—including Wellstone—spent less than the incumbent and won. Of course, all except Wellstone were running in House races, where a big disparity is somewhat easier for the challenger to overcome because the spending is smaller. All but one of these eight House challengers had considerably more than the $200,000 minimum suggested by Peter Fenn.

Republican Frank Riggs, who spent $262,809, defeated Rep. Douglas H. Bosco, D-Calif., who spent $438,541; Republican Wayne T. Gilchrest, $270,484, defeated Rep. Roy Dyson, D-Md., $689,175; Democrat Collin C. Peterson, $373,170, defeated Rep. Arlan Stangeland, R-Minn., $520,031; Democrat Joan Kelly Horn, $348,543, defeated Rep. Jack Buechner, R-Mo., $670,467; Democrat Pete Peterson, $348,544, defeated Rep. Bill Grant, R-Fla., $842,461; Democrat Tim Roemer, $475,368, defeated Rep. John Hiler, R-Ind., $717,601; Republican Rick Santorum, $250,877, defeated Rep. Doug Walgren, D-Pa., $720,606; Republican Scott L. Klug, $184,315, defeated Rep. Robert W. Kastenmeier, D-Wis., $371,914.

In many of these cases, however, the challengers succeeded not because of anything they themselves did but because of widely publicized mistakes by the incumbents. Campaign money can compensate for many weaknesses, but it seldom can mask a lawmaker's improper behavior or lack of interest in the electorate. Fortunately, money is still not the only determining factor in American politics.

Dyson's alleged involvement in a defense contracting scandal clearly helped Gilchrest, who won despite a lackluster campaign. Collin Peterson benefited from a report in the *St. Cloud Times* that Stangeland had made 341 telephone calls—all with his official credit card—to the home of a woman, Eva Jarvis. Pete Peterson was helped enormously by Grant's decision to switch from the Democratic party to the GOP.

Likewise, Horn and Santorum mounted extremely effective, negative campaigns that capitalized both on the weaknesses of their opponents and the growing anti-incumbent sentiment. Santorum's ads showed photos of Walgren's house in suburban Washington, D.C., and asserted that the incumbent had spent only twenty-nine days in his home district since his last election. Horn produced two ads that attacked Buechner for his reliance on the perks of office. Her toughest spot opened with a film clip of Buechner saying that congressional service amounted to "a public trust, not a public trough." It then cited Buechner's honoraria, overseas travel, $125,000 salary, and a cable television stock deal. It ended with a picture of hogs wallowing in the mud.

To a lesser degree, Klug also ran a negative campaign. He focused not so much on the individual shortcomings of his opponent but instead on Kastenmeier's thirty-two-year tenure in Congress, which he persuaded the voters was entirely too long.

Roemer might not have won without his strong ties to the party elite in Washington, D.C., and the "father-in-law factor." He received considerable assistance from special-interest groups seeking favor with his father-in-law, Sen. J. Bennett Johnston, D-La., chairman of the Senate Energy and Natural Resources Committee.

What helped Riggs was having a strong third-party candidate in the race, Peace and Freedom Party nominee Darlene G. Comingore. Riggs probably would not have beaten Bosco had Commingore not taken 15 percent of the vote away from the incumbent.

Not all challengers are underfunded. In 1990, there were twenty House and three Senate challengers who managed to spend almost as much—and, in some cases, more—than the incumbent. Seven of them won, but the majority lost. Once again, these results proved that while money is an important factor, it is not necessarily the only determining factor.

Those who spent almost as much or more and won were: Democrat Mike Kopetski, $859,862, who defeated Rep. Denny Smith, R-Ore., $881,387; Democrat James P. Moran, Jr., $952,253, who defeated Rep. Stan Parris, R-Va., $979,332; Democrat Dick Swett, $465,540, who defeated Rep. Chuck Douglas, R-N.H., $492,317; Socialist Bernard Sanders, $543,308, who defeated Rep. Peter Smith, R-Vt., $684,266; Republican Randy "Duke" Cunningham, $543,708, who defeated Rep. Jim Bates, D-Calif., $713,667; Republican Charles H.

Taylor, $533,517, who defeated Rep. James McClure Clarke, D-N.C., $453,032; and Democrat Calvin Dooley, $524,034, who defeated Rep. Chip Pashayan, R-Calif., $587,593.

From the beginning, Kopetski's race was viewed as a potential Democratic victory by national party officials in Washington, D.C. Smith, who served on the board of a local savings and loan, had been weakened politically by reports that he had sought a change in government policy that would have given all thrift directors immunity from civil suits. Likewise, Pashayan was seen as vulnerable not only because he had accepted savings and loan contributions, but also because he had not maintained close contact with voters.

The father-in-law factor also worked for Swett, whose campaign received contributions and assistance from his wife's father, Rep. Tom Lantos, D-Calif.

Like Riggs, Cunningham owed his victory primarily to third-party candidates on the ballot. In addition, he was able to capitalize upon sexual harassment charges that had been leveled against Bates two years earlier.

Cunningham also had the kind of campaign help that most challengers only dream of. Rep. Duncan Hunter, R-Calif., who represents a nearby San Diego district, did everything possible to enable Cunningham to beat Bates. "We raised more than $200,000 in political action committee money—a lot for a challenger—and it was largely because of a lot of hard work by Duncan Hunter," explained Frank Collins, Cunningham's chief of staff.

Hunter's support helped to attract other party luminaries to Cunningham's campaign. He held fund-raisers featuring Marilyn Quayle, wife of the vice president; Housing and Urban Development Secretary Jack Kemp; NRCC chairman Rep. Guy Vander Jagt, R-Mich.; pop singer Stephen Stills; and former astronaut Wally Schirra.

Ironically, the very thing that strengthens most incumbents—their personal, permanent political organization—begins to become something of a liability whenever the challenger is able to raise nearly as much money as the incumbent. A penny-pinching challenger can get more out of his campaign organization than a free-spending incumbent who is saddled with large overhead costs, such as plush offices, campaign cars, and a large staff.

In Minnesota, Stangeland was defeated, in part, by the burden of a permanent campaign organization. Although he outspent Peterson by nearly $147,000, he invested most of that spending edge in off-year purchases. In Kentucky, Rep. Carl C. Perkins, D-Ky., sank 72 percent of his funds into campaign overhead—mostly salaries and travel—and thus had little left to fend off GOP challenger Will T. Scott, who came within 2,000 votes of defeating the incumbent.

Worley demonstrated how much a challenger can accomplish with very little money. In planning his campaign against Gingrich, the Democrat decided not to buy any television time. Instead, he invested heavily in voter persuasion mailings designed by Campaign Performance Group. "We made a decision . . . early on that to buy TV was a waste, given Worley's limited resources," said Richard Schlackman, president of Campaign Performance Group. "If you dominate the medium, you can dominate. We couldn't dominate TV, so we decided to dominate the mail." With some financial help from the Georgia Democratic party, Worley was able to fund five mailers, which tried to paint Gingrich as a privileged member of the Washington establishment. One such brochure showed a beautifully set table in a restaurant and on it was a "gold card" engraved with Gingrich's picture and the words "membership has its privileges—and Newt Gingrich took every one of them." The brochure, which did not even mention Worley, concluded: "Vote 'no' on Newt Gingrich."

In Maine, Democrat Patrick K. McGowan nearly defeated Rep. Olympia J. Snowe by hoarding his funds for a last-minute burst of negative television advertising that stunned the incumbent and left her unable to respond.

Without sufficient money to run a top-notch campaign, most underfunded challengers must rely almost entirely on ingenuity and perseverance. Al Beverly, a Republican newcomer who unsuccessfully challenged Rep. George "Buddy" Darden, D-Ga., was clearly a candidate with most of those qualities. Operating out of a spare bedroom in his home, Beverly mounted the very best campaign that $18,697 could buy. His opponent spent $392,877.

Lacking a media consultant, Beverly took lessons from a friend on how to write a press release. As a result, he finished with a scrapbook full of press clippings. With the help of volunteers, he produced three reasonably polished thirty-second television commercials for a mere $400. He aired his ads on obscure cable television stations for as little as $1 each.

Although Beverly had no money for mail, he distributed huge

quantities of the brochures that he and his brother produced with their desktop publishing skills. Instead of mailing them, he stood in front of the local post office on April 15 and handed one to all those who came by to mail their income tax returns. On election day, he captured 40 percent of the vote.

Some challengers—especially those with personal wealth—make the same mistake as the most vulnerable incumbents: They spend too much money on unnecessary frills. They often invest early in big-name consultants in order to gain national recognition and then wind up without enough money to get them through the final days of the campaign.

Actor Ralph Waite, a Democrat, is a classic example. He spent $634,544—about half of it his own money—in a futile effort to oust Rep. Al McCandless, D-Calif. His campaign spending on salaries and consultants cost him about $492,000 overall. He even paid $925-a-month rent on a house where his campaign employees lived.

Democrat Reid Hughes squandered some of his money on expensive consultants in an attempt to defeat Rep. Craig T. James, R-Fla. Hughes paid his media consultants, Trippi & Associates of Alexandria, Va., more than $629,000 to design and place his ads; James relied on the NRCC to produce his ads.

Also in Florida, Scott Shore, a young Republican business consultant who challenged Rep. Harry A. Johnston, D-Fla., had $247,991 to spend, but he spent it too early and had little left for television immediately before the election.

Republican Jim Salomon's spending was more in line with the budgets of most incumbents. In his campaign against Rep. Anthony C. Beilenson, D-Calif., he employed a long list of campaign consultants. In addition, he spent $55,000 on broadcast advertising, about half of it to buy a small amount of television time in the vast Los Angeles market.

The most successful challengers carefully husband their money until the final weeks of the election. "A lot of money gets wasted in campaigns," says Jay Hakes, who managed Pete Peterson's campaign. "If you raise the money early, you spend it before you need it. I told Pete, 'You're lucky that you didn't raise that money early, you would have just wasted it.'"

At least seven GOP challengers in 1990 either paid themselves salaries or used their campaign funds for living expenses. They were

Terry Ketchel in Florida, who paid himself $6,834; Joe Hoffman in Georgia, $14,607; Mike Pence in Indiana, $13,514; Rick Hawks in Indiana, $15,974; Ted Blanton in North Carolina, $20,678; Harry M. Singleton in Washington, D.C., $8,354; and Ken Bell in North Carolina, $3,021. The Federal Election Commission (FEC) declined to rule on the legality of these expenditures, even though they were challenged by the Democratic Congressional Campaign Committee. Instead, the FEC promised to tackle the issue in future rule making. These payments became a major issue in Pence's campaign against Rep. Philip R. Sharp, D-Ind., undercutting his effort to make ethics and political action committee (PAC) contributions an issue.

Under normal circumstances, the national parties focus their attention on candidates for open seats and in special elections where there is no incumbent on the ballot. As a result, these contestants usually get the kind of support from PACs and rich contributors that normally goes only to incumbents. In the House, these are usually the most expensive races. In the Senate, however, open seat races were not as expensive in 1990 as many of the battles involving an incumbent and challenger.

While most ordinary challengers were begging for money, open seat contenders such as Rosa DeLauro, D-Conn., got PAC contributions in some cases without even asking. Of the nearly $1 million that DeLauro raised, more than $400,000 of it came from PACs. She also raised $134,375 in large, out-of-state contributions.

While open seat races attracted big contributions, money appeared to be somewhat less important to the outcome. More than one-third of the twenty-nine winners in open seat races spent less money than their opponents in 1990. Among other things, such contestants got more media attention than ordinary challengers, and thus their name identification was not entirely dependent upon money. Even the most underfunded candidate in these races normally had more than a minimal amount of money to compete.

In the most expensive race for an open House seat, Republican Dick Zimmer beat Democrat Marguerite Chandler. Zimmer spent $1.33 million and Chandler spent $1.29 million.

Open-seat winners who spent less were Gary Franks, R-Conn., who was outspent by $263,990; Bill Orton, D-Utah, outspent by $192,451; Wayne Allard, R-Colo., outspent by $139,026; Chet Edwards, D-Texas, outspent by $128,313; Jim Nussle, R-Iowa, outspent by

$106,117; John W. Cox, Jr., D-Ill., outspent by $87,304; Charles Luken, D-Ohio, outspent by $27,868; and Larry LaRocco, D-Idaho, outspent by $20,857.

One of the most unusual campaign expenditures was made in an open seat race. Republican Mike Liu in Hawaii paid $75 to Rev. Claude DuTeil to bless his campaign headquarters. But the blessing did not bring success to Liu, who lost to Rep. Neil Abercrombie, D-Hawaii.

The real anomalies in the current campaign finance system are those incumbents who spend less than their challengers, even though the money is clearly available to them. Eleven sitting members of Congress survived challenges by better-funded opponents in 1990. Most of them were incumbents who simply did not indulge in the typical extravagances of campaign financing—people such as Beilenson in California.

In the 1990 election, Beilenson's constituents—well-known, wealthy people such as movie mogul Lew Wasserman and rock singer Don Henley—contributed more than $4 million to candidates all across the country. But Beilenson raised only $178,300 from big givers and $128,950 of it came from his own constituents. He took no PAC money.

Incumbents who survived better-funded challenges included Beilenson, who spent $160,833 less than Salomon; James, who spent $556,624 less than Hughes; McCandless, who spent $62,095 less than Waite; Rep. Earl Hutto, D-Fla., who spent $10,851 less than Ketchel; George E. Sangmeister, D-Ill., who spent $193,867 less than Republican Manny Hoffman; Rep. Jim A. Jontz, D-Ind., who spent $98,508 less than Republican John Arthur Johnson; Rep. William H. Natcher, D-Ky., who spent $37,452 less than Republican Martin A. Tori; Rep. Ted Weiss, D-N.Y., who spent $364,640 less than Republican William W. Koeppel; David Price, D-N.C., who spent $10,407 less than Republican John Carrington; and Bill Sarpalius, D-Texas, who spent $93,711 less than Republican Dick Waterfield.

No incumbent survived a bigger spending disadvantage in 1990 than James, a freshman from Florida. His wife, Kitty, who helped to run the campaign, attributes his victory to frugality. "In a political campaign, you have to make every dollar count," she said. "We made every penny count." While some congressional spouses such as Carol

Hubbard were earning thousands of dollars doing campaign tasks, Mrs. James took no payment for her work.

Like Beilenson, McCandless had always prided himself on running inexpensive campaigns. "The staff would cringe whenever he'd stand up at PAC fund-raisers and say, 'I really don't need a lot of money,'" recalled McCandless's administrative assistant, Signy Ellerton. "Our campaigns were short. The district field rep would go off congressional payroll three or four weeks before the election to run the campaign. And that was it—every year."

So when McCandless's staff learned in the summer of 1990 that Waite, a well-known actor who had played the role of the father on "The Waltons" television drama, was spending large amounts of his own money to win the Democratic primary, they were stunned. Even though McCandless was forced to enter the modern age of campaigning in 1990, his spending remained modest. It was late August before he opened a campaign office, assembled a staff, and hired a cadre of consultants.

The incumbent who spent the least in 1990 was Natcher, the only member of the 102nd Congress who has never accepted donations from anyone for his reelection campaigns. He financed his $6,769 campaign with his own money. He did not run television ads. He never used his congressional staff members for political work. If he entertained constituents, he did not do it at the expense of the campaign.

The most remarkable incumbent was Rep. Andrew Jacobs, Jr., D-Ind., who spent only $14,670, even though he has never had a particularly secure district and was even swept out of office for one term in 1972 during Richard M. Nixon's presidential landslide. In 1990, he held no fund-raisers and took no PAC money.

The survival of underfunded incumbents such as Jacobs calls into question the basic assumption that so many other members of Congress make about the political necessity of having an elaborate, well-funded, permanent political machine.

Table 4-1 Coordinated Expenditures by Federal Party Committees on Behalf of House Candidates: The Top Twenty-Five Beneficiaries

Rank	Challengers	Coordinated Expenditures	Incumbents	Coordinated Expenditures
1	George D. Wingert, D-Kan.	$57,393	Craig Thomas, R-Wyo.	$84,252
2	John Doolittle, R-Calif.	50,280	Peter Smith, R-Vt.	83,954
3	Joe Dial, R-Texas	50,279	Jill L. Long, D-Ind.	53,632
4	Rick Hawks, R-Ind.	50,270	Susan Molinari, R-N.Y.	50,080
5	Thomas Scott, R-Conn.	50,182	Denny Smith, R-Ore.	50,000
6	John W. Hallock, R-Ill.	50,152	Jim McCrery, R-La.	49,651
7	Bob Hammock, R-Calif.	50,140	John Hiler, R-Ind.	49,498
8	William Tolley, R-Fla.	50,077	James M. Inhofe, R-Okla.	49,423
9	Oliver Luck, R-W.Va.	50,000	Al McCandless, R-Calif.	49,396
10	David F. Emery, R-Maine	50,000	Arlan Stangeland, R-Minn.	49,277
11	Genevieve Atwood, R-Utah	50,000	Bill Grant, R-Fla.	49,000
12	Daniel J. Mangini, R-N.J.	49,995	Stan Parris, R-Va.	48,358
13	Dick Zimmer, R-N.J.	49,990	Chip Pashayan, R-Calif.	48,222
14	Ally Milder, R-Neb.	49,774	Ileana Ros-Lehtinen, R-Fla.	45,489
15	J. Kenneth Blackwell, R-Ohio	49,700	Craig T. James, R-Fla.	45,059
16	John Linder, R-Ga.	49,548	Bill Sarpalius, D-Texas	44,055
17	Dick Waterfield, R-Texas	49,523	Peter Hoagland, D-Neb.	39,531
18	Bill Barrett, R-Neb.	49,519	Pete Geren, D-Texas	33,333
19	Wayne Allard, R-Colo.	49,461	James McClure Clarke, D-N.C.	31,989
20	Randy "Duke" Cunningham, R-Calif.	49,271	Cliff Stearns, R-Fla.	29,218
21	Charles H. Taylor, R-N.C.	49,162	Don Young, R-Alaska	29,013
22	Walter W. Dudycz, R-Ill.	49,076	Jolene Unsoeld, D-Wash.	27,984
23	Wayne T. Gilchrest, R-Md.	48,909	Roy Dyson, D-Md.	24,789
24	Gary Franks, R-Conn.	48,896	Harley O. Staggers, Jr., D-W.Va.	24,779
25	John F. MacGovern, R-Mass.	48,748	John Miller, R-Wash.	24,723

Note: Totals include coordinated expenditures for special elections.

Table 4-2 Coordinated Expenditures by Federal Party Committees on Behalf of Senate Candidates: The Top Twenty-Five Beneficiaries

Rank	Challengers	Coordinated Expenditures	Incumbents	Coordinated Expenditures
1	Lynn Martin, R-Ill.	$869,664	Phil Gramm, R-Texas	$1,090,387
2	Bill Schuette, R-Mich.	685,967	Paul Simon, D-Ill.	871,159
3	Harvey B. Gantt, D-N.C.	489,699	Jesse Helms, R-N.C.	495,000
4	Jim Rappaport, R-Mass.	460,163	John Kerry, D-Mass.	458,663
5	Christine Todd Whitman, R-N.J.	402,728	Daniel R. Coats, R-Ind.	415,614
6	Bill Cabaniss, R-Ala.	302,686	Rudy Boschwitz, R-Minn.	323,975
7	Harvey I. Sloane, D-Ky.	270,739	Bill Bradley, D-N.J.	299,702
8	Hank Brown, R-Colo.	231,155	Carl Levin, D-Mich.	280,164
9	Tom Tauke, R-Iowa	212,779	Mitch McConnell, R-Ky.	277,546
10	Harry Lonsdale, D-Ore.	211,989	Strom Thurmond, R-S.C.	241,689
11	Paul Wellstone, D-Minn.	130,000	Mark O. Hatfield, R-Ore.	211,695
12	Hugh Parmer, D-Texas	120,000	Tom Harkin, D-Iowa	187,792
13	Hal Daub, R-Neb.	118,285	Howell Heflin, D-Ala.	134,811
14	Patricia Saiki, R-Hawaii	105,560	J. Bennett Johnston, D-La.	125,500
15	Baron P. Hill, D-Ind.	102,176	Pete V. Domenici, R-N.M.	108,001
16	Jane Brady, R-Del.	100,560	Jim Exon, D-Neb.	104,304
17	Robert C. Smith, R-N.H.	100,560	Ted Stevens, R-Alaska	100,560
18	Larry E. Craig, R-Idaho	100,274	William S. Cohen, R-Maine	100,560
19	Claudine Schneider, R-R.I.	100,209	Larry Pressler, R-S.D.	99,888
20	John A. Durkin, D-N.H.	99,300	Daniel K. Akaka, D-Hawaii	90,000
21	Ron J. Twilegar, D-Idaho	99,060	John W. Warner, R-Va.	86,418
22	Allen C. Kolstad, R-Mont.	96,951	Alan K. Simpson, R-Wyo.	84,446
23	Neil Rolde, D-Maine	87,884	John D. Rockefeller IV, D-W.Va.	73,613
24	Ted Muenster, D-S.D.	84,692	Nancy Landon Kassebaum, R-Kan.	52,970
25	Josie Heath, D-Colo.	84,254	Joseph R. Biden, Jr., D-Del.	50,000

CHAPTER 5

Political Consultants
Thriving on Special-Interest Money

Enshrined in the lobby of Mal Warwick's office in Berkeley, Calif., is a tiny, outmoded computer terminal that he first installed in his kitchen in 1970. It is the machine that launched Warwick's multimillion-dollar career as a direct-mail political fundraiser.

Warwick acquired the computer to help raise money for a friend, Ronald V. Dellums, a radical black Democrat first elected to Congress from Berkeley in 1970. Dellums, whose supporters were primarily students, intellectuals, and blacks, had no way of raising money from traditional party sources. So Warwick came up with the idea of soliciting small donations by mail from a wide group of like-minded liberals.

"I wasn't even familiar with the term direct mail back then," recalled Warwick. "But we knew we weren't going to raise hundreds of thousands of dollars by holding barbecues and celebrity cocktail parties."

Today, Warwick runs a highly successful direct-mail fund-raising empire for liberal causes and candidates that includes a number of spinoff firms. While he still raises money for Dellums, Warwick also has acquired a long list of other Democratic clients, including Sen. Tom Harkin, D-Iowa, who used his services in the 1992 presidential campaign.

Warwick's remarkable success story vividly illustrates how political consulting has grown into a multibillion-dollar industry in recent years. Over the past two decades, many people involved in running campaigns have decided to use their expertise to go into business for themselves.

THE GROWTH OF POLITICAL CONSULTING

In every election, an increasing number of candidates hire professionals to help run their races. Modern political campaigns demand technical skills that most candidates do not possess. Today's political entrepreneurs find it cheaper and more efficient to contract out many of the functions of a political campaign.

The political consulting industry, which includes media specialists, professional fund-raisers, pollsters, and general campaign consultants, would never have grown so rapidly had there not been a dramatic increase in the amount of special-interest money available to political candidates. Consultants are, in many cases, another luxury available to candidates because of their easy access to millions of dollars of campaign contributions.

No one knows precisely how big the political consulting industry is in terms of total revenues. Most consulting firms are privately held and do not publish annual earnings reports. But our research enabled us to quantify, for the first time, how much was spent on consultants in a congressional election.

In the 1990 congressional elections, political consultants were responsible for more than $188 million, or 45 percent of all the spending in those races. This included $116.7 million for media work, $38 million for fund raising, and $12.6 million for polling. Of course, congressional races represent just a portion of the total revenues of political consultants, who also work in local, state, and presidential races.

Predictably, well-known media consultants earned the most money (see Table 5-1). In the 1990 campaign, Squier/Eskew Communications of Washington, D.C., billed nearly $8.2 million in business for congressional candidates, including Sens. Harkin, Howell Heflin, D-Ala., Joseph R. Biden, Jr., D-Del., Daniel K. Akaka, D-Hawaii, Claiborne Pell, D-R.I., Al Gore, D-Tenn., and John D. Rockefeller IV, D-W. Va. The Sawyer/Miller Group of New York, which has since left the political consulting business, took in $4.7 million—all of it to assist Harvey B. Gantt, the Democratic candidate for senator in North Carolina.

But even though media specialists took away more money than other consultants, the real growth in recent years has been in the other forms of political consulting, particularly in direct-mail fund raising. Coyle, McConnell, & O'Brien of Washington, D.C., a leading Democratic direct-mail fund-raising firm that did not exist until 1985, grossed nearly $3 million in the 1990 cycle for its work on behalf of congressional candidates, including Sens. Harkin, John Kerry, D-Mass., and Paul Simon, D-Ill.

Polling has been a hot growth area in recent years. During the 1990 cycle, Sen. Bill Bradley, D-N.J., paid a single pollster, Joe Peritz & Associates, more than $900,000. Very few campaigns did not have their own pollster. In all, ten different pollsters earned more than $500,000 each by working in 1990 congressional races.

Although consultants are often criticized for their impact on American politics, there is no question that they can make the difference between success or failure for political candidates. Rep. Al McCandless, R-Calif., who never previously relied on consultants, might have been defeated in 1990 had he not received about $300,000 of last-minute consulting advice, including $189,680 of media work by Russo, Marsh, & Associates Inc. of Sacramento.

Media specialists have the equipment, staff, and experience to produce polished television commercials that the average politician could not duplicate. Professional time-buyers know more than any politician about how to get lower advertising rates from television and radio stations. Professional pollsters not only have the personnel to conduct opinion research, but they also have the experience necessary to use those results to help redirect campaign strategy. Unlike most candidates, particularly challengers, professional fund-raisers know who to ask for contributions and have practiced the right pitch that will cause people to give.

As a result, it is not unusual for a well-financed incumbent to have multiple consultants. Majority Leader Richard A. Gephardt, D-Mo., for example, employed eleven different consultants during the 1990 cycle at a total cost of $545,555. They included the Washington, D.C., media firm of Doak, Shrum & Associates, which developed and placed three ads at a cost of $365,566; the polling firm of Mellman and Lazarus, Inc., which billed $52,174; Malchow & Co., which billed $27,092 for its direct-mail fund-raising services; and Telephone Contact Inc., which handled promotional mailings for $55,202.

In the 1990 cycle, the House candidates who spent most on consultants were Democrat Reid Hughes of Florida, $937,235; Rep. Ileana Ros-Lehtinen, R-Fla., $856,865; Rep. Jill L. Long, D-Ind., $807,447; Rep. Robert K. Dornan, R-Calif., $793,152; Democrat Marguerite Chandler of New Jersey, $752,394; and Rep. Dick Zimmer, R-N.J., $694,204 (see Table 5-2). Ros-Lehtinen and Long both ran in special elections to fill House vacancies as well as primary and general elections.

In the Senate, Sen. Jesse Helms, R-N.C., employed thirty different consultants at a total cost of more than $10.6 million, including $4.3 million to Campaign Management Inc. of Raleigh for media consulting, $1.1 million to Jefferson Marketing of Raleigh, more than $1.3 million to Bruce W. Eberle of Vienna, Va., and nearly $1.3 million to Computer Operations of Raleigh for direct-mail fund raising. Helms's highest paid consultants were all related in one way or another to his conservative political consulting empire headquartered in Raleigh.

Other Senate candidates who spent heavily on consultants were Sen. Phil Gramm, R-Texas, $7.1 million; Gantt, $5.5 million; Simon, $5.4 million; Sen. Carl Levin, D-Mich., $5.2 million; and Kerry, $4.5 million.

Incumbents usually retained big-name consultants at the beginning of the election cycle as a kind of insurance policy against an unexpectedly strong opponent. "Folks are hiring earlier and earlier," observed media consultant Peter Fenn. Consultants who have been successful in recent, high-profile races are particularly in demand at the start of each cycle.

If no real race develops, the consultants get paid anyway. Rep. Sam M. Gibbons, D-Fla., has kept Squier/Eskew on retainer for a number of cycles on the assumption that he will someday have a serious challenge. In 1990, Gibbons spent $47,720 to develop five television spots, only three of which actually ran. "The joke around here is we make home movies for Sam Gibbons," said Robert D. Squier, partner at Squier/Eskew.

Challengers, on the the other hand, try to retain big-name consultants in order to enhance their credibility among political action committee (PAC) managers and other contributors. Doug Bailey, a well-known former GOP media consultant, said "the biggest change of all" in political consulting over the past twenty years is that consultants now help to enhance the reputation of a candidate.

"Years ago, a client who hired an out-of-state consultant tried to hide the consultant because he feared it could be a potential issue in his campaign," Bailey recalled. "A candidate had to really want professional advice to take that risk. Now, a candidate will hire a consultant and hold a news conference to announce it. Even the party does not think you are serious if you don't have the right consultant."

As a result, consultants often act as "kingmakers" in congressional elections. "It's a little bit like an animal chasing its tail," acknowledged Squier, who boasted that his own choice of clients "carries some weight" when PAC managers are trying to decide which challengers to support.

Consultants are sometimes accused of overcharging, providing services that candidates do not need, spawning too many negative campaigns, and providing candidates with standard advice that does not work in every situation. Although most consultants deny these charges, they acknowledge that there are some unqualified or unethical practitioners in their trade.

At a minimum, consultants are in the business of selling themselves. "This business is about hucksters and who can best sell the con," said Neal Oxman, president of Campaign Group Inc., a media consulting firm headquartered in Philadelphia.

For some candidates, particularly challengers, hiring consultants can be a risky investment. Consulting costs can soak up so much of a candidate's available funds at the beginning of the race that the campaign has little left to spend immediately prior to the election, when it is often needed the most.

Likewise, candidates that select big-name consultants often join a long list of clients. Consultants begin to lose their effectiveness when they take on too many clients. Lacking a sustained, personal relationship with the candidate, the consultant is likely to offer a "cookie cutter" strategy that is not well-suited to the client.

"The modern consultant does not spend enough consecutive time with the candidate," said Bailey. "He's consulting in Atlanta on Monday, in Nashville on Tuesday, in Chicago on Wednesday. His tendency is to give the same answers in Chicago on Wednesday that he gave in Atlanta on Monday."

Whenever one candidate hires large numbers of consultants, the campaign can suffer from what media consultant Peter Fenn calls "group grope," with each consultant trying to lead in a different direction. "You've got paralysis," Fenn said. "No one is making decisions. The more people you have making decisions about the campaign, the worse you are."

To avoid that problem, some candidates hire yet another consultant—either a campaign management specialist or a general strategist—or they put their media consultant or the pollster in charge of the overall strategy. Some firms also provide a combination of services, including general consulting, media advice, and polling.

In the 1990 cycle, the highest paid campaign management consultant was MaryAlice Erickson from Campaigns & Elections Inc. of Peoria, Ill., who took in a total of $291,728, most of it running the office of Minority Leader Robert H. Michel, R-Ill. Erickson had managed Michel's campaign as an employee before she went into business for herself in 1986. Erickson then hired other consultants to help her.

Despite the proliferation of consulting firms, some politicians still believe that a small, experienced campaign staff can run a campaign without consultants. Few candidates in contested races are willing to test that theory, however. Not surprisingly, the consultants scoff at the idea that candidates can make it without them.

"I would like to say that it's a charming idea," said Squier. "But it sounds to me like somebody saying, 'I had a brain tumor and we decided that instead of going to the hospital, we could take it out ourselves on the kitchen table.'"

MEDIA CONSULTANTS

Media consultants dominate most congressional campaigns. They charge higher fees for their work than other consultants, and they usually have more influence over campaign strategy than other professionals hired by the candidate.

"We don't take races where we're viewed as functionaries," said Fenn, whose firm specializing in House races took in more than $3.6 million in the 1990 elections. He said most of his clients look to him to do more than produce television spots. "They want us to help develop the theme, the message of the campaign. We even do media training."

For their advice on strategy, most top media consultants demand a retainer from the candidate, either a large sum paid at the outset of the campaign or a monthly fee. Squier, for example, charged an initial fee of $70,000 for Senate candidates and $25,000 for House candidates in the 1990 elections. He said his fee was somewhat higher than others because he did not charge for the cost of producing the television ads.

No matter how their rates are structured, media consultants seldom make their biggest profit on the retainer or production costs. Their profit is earned primarily through a 15 percent surcharge they levy on all television time purchased for airing the candidate's ads.

If media consulting firms do not have specialists on their own payroll to buy the television time, they rely on outside time-buyers, who then share the commission. Cathy Farrell, whose firm, Farrell Media Inc. of New York, purchased more than $5.4 million in air time for media consultant Roger Ailes during the 1990 election, said she usually got a 3 or 4 percent commission and Ailes took 11 to 12 percent.

Because their profits are based on volume, media consultants are often suspected of encouraging candidates to do more advertising than they actually need. While very few candidates spend as much as half of their budget on advertising, consultants usually advise them to spend more than that—sometimes as much as 75 percent.

Predictably, media consultants earn most of their money in hotly contested Senate races, where advertising costs for incumbents averaged $2.3 million in the 1990 elections. In Kentucky, Sen. Mitch McConnell, R-Ky., and the Republican party paid more than $250,000 to Ailes for advice and production and about $3 million to Farrell for time buys.

House races, even the most hotly contested ones, are much less lucrative for media consultants. In a $2.6 million matchup between Chandler and Republican Dick Zimmer in New Jersey, media consultant Smith & Harroff Inc. of Alexandria, Va., received $484,243 for work on the Zimmer campaign.

During the 1990 election cycle, the media consulting industry appeared to be changing, both in practice and personnel. Many big-name firms that dominated the industry, such as Ailes and the Sawyer/Miller Group, were preparing to phase out of politics and move into corporate work. New firms run by younger professionals, such as Frank Greer, Don Sipple, and Alex Castellanos, were expanding their share of the political consulting business. "There are a lot of new people around who are doing a good job," said Farrell.

The type of ads produced for congressional candidates was changing, too. In addition to old-fashioned biographical commercials filled with platitudes about the candidates' qualifications, consultants were routinely producing comparison ads and negative spots that attacked the qualifications or the integrity of the opponents.

Consultants were quick to defend negative advertising against those who contend that resorting to this type of attack has devalued the political debate. "If I'm telling the truth about my opponent, then I'm serving the process," insisted Squier.

Even positive ads were different than they had been in the past. "More and more," said Fenn, "we're going to third-party endorsements or analysis in our ads, not just the candidate making promises. When a newspaper says something good for your side, it gets lifted and put into the next ad. It's effective."

In addition, the television industry itself has been changing, calling for new strategies on the part of media consultants. Cable television offered lower rates and increased opportunities for targeting ads to specific audiences. But remote control channel-changers made it easier for viewers to skip the commercials, thereby causing consultants to recommend an increase in the number of buys on cable as well as broadcast stations in order to reach the same number of voters.

Even radio, a longtime staple of congressional campaigns in urban areas where television is too expensive, was considered less effective as a result of technology that allowed listeners to automatically scan the channels.

Among media consultants, the unsung heroes appeared to be those who specialized in voter persuasion mail. Those candidates who could not afford a heavy television blitz were often able to use the mail effectively to contact likely voters (see Table 5-3).

Democratic candidate David Worley, for example, chose to invest all his money on mailings after Squier's firm advised him that he didn't have enough money to use television advertising effectively against House Minority Whip Newt Gingrich, R-Ga. Worley paid $7,500 to Squier for media advice and $64,695 to Campaign Performance Group of Washington, D.C., which produced his mailings.

Most campaigns used a combination of different media for advertising. In Democrat Tim Roemer's successful race against Rep.

John Hiler, R-Ind., Roemer's total media costs in the general election were as follows: $114,467 in television air time, $30,557 in radio air time, $7,345 in mailings, $35,632 in production costs paid by the campaign, and $20,164 in production costs paid by the party.

Media consultants sometimes make blunders. In Roemer's race, Hiler ran an ad seven months before the election attacking the young Democrat as a "carpetbagger" whose campaign was financed largely with PAC money. The ad, produced by Mike Murphy Media Inc. of Washington, D.C., opened the way for Roemer to respond with an ad that pointed out how Hiler himself had taken large amounts of PAC money.

John Gautier, Hiler's former aide who later went to work for Murphy, recalled that "everybody thought we were nuts" when they raised the issue of PAC contributions. He said the PAC issue was not effective, but he doubted it directly contributed to Hiler's defeat.

Some media consultants are not familiar enough with their clients to produce television ads that reflect the clients' strengths or avoid their weaknesses. Some consultants appear to use the same ads in every race. Others make the mistake of talking down to their audience or making claims in their commercials that cannot be supported.

As Squier sees it, some candidates are hurt more than they are helped by professional media advice. "There are people in this town that I wouldn't hire to do a dog food ad!" he said.

FUND-RAISING CONSULTANTS

As the sources of campaign contributions have changed over the past two decades, so has the process of fund raising. No longer can candidates depend on a business partner, a relative, or an old college chum to manage their fund raising. Because most candidates—particularly challengers—are not familiar with PAC managers and other special-interest donors, they must turn for help to professional fund-raisers who know how to approach donors who might be interested in funding the campaign.

"PAC fund raising—that's not a form of fund raising that can be done by your brother-in-law back in Omaha," remarked Bailey.

Even those candidates who still rely on small, individual donors instead of special interests for their money find they now need the help of professionals skilled in the techniques of direct mail and telemarketing. In 1990, a majority of House and Senate candidates hired at least one fund-raiser.

Linda Davis, a well-known Democratic fund-raiser, recalled that when she founded her firm, Creative Campaign Consultant, in 1981 "there weren't a lot of people focusing on fund raising for Democrats." In those days, she said, consultant Matt Reese, who paid more attention than most to fund raising, would give candidates "a little section in his handbook" on the subject.

Davis's firm is one of dozens of small companies in Washington, D.C., and elsewhere that specialize in raising money from special interests. During the 1990 cycle, firms such as these billed congressional candidates a total of $10.5 million for their work (see Table 5-4).

Davis, whose firm received $432,860 from congressional candidates in the 1990 election, is a specialist in PAC fund raising. For a retainer fee of between $1,500 and $2,000 a month, plus expenses, she contacted PAC managers on behalf of her 1990 clients and staged frequent fund-raising parties to which special-interest representatives were invited. For parties, she rented the hall, hired the caterer, and sent out the invitations.

While Davis and her ilk concentrated on funding sources in Washington, D.C., firms such as Barbara Silby & Associates in Potomac, Md., and Amy Zisook & Associates in Chicago, specialized in hosting fund-raising events beyond the Beltway.

Silby, who has since retired from the fund-raising business, said she specialized in introducing her clients to like-minded donors in Los Angeles and other big cities around the country. Whenever Silby took a client to a distant city for fund raising, she said, she always arranged a series of one-on-one meetings and small group sessions for her client as well as a gala fund-raising party in the home of a prominent local citizen. "I look at the client, his record, his personality, and how much money he has to raise, then we decide where we're going. West LA tends to give to my more liberal clients. Challengers don't do as well there unless they're coming in like a Harvey Gantt, where there's a real bad guy on the other side."

In addition, almost all Senate candidates employed consultants to do direct mail or telemarketing. Some House candidates did likewise, but many chose to do it themselves. The Republican and Democratic parties also relied heavily on direct-mail and telemarketing consultants.

Direct-mail fund raising is an expensive way to raise money. Direct-mail fund-raising firms billed $22.4 million for their work for congressional candidates during the 1990 cycle (see Table 5-5). Some experts believe that this level of spending will not be matched in future years because of the growing expenses involved in contacting potential donors by mail.

Frank O'Brien, a partner in the Washington, D.C.-based direct-mail fund-raising firm of Coyle, McConnell, & O'Brien, explained that the rising costs of postage and printing, combined with declining response rates, have raised the barriers for politicians seeking to initiate direct-mail fund raising.

To run a successful direct-mail fund-raising campaign, candidates must be prepared to invest between 35 and 40 percent of their receipts in an ongoing process. Although the costs of direct-mail campaigns vary, Coyle, McConnell, & O'Brien generally charges each client a retainer of between $5,000 and $10,000 a month, a production fee for the mailings, and between $25,000 and $35,000 for each new letter that the firm writes on the candidate's behalf.

As costly as direct-mail fund raising can be, it is still not as expensive as telemarketing. Michael P. Gordon, president of Gordon & Schwenkmeyer Inc. of El Segundo, Calif., said that even the most successful telemarketing effort initially costs 50 cents for every dollar it raises for political candidates.

In the 1990 election cycle, Gordon & Schwenkmeyer, which charged its clients $24 an hour for the work of each person making telephone calls, billed congressional candidates a total of $944,288. Their clients included Sens. Simon, Kerry, Levin, and Max Baucus, D-Mont.

Although telemarketing appeared to be increasingly popular among candidates in contested Senate races, Gordon acknowledged that some incumbent senators become skittish about it when they get complaints from supporters who object to being disturbed at home.

While some fund-raisers demand a percentage of the money they raise, most view commissions as unethical. Some contributors, such as labor union PACs, refuse to give money to candidates who are paying fund-raisers a percentage of the donations.

POLLSTERS

Polling is another fast-growing field in the political consulting business. Just a decade ago, many members of Congress—particularly those in the House—did little or no polling. In 1990, there were very few incumbents who did not hire at least one pollster, even if only a hometown marketing firm, to keep tabs on voter sentiment prior to the election.

A decade ago, Cooper & Secrest Associates of Alexandria, Va., a firm that pioneered polling for congressional campaigns, seldom did more than a midsummer poll for most of its clients. This was perhaps followed by a few tracking polls in the fall. The last poll usually was conducted no later than early October—more than a month before the election. Sometimes the interviewing was done by volunteers supplied by the candidate. Now all of their interviewing is done by permanent employees of the company. A typical incumbent pays for a benchmark poll early in the election year, another poll in the late summer, and perhaps as many as four post-Labor Day tracking polls.

The popularity of polling is reflected in the earnings of the pollsters who worked for congressional candidates in the 1990 election (see Table 5-6). Cooper & Secrest billed candidates and national Democratic committees a total of $1,482,656 in congressional races; Greenberg-Lake of Washington, D.C., billed $1,438,385; Peter D. Hart Strategic Research of Washington billed $1,112,240.

Critics believe that some of this money is being wasted by incumbents who should rely more upon their own political instincts than upon poll results.

"There is no question that polling costs have gone up, and the amount of polling that a campaign does is just out of sight, compared with what it should be," said Bailey. "I'm not sure that it's produced better campaigns, but it certainly has produced more polling."

Still, polling is one of the cheaper items in the modern congressional campaign budget. Even though polling costs have risen, they still represent less than 3 percent of the costs of an average congressional campaign. Pollsters' profit margins are understood to be lower than those of other political consultants, primarily because they must employ large numbers of interviewers and other personnel.

GENERAL AND CAMPAIGN
MANAGEMENT CONSULTANTS

It is sometimes called the "California model," but many candidates in cities and towns all over the country—including Peoria—use it to organize their election bids: they hire a single consultant to manage the campaign. In California, for example, Democrat Calvin Dooley hired Directions, a Sacramento consulting firm headed by Rose King, to run his campaign. King sent several of her assistants to operate Dooley's headquarters in Visalia, Calif., but she called the shots from her office in Sacramento.

"I am responsible for everything—the media, the management, the message," King explained during the 1990 campaign. "I contract with the media guy in Fresno. I contract with a pollster. I do all of the script-writing myself. . . . Primarily, my job is managing the spending of the money. My job is spending it and spending it wisely." For her efforts, which helped Dooley to unseat Rep. Chip Pashayan, R-Calif., King received $85,723—$35,000 of it for consulting.

Likewise, Erickson not only ran Michel's campaign, but she managed his permanent campaign organization as well. Her responsibilities included running a small, in-state direct-mail fund-raising program, arranging fund-raising events, publishing a newsletter for supporters, mailing out 10,000 Christmas cards, sending congratulations to recent graduates, and contracting with other consultants, including a general strategist.

Many of the top campaign management consultants were headquartered in California (see Table 5-7). They included Western Pacific Research Inc. of Bakersfield, which did $209,404 worth of business in 1990; Clinton Reilly Campaigns of San Francisco, which took in $95,124; and Whitehurst & Nelson of San Francisco, which received $87,211. Other top firms included Jenson & Associates of Austin, Texas, which received $194,996, and Eddie Mahe, Jr. & Associates Inc. of Washington, D.C., which brought in $162,865.

In Boston, the firm of Marttila & Kiley Inc. was paid a total of $413,774 to handle a variety of tasks for Kerry's campaign, including $252,518 for general consulting (see Table 5-8).

STAKE IN THE STATUS QUO

No doubt, American politics would be very different without the vast army of campaign consultants that has been organized in both parties over the past two decades. Their impact on political advertising, campaign strategy, and fund-raising practices cannot be overestimated.

The growth in political consulting can be traced back to one primary cause: the availability of large sums of special-interest money. With millions of dollars being pumped into the system each year, it is understandable that enterprising professionals are trying to reap the benefits.

If campaign spending were limited by legislation, the political consulting industry would probably shrink overnight. Understandably, political consultants represent a strong force on behalf of preserving the status quo.

Table 5-1 The Top Fifteen Media Consultants in the 1990 Congressional Races

			Payments		
Rank	Company	City	From Candidate	From Party	Total
1	Squier/Eskew Communications	Washington, D.C.	$7,864,761	$ 355,613	$8,220,374
2	Farrell Media Inc.	New York, N.Y.	4,359,283	1,089,254	5,448,537
3	National Media Inc.	Alexandria, Va.	4,162,234	1,113,351	5,275,585
4	Campaign Management Inc.	Raleigh, N.C.	4,317,361	495,000	4,812,361
5	Pro Media, Inc.	Needham, Mass.	4,674,387	125,000	4,799,387
6	Sawyer/Miller Group	New York, N.Y.	4,390,830	330,000	4,720,830
7	John Franzen Multimedia	Washington, D.C.	3,720,384	125,000	3,845,384
8	Fenn & King Communications	Washington, D.C.	3,621,375	9,785	3,631,160
9	Doak, Shrum & Associates	Washington, D.C.	2,536,747	871,159	3,407,906
10	Creative Media Planning	New York, N.Y.	2,291,312	337,890	2,629,203
11	Raymond D. Strother Ltd.	Washington, D.C.	2,319,359	77,072	2,396,431
12	Greer, Margolis, Mitchell & Associates Inc.	Washington, D.C.	2,168,526	220,000	2,388,526
13	Trippi & Associates	Alexandria, Va.	2,060,974	301,296	2,362,270
14	Western International Media	Los Angeles, Calif.	1,978,313	298,402	2,276,715
15	Campaign Group Inc.	Philadelphia, Pa.	2,247,736	—	2,247,736

Table 5-2 The Top Twenty-Five Spenders in the 1990 Congressional Races: Consultants

Rank	House		Senate	
	Candidate	Expenditures	Candidate	Expenditures
1	Reid Hughes, D-Fla.	$937,235	Jesse Helms, R-N.C.	$10,641,690
2	Ileana Ros-Lehtinen, R-Fla.	856,865	Phil Gramm, R-Texas	7,065,509
3	Jill L. Long, D-Ind.	807,447	Harvey B. Gantt, D-N.C.	5,484,725
4	Robert K. Dornan, R-Calif.	793,152	Paul Simon, D-Ill.	5,425,651
5	Marguerite Chandler, D-N.J.	752,394	Carl Levin, D-Mich.	5,181,938
6	Dick Zimmer, R-N.J.	694,204	John Kerry, D-Mass.	4,511,338
7	David E. Bonior, D-Mich.	663,145	Bill Bradley, D-N.J.	4,345,748
8	John Carrington, R-N.C.	602,931	J. Bennett Johnston, D-La.	3,782,425
9	Sidney R. Yates, D-Ill.	555,624	Mitch McConnell, R-Ky.	3,626,467
10	Gary Condit, D-Calif.	551,377	Rudy Boschwitz, R-Minn.	3,298,871
11	Newt Gingrich, R-Ga.	549,205	Tom Harkin, D-Iowa	3,280,779
12	Richard A. Gephardt, D-Mo.	545,555	Lynn Martin, R-Ill.	2,755,969
13	Jim Ramstad, R-Minn.	542,459	Howell Heflin, D-Ala.	2,243,193
14	Jim Bacchus, D-Fla.	539,903	Hank Brown, R-Colo.	2,191,153
15	Rosa DeLauro, D-Conn.	533,026	Daniel R. Coats, R-Ind.	2,186,304
16	David E. Price, D-N.C.	525,222	Tom Tauke, R-Iowa	1,745,638
17	Philip R. Sharp, D-Ind.	514,655	Jim Exon, D-Neb.	1,523,328
18	Glen Browder, D-Ala.	508,772	Claiborne Pell, D-R.I.	1,507,022
19	Jack Buechner, R-Mo.	472,272	Claudine Schneider, R-R.I.	1,496,526
20	Toby Moffett, D-Conn.	468,573	Patricia Saiki, R-Hawaii	1,457,947
21	H. James Saxton, R-N.J.	454,178	Jim Rappaport, R-Mass.	1,376,950
22	Chester G. Atkins, D-Mass.	437,981	Bill Schuette, R-Mich.	1,228,985
23	George E. Brown, Jr., D-Calif.	433,752	Mark O. Hatfield, R-Ore.	1,190,702
24	Doug Barnard, Jr., D-Ga.	417,136	Max Baucus, D-Mont.	1,127,741
25	Roy Dyson, D-Md.	412,583	John D. Rockefeller IV, D-W.Va.	1,095,641

Note: Totals for the House are for the entire two-year cycle, including special elections; totals for the Senate are for the entire six-year cycle.

Table 5-3 The Top Fifteen Promotional Mail Consultants in the 1990 Congressional Races

Rank	Company	City	Payments From Candidate	Payments From Party	Total
1	Campaign Performance Group	Washington, D.C.	$1,281,481	$ 26,940	$1,308,421
2	Bates & Associates	Washington, D.C.	640,574	—	640,574
3	Welch Communications	Arlington, Va.	307,653	139,379	447,032
4	Russo, Marsh, & Associates Inc.	Sacramento, Calif.	230,767	186,775	417,541
5	James R. Foster & Associates	Carrollton, Texas	213,809	148,492	362,301
6	Odell Roper & Associates Inc.	Golden, Calif.	300,431	—	300,431
7	The November Group Inc.	Washington, D.C.	291,768	—	291,768
8	Below, Tobe & Associates, Inc.	Bethesda, Md.	242,468	1,914	244,382
9	Whitehurst & Nelson	San Francisco, Calif.	212,320	6,000	218,320
10	Quinn & Associates	Columbia, S.C.	—	206,845	206,845
11	Clinton Reilly Campaigns	San Francisco, Calif.	195,619	—	195,619
12	Public Office Corp.	Washington, D.C.	187,371	—	187,371
13	Campaign Strategies Inc.	Houston, Texas	178,366	—	178,366
14	Lukens Co.	Arlington, Va.	41,657	127,727	169,384
15	Karl Rove & Company	Austin, Texas	105,863	52,534	158,397

Table 5-4 The Top Fifteen Fund-Raising Event Consultants in the 1990 Congressional Races

| Rank | Company | City | Payments | | Total |
			From Candidate	From Party	
1	Steven H. Gordon & Associates	St. Paul, Minn.	$524,877	—	$524,877
2	PM Consulting Corp.	Washington, D.C.	502,905	—	502,905
3	Creative Campaign Consultant	Washington, D.C.	432,860	—	432,860
4	Barbara Klein Associates	Washington, D.C.	302,817	—	302,817
5	Amy Zisook & Assocoates	Chicago, Ill.	294,156	—	294,156
6	Barbara Silby & Associates	Potomac, Md.	251,726	$ 2,250	253,976
7	Paula Levine	Washington, D.C.	237,416	11,800	249,216
8	Dan Morgan & Associates	Arlington, Va.	244,832	—	244,832
9	Patricia Hurley	Chicago, Ill.	242,326	—	242,326
10	Erickson & Co.	Washington, D.C.	215,279	—	215,279
11	Robert H. Bassin Associates Inc.	Washington, D.C.	194,696	18,000	212,696
12	Hammelman Associates	Arlington, Va.	211,040	—	211,040
13	Fraioli/Jost	Washington, D.C.	194,961	—	194,961
14	Sheehan Associates Inc.	Washington, D.C.	163,982	—	163,982
15	Jim Wise Associates	Alexandria, Va.	149,108	—	149,108

Table 5-5 The Top Fifteen Fund-Raising Direct-Mail Consultants in the 1990 Congressional Races

Rank	Company	City	Payments		Total
			From Candidate	From Party	
1	Coyle, McConnell, & O'Brien	Washington, D.C.	$2,979,081	—	$2,979,081
2	A.B. Data Ltd.	Milwaukee, Wis.	2,260,655	—	2,260,655
3	Response Dynamics	Vienna, Va.	1,872,116	—	1,872,116
4	Karl Rove & Company	Austin, Texas	1,757,293	—	1,757,293
5	Bruce W. Eberle & Associates Inc.	Vienna, Va.	1,338,783	—	1,338,783
6	Computer Operations	Raleigh, N.C.	1,246,726	—	1,246,726
7	Jefferson Marketing	Raleigh, N.C.	1,129,028	—	1,129,028
8	Odell Roper & Associates Inc.	Golden, Colo.	1,102,294	—	1,102,294
9	James R. Foster & Associates	Carrollton, Texas	713,230	—	713,230
10	Direct Mail Specialists	Ocean Springs, Miss.	631,609	—	631,609
11	Discount Paper Broker	Raleigh, N.C.	603,142	—	603,142
12	PM Consulting Corp.	Washington, D.C.	545,252	—	545,252
13	Sam K. Pate Associates Inc.	Forest, Va.	522,009	—	522,009
14	Communication Specialists	Austin, Texas	398,973	—	398,973
15	Gold Communications Co. Inc.	Austin, Texas	327,830	—	327,830

Table 5-6 The Top Fifteen Pollsters in the 1990 Congressional Races

| Rank | Company | City | Payments | | Total |
			From Candidate	From Party	
1	Cooper & Secrest Associates	Alexandria, Va.	$1,476,906	$ 5,750	$1,482,656
2	Greenberg-Lake	Washington, D.C.	1,400,885	37,500	1,438,385
3	Peter D. Hart Strategic Research	Washington, D.C.	1,053,704	58,536	1,112,240
4	Mellman & Lazarus Inc.	Washington, D.C.	900,214	108,385	1,008,600
5	Tarrance & Associates	Houston, Texas	1,001,338	4,500	1,005,838
6	Joe Peritz & Associates	Wilton, Conn.	913,491	—	913,491
7	Hickman-Maslin Research Inc.	Washington, D.C.	761,089	7,000	768,089
8	American Viewpoint	Alexandria, Va.	681,033	27,893	708,926
9	Wirthlin Group	McLean, Va.	667,516	7,500	675,016
10	Donilan & Petts	Washington, D.C.	562,530	56,510	619,040
11	Marttila & Kiley Inc.	Boston, Mass.	399,671	11,000	410,671
12	Lawrence Research	Santa Ana, Calif.	376,862	—	376,862
13	Penn & Schoen Associates	New York, N.Y.	347,574	28,000	375,574
14	Market Strategies Inc.	Southfield, Mich.	372,531	—	372,531
15	Arthur J. Finkelstein & Associates	New York, N.Y.	364,170	—	364,170

Table 5-7 The Top Fifteen Management Consultants in the 1990 Congressional Races

| Rank | Company | City | Payments | | Total |
			From Candidate	From Party	
1	Campaigns & Elections Inc.	Peoria, Ill.	$291,728	—	$291,728
2	Western Pacific Research Inc.	Bakersfield, Calif.	209,404	—	209,404
3	Jenson & Associates	Austin, Texas	194,996	—	194,996
4	Eddie Mahe, Jr. & Associates Inc.	Washington, D.C.	162,865	—	162,865
5	Carol Reed Associates Inc.	Dallas, Texas	144,677	—	144,677
6	Clinton Reilly Campaigns	San Francisco, Calif.	95,124	—	95,124
7	Whitehurst & Nelson	San Francisco, Calif.	87,211	—	87,211
8	Research/Strategy/Management	Washington, D.C.	85,925	—	85,925
9	Townsend & Company	Sacramento, Calif.	75,864	—	75,864
10	Attention! Inc.	Naperville, Ill.	75,480	—	75,480
11	Kuwata Communications	Santa Monica, Calif.	71,069	—	71,069
12	Campaign Strategies, Inc.	Houston, Texas	69,894	—	69,894
13	Anne Stanley	Alexandria, Va.	69,362	—	69,362
14	Ed Brookover	Burke, Va.	59,689	—	59,689
15	Directions	Anchorage, Alaska	58,458	—	58,458

Table 5-8 The Top Fifteen General Consultants in the 1990 Congressional Races

Rank	Company	City	Payments From Candidate	Payments From Party	Total
1	Marttila & Kiley Inc.	Boston, Mass.	$252,518	—	$252,518
2	Coldwater Corp.	Ann Arbor, Mich.	194,277	—	194,277
3	Campaign Consultants Inc.	Alexandria, Va.	168,988	—	168,988
4	Jim Robinson Associates	Sioux Falls, S.D.	124,542	$23,704	148,246
5	Research/Strategy/Management	Washington, D.C.	133,770	—	133,770
6	Tony Payton & Associates	Arlington, Va.	126,967	—	126,967
7	Joe Gaylord	Washington, D.C.	97,311	—	97,311
8	Rivers Trainor Doyle	Providence, R.I.	97,196	—	97,196
9	Colorado Media Group Inc.	Englewood, Colo.	93,992	—	93,992
10	Clinton Reilly Campaigns	San Francisco, Calif.	89,004	—	89,004
11	Sante Fe Associates	Sarasota, Fla.	87,620	—	87,620
12	Ed Brookover	Burke, Va.	85,997	—	85,997
13	The DCM Group	McLean, Va.	83,682	—	83,682
14	Randy Hinaman	Alexandria, Va.	76,300	—	76,300
15	The Cottington Company	Alexandria, Va.	75,430	—	75,430

CHAPTER 6

Television
At What Cost?

In Senate elections, television advertising costs consume the
majority of a candidate's budget. Such costs constitute the
fastest growing item in that budget. If these costs were
significantly curtailed, the budget of each candidate would be
dwarfed.
Sen. William V. Roth, Jr., R-Del., in a 1990 Senate speech

Perhaps the biggest misconception in American politics today is
the notion that candidates spend most of their campaign funds
on television advertising. For years, rising television advertising
rates have been blamed for driving up the cost of political advertising,
particularly for Senate candidates. Some senators will even tell you
that they spend as much as 75 percent of their campaign funds on
broadcast ads.

The impact of television costs on campaigns has been wildly exaggerated. In the 1990 election, only 29 percent of the money spent by
congressional candidates went for radio and television advertising and
media consultants. On average, broadcast advertising accounted for
35 percent of the money spent by Senate candidates and 23 percent of
the money spent by House candidates.

These findings came as a shock to many people, even those who
would be expected to be familiar with the true costs of campaign
advertising. "I'm surprised by that," said Sen. John C. Danforth,
R-Mo., a leading advocate for legislation to cut broadcast costs. "It
is certainly not the conventional wisdom." Democratic media consultant Frank Greer, of the Washington, D.C.-based firm Greer,
Margolis, Mitchell & Associates, Inc., remarked: "If you had asked
me how much was spent on media, I would have guessed 75 percent."

There are several reasons why these and many other experts have
overestimated the true costs of television ads. First of all, advertising
did represent the biggest single expenditure for the average Senate

campaign, even though overhead and fund-raising costs were close behind. In addition, media consultants have always recommended that candidates spend as much as possible on broadcast advertising, and it long has been assumed that the candidates were following that advice. Among media consultants, it is unchallenged dogma that successful Senate candidates never spend less than 75 percent of their money on television in a close race or 50 percent of their money on television in all other races.

Even in extremely close races, where the winner received 60 percent or less of the vote, the average spending on all media—television, radio, newspapers, and billboards—did not exceed 36 percent. In fact, not one Senate candidate in 1990 spent as much as 75 percent of his campaign treasury on media. Only three candidates—Sen. Mitch McConnell, R-Ky.; Democrat Harvey B. Gantt, who unsuccessfully challenged Sen. Jesse Helms, R-N.C.; and Democrat Harry Lonsdale, who unsuccessfully challenged Sen. Mark O. Hatfield, R-Ore.—spent as much as 60 percent of their funds on ads. Only seven other Senate candidates spent at least 50 percent of their treasuries on media.

Of course, there were no 1990 Senate contests in California or New York, two places where statewide candidates are thought to depend most heavily on television advertising. Still, there was no shortage in 1990 of well-financed races in states such as Texas, Michigan, New Jersey, Hawaii, and Illinois, where campaign advertising is expensive.

These findings raise questions about the necessity of efforts by some members of Congress to reduce campaign costs by legislating lower television ad rates. The 102nd Congress passed—and President George Bush vetoed—a campaign finance reform bill that, among other things, would have guaranteed a 50 percent broadcast discount in the final forty-five days of the election to candidates who agreed to abide by very liberal spending limits.

Television discounts undoubtedly would help to lower campaign costs. Danforth argued that "any reduction in the costs of campaigns is an advantage." But it probably would not create the huge windfall anticipated by some proponents of cut-rate media. Nor would it necessarily bring down overall campaign costs. On the contrary, if broadcast costs were lowered, members of Congress would probably invest the savings either in buying more television time or in building a stronger, more elaborate permanent campaign organization.

"Candidates will continue to raise as much money as they can and spend as much as they need to win," said Michael J. Conly, senior vice president of Hartke-Hanks Communications of San Antonio, Texas, and an active member of the National Association of Broadcasters (NAB). "It is entirely likely that any savings from broadcast expenses will easily be spent in other ways." *

Television advertising rates did decline slightly immediately prior to the 1990 election as a result of pressure brought to bear on station owners by the Federal Communications Commission (FCC). The price break was greeted by candidates as an opportunity to buy more television air time to compensate for the declining number of viewers now watching each channel.

"What [a lower rate] means is that we can do more television or do more effective television," said Greg Stevens, who did political advertising for media consultant Roger Ailes in the 1990 election. "It means that candidates will get more bang for their buck."

Until recently, complaints about the high costs of television advertising have provided a strong impetus within Congress for enacting campaign finance reform. But the decline in rates, combined with the results of the survey on television expenditures first published in the *Los Angeles Times* in March 1991, have somewhat dampened the crusade for television discounts.

Even though television expenditures were not as big as most experts thought, candidates for Congress still spent incredibly large sums on political advertising. As Danforth noted, "Thirty-five percent of a Senate campaign in the state of Missouri is a whole lot of dough."

In all, congressional candidates spent about $119 million on broadcast advertising in the 1990 election, and many media consultants made a handsome living from their work on these campaigns. Broadcast costs comprised the bulk of most candidates' total advertising expenditures (see Tables 6-1 and 6-2).

In Senate races, Helms spent more than $5 million on broadcast costs; his challenger, Gantt, $4.4 million; Sen. Carl Levin, D-Mich., $3.9 million; Sen. Bill Bradley, D-N.J., $3.3 million; McConnell, $3.1 million; Sen. J. Bennett Johnston, D-La., $3.1 million; and Sen. Phil Gramm, R-Texas, nearly $3.1 million.

* Michael J. Conly, senior vice president, Hartke-Hanks Communications, testimony before Senate Rules and Administration Committee, March 14, 1991.

The Helms race demonstrates vividly why advertising costs are not a higher percentage of a candidate's total spending. Even though he invested $5 million in broadcast media, it amounted to only 28 percent of his total budget because he spent more than $11.4 million—or 64 percent of his total outlays—on fund raising. Like Helms, three other big spenders in the 1990 race—Sens. Paul Simon, D-Ill., Bradley, and Gramm—devoted less than 30 percent of their funds to broadcast advertising.

In the House, the leading spenders on television advertising were two challengers who lost, North Carolina Republican John Carrington and Florida Democrat Reid Hughes. Carrington spent $682,657, or 82 percent of his money, on broadcast advertising; Hughes spent $648,160, or 55 percent. Rep. Ileana Ros-Lehtinen, R-Fla., spent $712,428 on both her 1989 special election and her 1990 race.

Rep. Claude Harris, D-Ala., was one of the few House incumbents who spent as much as 60 percent of his funds on media. In his case, however, 60 percent was a mere $140,000. Harris decided to spend a lot of money on broadcast advertising because he feared the reelection of Republican governor Guy Hunt would help all Republicans, including his opponent.

Many well-funded House incumbents never do any television advertising. This is especially common in large metropolitan areas containing numerous congressional districts. Many House members see it as a waste of money to buy advertising on major television stations when voters in their district comprise just a fraction of the viewing audience. These candidates normally rely on lower-priced advertising on radio or cable stations, if they use any broadcast media at all. In 1990, 182 House members spent less than $10,000 on broadcast advertising, including 127 incumbents who spent nothing on such ads.

In the Senate, however, candidates who have no opposition still may use broadcast advertising during an election. Often this occurs because senators retain their media consultants before they know whether or not they will have an opponent. Sen. John W. Warner, R-Va., for example, spent $237,158 on broadcast advertising even though he had no Democratic challenger. He never ran the television ads that he produced.

When it comes to buying television advertising, Senate challengers are normally at a big disadvantage. Although Gantt spent nearly as much as Helms, he was an exception. On average, incumbents spent twice what challengers spent on broadcast advertising. Levin bought nearly five times—or nearly $3.1 million—more on advertising than his opponent, Rep. Bill Schuette, R-Mich. Bradley barely defeated his challenger, Christine Todd Whitman, even though he spent $3.3 million on broadcast advertising compared with her $178,130.

It is not impossible for challengers who spend less on television to win, of course, as Democrat Paul Wellstone proved in his race against Sen. Rudy Boschwitz, R-Minn. Boschwitz spent nearly $1.6 million on media to Wellstone's $575,918. Yet despite his spending disadvantage, Wellstone had the help of an unusually inexpensive and highly inventive media consultant, Northwoods Advertising, which since has won awards for devising ads that made a virtue out of the challenger's lack of funding.

Likewise, Democrat Pete Peterson unseated incumbent Rep. Bill Grant, R-Fla., with low-cost television ads produced primarily with volunteer help. Peterson spent less than $82,000 on broadcast advertising; Grant spent more than $259,000. One of Peterson's most effective ads, which cost only $1,800 to produce, showed an acrobat doing back flips in front of the state capital while a voice-over explained how Grant had switched from the Democratic party to the GOP. It was later designated by a local newspaper as the best ad of the political season.

But few challengers approach television advertising like Wellstone or Peterson. Most seek out high-paid consultants to handle their media campaign.

Despite a few notable exceptions in the 1990 cycle, television advertising still appears to affect the outcome of hotly contested congressional races more than any other single expenditure. With $3.1 million to spend on advertising, Johnston had the resources necessary to run repeated ads showing an old film clip of his challenger, David Duke, making a Nazi-style salute to a burning cross. Media adviser John Franzen of the Washington, D.C.-based firm of John Franzen Multimedia, estimated that the average Louisiana household saw that ad eight times. In fact, Franzen credited the ad with turning the tide against Duke. In addition, Johnston's huge war chest enabled Franzen to produce forty-two different spots for the Democratic incumbent, many of them customized for particular regions of Louisiana where accents and attitudes are different.

In North Carolina, Rep. W. G. "Bill" Hefner, D-N.C., used television particularly effectively against his Republican challenger, Ted Blanton. Hefner's ads succeeded in making Blanton the issue in the election by attacking him for using his campaign treasury to pay $20,678 in personal expenses. In a scathing negative ad, Hefner charged that Blanton "even used it to pay for baby sitters."

Nobody knows better the power of television advertising than McConnell, who captured his Senate seat in 1984 with the help of a television spot that spoofed incumbent Walter "Dee" Huddleston's low voting record by showing bloodhounds searching for him. In 1990, McConnell ran an aggressive media campaign against his challenger, former Louisville mayor Harvey I. Sloane. He began planning his media strategy eighteen months before the 1990 general election by hiring Ailes Communications of New York for early consultations at a cost of $180,000. He ultimately retooled his old bloodhound ad for maximum impact. In the final analysis, McConnell spent $3.1 million on media, compared to Sloane's $606,261.

During the past few years, there has been a lively debate between members of Congress and the nation's broadcasters over who is responsible for rising campaign costs. Congress blamed broadcast rates; the broadcasters insisted they were not to blame. Both sides even produced studies to support their own points of view.

Our findings were generally consistent with studies conducted by the National Association of Broadcasters after the 1986 and 1988 congressional elections, which also were based on spending reports submitted to the Federal Election Commission. In 1986, the NAB study found, House members spent an average of 15.8 percent on broadcast advertising and Senate candidates spent an average of 34 percent. In 1988, the NAB's figures were 19.3 percent for the House and 41.1 percent for the Senate. At the time they were first made public, the NAB studies were widely ridiculed by members of Congress for being biased in favor of the broadcasters.

Our survey contradicted a study published in September 1990 by the Congressional Research Service (CRS), a branch of the Library of Congress that provides members of Congress and committees with information. The CRS study set the level of spending on broadcast advertising at 53.5 percent for Senate races and 39.5 percent for House races. The study was based on questionnaires filled out by major party candidates in competitive races in the 1988 election.

Whatever reduction has already occurred in broadcast rates for political candidates can be attributed to the relentless pressure that members of Congress have put on broadcasters and the FCC. Shortly before the 1990 election, the FCC responded to that pressure by conducting a surprise audit of thirty radio and television stations in five major metropolitan markets. The agency found many instances in which candidates were required to pay higher rates for comparable time than commercial advertisers. For example, the FCC found that one station had charged political candidates $4,000 for the same spot that was selling for between $575 and $2,500 to commercial clients.

The investigation sent a shock wave through the broadcasting industry, causing a quick drop of as much as 50 percent in the political ad rates of some stations right before the 1990 election and prompting a spate of lawsuits by politicians who accused television stations of overcharging.

In the view of most politicians, the broadcasters had been ignoring a 1972 law that required them to give candidates the lowest unit rate charged to commercial advertisers. Politicians are often frustrated because the stations no longer set fixed rates for broadcast time. Instead, the broadcasters tend to auction off valuable time slots and they charge higher rates for time slots that cannot be preempted by a higher paying advertiser.

Commercial advertisers generally do not object to being preempted, but politicians do not want to be preempted in the days immediately prior to an election. Politicians also claim that the broadcasters do not disclose all the pricing options to political advertisers. Danforth has argued that some television stations have been setting arbitrary rates for candidates, depending on whether the station executives support the candidate.

As a result of the FCC's intervention, television ad rates are likely to continue to be lower for political advertisers in the foreseeable future, at least through the 1992 elections. On December 12, 1991, the FCC announced that it had decided to take jurisdiction in lawsuits involving rate disputes between politicians and broadcasters, and the agency established expedited procedures for adjudicating these cases.

According to Robert S. Kahn, an Atlanta lawyer and Democratic party leader who has represented politicians in these suits, the lower rates are likely to ease tensions between politicians and broadcasters for a while. "If the stations have any sense they are going to look pretty clean for the next couple of years," Kahn said. "Broadcasters would be crazy to allow some of their old tricks."

As for the broadcasters, they claim that the problem stems from greed and ignorance on the part of media consultants, who were not seeking lower advertising rates from the television stations because their fees are based on a percentage of the overall expenditures.

"A good case can be made that it is the consultants who are as responsible as anyone for the increase in campaign spending, particularly for TV advertising," said Conly. "Working on commissions based on how much advertising is bought, these consultants have a built-in incentive to use TV more so as to increase their own piece of the pie. . . . Time-buying becomes a double hit for consultants. They urge candidates to buy more time, which increases their commission, and they insist that the spots be fixed, which raises the cost even higher."

To some extent, candidates for Congress wasted money on campaign advertising. Challengers hired big-name media consultants in an effort to get the attention of the political establishment in Washington, D.C. As political analyst Norman J. Ornstein put it, "One of the ways you can sell yourself to PACs is to say, 'I've hired Doak and Shrum.'" All too frequently, they spend too much early in the campaign to pay these consultants and then have little money left to air their ads in the crucial final days.

In Colorado, the open seat race between Republican Wayne Allard and Democrat Dick Bond hinged on the decisions they made about television advertising. Bond invested heavily in media consultants early in the race; Allard saved his money for last-minute media buys. Allard's last-minute ads on Denver television were thought to be crucial in his victory.

At the same time, there were many examples in the 1990 election of candidates who produced effective television advertising without relying on big-name media consultants, much as Wellstone and Peterson did. One common technique is for candidates to buy prefabricated ads supplied by their party organization and then to provide their own voice-over. Like many others, Rep. Glenn Poshard, D-Ill., made his ads cheaply by filming them at Harriman Communications Center, the Democratic broadcast studios on Capitol Hill. "I just sat down in front of the camera and talked," he recalled. "It wasn't very fancy."

Likewise, Democratic House candidate Thomas H. Andrews of

Maine, lacking enough money to produce a normal ad, made two ads out of black-and-white still photographs with a voice-over. "After the primary," recalled Dennis Bailey, Andrews's press secretary, "there were newspaper articles written about our craftiness in putting together this simple, family album video, but in reality it was done for entirely budgetary reasons."

Cable television advertising offers a low-cost alternative that has become increasingly popular among political candidates, particularly underfunded challengers. *Cable World* magazine predicted that the industry would receive $100 million in political advertising during the 1992 election cycle as a result of a gradual shift away from the major broadcast channels.

Some candidates were already using cable frequently in 1990. "Out here in the hinterlands, there are cable outlets where you can buy a thirty-second spot for $1," explained Michael Daly, district chief of staff for Rep. Richard J. Durbin, D-Ill. "They frequently have a minimum number of spots you have to buy, say 200, but that's still only $200."

Cable also was being used increasingly by congressional candidates in big metropolitan areas, who have never found advertising on the major television broadcast outlets to be cost-effective. Not only did many candidates see cable advertising as cheap, but it provided them an opportunity to target certain types of voters concentrated in their districts. Hispanic candidates, for example, said it was to their advantage to advertise on Spanish-language cable stations.

Some candidates were even mailing videotaped advertisements to their potential supporters, figuring that this was cheaper than the traditional broadcast advertising.

Television advertising was by no means limited to candidates with opposition. Unopposed incumbents spent a total of nearly $1 million on radio and television advertising in 1990. Some said they felt compelled to advertise on television just to keep their name firmly imbedded in the public consciousness. "There were points during the campaign when we discussed not doing any advertising," recalled Ron Hardman, chief of staff to Rep. John T. Myers, R-Ind. "But we found that many people didn't realize we were running again because of the lack of a real campaign. It was a reminder that we were on the ticket."

In fact, some incumbents appeared to advertise on television simply because they had the money to do so. Rep. Richard Baker, R-La., paid National Media of Alexandria, Va., $10,400 to produce ads for his campaign, even though he has not had an opponent since he was first elected in 1986. "They were 'thank you' spots," explained Tim Carpenter, a staff assistant. "We wanted people to know that we don't take this position for granted. And we wanted to stay visible."

A few candidates reported spending money on advertising simply to curry favor with the local broadcasters and newspaper publishers, whose endorsement was helpful to them.

Even though he faced a challenger with no money, Rep. Alex Mc-Millan, R-N.C., spent more than $200,000 on advertising because he feared he might otherwise suffer voter backlash as a side effect of the contentious senatorial battle being waged in his state. These ads were run simply to separate him from the highly publicized Helms and Gantt race. "We felt like a runt in the back of the classroom waving our arms saying, 'Hey, don't forget about me,'" said Jay Severin, McMillan's media consultant.

While many members of Congress do not rely heavily on television advertising—at least not as heavily as they often claim they do—they certainly do not hesitate to use it whenever they perceive a need of any kind. With ready access to special-interest money, the costs of television advertising are of little consequence to most incumbents when they weigh the question of whether to air broadcast ads.

Table 6-1 The Top Twenty-Five Spenders in the 1990 Congressional Races: Total Advertising

Rank	House		Senate	
	Candidate	Expenditures	Candidate	Expenditures
1	Ileana Ros-Lehtinen, R-Fla.	$767,315	Jesse Helms, R-N.C.	$5,050,706
2	John Carrington, R-Fla.	692,811	Harvey B. Gantt, D-N.C.	4,667,433
3	Reid Hughes, D-Fla.	653,080	Carl Levin, D-Mich.	3,895,859
4	David E. Bonior, D-Mich.	552,749	Bill Bradley, D-N.J.	3,316,678
5	Pete Geren, D-Texas	547,281	Mitch McConnell, R-Ky.	3,190,153
6	Craig Thomas, R-Wyo.	529,462	Jim Rappaport, R-Mass.	3,151,580
7	Patsy T. Mink, D-Hawaii	521,221	J. Bennett Johnston, D-La.	3,083,711
8	Jim Ramstad, R-Minn.	474,534	Phil Gramm, R-Texas	3,064,318
9	Philip R. Sharp, D-Ind.	459,038	Paul Simon, D-Ill.	2,326,879
10	Wayne Owens, D-Utah	456,449	Howell Heflin, D-Ala.	2,002,861
11	Charles Luken, D-Ohio	455,503	Tom Harkin, D-Iowa	1,945,204
12	Jack Buechner, R-Mo.	446,154	John Kerry, D-Mass.	1,852,713
13	Dick Zimmer, R-N.J.	429,336	Lynn Martin, R-Ill.	1,701,015
14	David Price, D-N.C.	425,016	Hank Brown, R-Colo.	1,697,906
15	Jolene Unsoeld, D-Wash.	423,700	Rudy Boschwitz, R-Minn.	1,615,724
16	Sidney R. Yates, D-Ill.	419,743	Daniel R. Coats, R-Ind.	1,349,554
17	Toby Moffett, D-Conn.	412,830	Tom Tauke, R-Iowa	1,318,452
18	Bill Zeliff, R-N.H.	412,714	Claudine Schneider, R-R.I.	1,245,737
19	James P. Moran, Jr., D-Va.	407,329	Patricia Saiki, R-Hawaii	1,213,771
20	John F. Reed, D-R.I.	405,855	Jim Exon, D-Neb.	1,186,844
21	Charles Wilson, D-Texas	394,180	Claiborne Pell, D-R.I.	1,121,793
22	D. French Slaughter, Jr., R-Va.	392,625	Mark O. Hatfield, R-Ore.	1,037,439
23	Richard A. Gephardt, D-Mo.	384,883	Neil Rolde, D-Maine	898,137
24	Rosa DeLauro, D-Conn.	378,585	Max Baucus, D-Mont.	895,422
25	Marguerite Chandler, D-N.J.	378,553	Harry Lonsdale, D-Ore.	867,706

Note: Totals for the House are for the entire two-year cycle, including special elections; totals for the Senate are for the entire six-year cycle.

Table 6-2 The Top Twenty-Five Spenders in the 1990 Congressional Races: Radio and Television Advertising

Rank	House Candidate	Expenditures	Senate Candidate	Expenditures
1	Ileana Ros-Lehtinen, R-Fla.	$712,428	Jesse Helms, R-N.C.	$5,023,452
2	John Carrington, R-N.C.	682,657	Harvey B. Gantt, D-N.C.	4,395,016
3	Reid Hughes, D-Fla.	648,160	Carl Levin, D-Mich.	3,885,827
4	David E. Bonior, D-Mich.	543,823	Bill Bradley, D-N.J.	3,314,628
5	Pete Geren, D-Texas	525,333	Mitch McConnell, R-Ky.	3,122,009
6	Craig Thomas, R-Wyo.	503,167	J. Bennett Johnston, D-La.	3,077,133
7	Philip R. Sharp, D-Ind.	456,179	Phil Gramm, R-Texas	3,050,927
8	Charles Luken, D-Ohio	453,261	Jim Rappaport, R-Mass.	2,856,178
9	Patsy T. Mink, D-Hawaii	448,686	Paul Simon, D-Ill.	2,309,272
10	Jack Buechner, R-Mo.	441,190	Howell Heflin, D-Ala.	1,990,542
11	Dick Zimmer, R-N.J.	428,906	Tom Harkin, D-Iowa	1,925,233
12	Wayne Owens, D-Utah	426,397	John Kerry, D-Mass.	1,821,728
13	David Price, D-N.C.	416,569	Lynn Martin, R-Ill.	1,674,455
14	Jolene Unsoeld, D-Wash.	412,967	Hank Brown, R-Colo.	1,661,529
15	Jim Ramstad, R-Minn.	404,444	Rudy Boschwitz, R-Minn.	1,579,136
16	James P. Moran, Jr., D-Va.	402,000	Daniel R. Coats, R-Ind.	1,347,202
17	John F. Reed, D-R.I.	398,857	Tom Tauke, R-Iowa	1,290,915
18	Toby Moffett, D-Conn.	395,712	Claudine Schneider, R-R.I.	1,237,610
19	D. French Slaughter, Jr., R-Va.	391,369	Patricia Saiki, R-Hawaii	1,197,157
20	Richard A. Gephardt, D-Mo.	382,713	Jim Exon, D-Neb.	1,173,100
21	Marguerite Chandler, D-N.J.	376,624	Claiborne Pell, D-R.I.	1,108,499
22	Rosa DeLauro, D-Conn.	372,145	Mark O. Hatfield, R-Ore.	957,016
23	Jim Bacchus, D-Fla.	367,111	Harry Lonsdale, D-Ore.	866,495
24	Jill L. Long, D-Ind.	361,772	Neil Rolde, D-Maine	850,000
25	J. Kenneth Blackwell, R-Ohio	355,188	Max Baucus, D-Mont.	843,431

Note: Totals for the House are for the entire two-year cycle, including special elections; totals for the Senate are for the entire six-year cycle.

CHAPTER 7

Fund Raising
More Than Money

R
ep. Stephen J. Solarz, D-N.Y., represents a heavily Jewish district in Brooklyn, N.Y., but many of his most loyal supporters are not Jewish and they live nowhere near Brooklyn. They are the more than 18,000 Asian-Americans across the United States who regularly send him campaign contributions.

Solarz, chairman of the House subcommittee on Asian and Pacific Affairs, has fostered a sizable Asian-American following by implementing one of the most savvy direct-mail fund-raising schemes currently in operation in Congress. Not only did it enable him to raise more than $600,000 in small donations during 1990, but it also provided him with an unshakable, national political base.

While Solarz's direct-mail fund raising was more sophisticated than most, many members of Congress use fund raising as a tool to extend their influence as well as to fatten their campaign treasuries. In modern congressional politics, fund raising is an integral part of incumbents' strategy to build and enlarge their own permanent political machines.

Fund raising provides both the money and the contacts important to any politician who wants to be successful. As a result, the economics of successful fund raising are more complex than one might expect. It is not always a simple matter of spending as little money as possible to raise as much as possible, although some members of Congress do view it that way. Fund-raising costs frequently reflect political objectives that go beyond the goal of simply raising money for a campaign.

For members of Congress who are considering running for higher office, national fund raising is often their only avenue for building a broader constituency. Fund raising is usually the first step in identifying potential supporters and people who also might be willing to raise money for the candidate. In the 1990 campaign cycle, for example, the first sign that three California Democrats—Reps. Mel Levine, Barbara Boxer, and Robert T. Matsui—were preparing to run for the Senate came when they began seeking money from a diverse group of people beyond their districts and home state.

Solarz's prodigious fund raising also has caused widespread speculation that he might be quietly plotting to run for the Senate in a few years.

For those who see themselves representing a minority view in Congress, usually either on the far right or left, nationwide fund raising is the way to demonstrate the power and popularity of their ideas. No one doubts that Sen. Jesse Helms's influence in Congress has been enhanced by the millions of dollars of contributions that the North Carolina Republican routinely raises from conservatives around the country.

That is clearly why Rep. William E. Dannemeyer, R-Calif., experimented with direct mail in 1990. Not only was he considering a Senate bid, but his direct-mail program also enabled him to generate support for his conservative views on the AIDS crisis. Because his ideas make him vulnerable to attack, Dannemeyer said, "I figured I'd better expand my own constituency beyond the boundaries of my district."

Almost by definition, candidates who depend heavily upon political action committee contributions receive much of their money from out of state, since most PACs are headquartered in Washington, D.C., and the decisions are made there. But many candidates also tour the big cities seeking contributions of up to $2,000 each from wealthy individuals, usually corporate executives, investment bankers, or partners in major law firms—another fast-growing source of special-interest money.

In 1990, about 350 congressional candidates, most of them incumbents, financed their campaigns primarily with large contributions ($200 or more) coming from individuals and PACs located beyond the borders of their own states. Sen. Bill Bradley, D-N.J., received nearly $5 million in out-of-state individual and PAC contributions in

1990—more than $900,000 of it from Californians and nearly $1.8 million from New York residents. His out-of-state receipts exceeded those of all other congressional candidates (see Table 7-1).

Some House candidates raised virtually all their money outside their home states in 1990. Rep. William J. Coyne, D-Pa., received 93 percent of his funds from out-of-state sources. Democrat Dick Swett, a challenger who upset Rep. Chuck Douglas, R-N.H., received 88 percent of his money from out-of-state sources, much of it raised for him by his father-in-law, Rep. Tom Lantos, D-Calif. Other representatives whose funds came primarily from out-of-state sources were: Bernard J. Dwyer, D-N.J., 89 percent; William L. Clay, D-Mo., 87 percent; Jim McDermott, D-Wash., 87 percent; Mary Rose Oakar, D-Ohio, 87 percent; and John D. Dingell, D-Mich., 87 percent.

Even Levine, who represented an affluent Los Angeles district centered in Santa Monica, did not raise the bulk of his money within his own district. Instead, he raised most of it in nearby Beverly Hills.

This search for out-of-state and out-of-district money has prompted an outcry from reformers, who properly reason that it has caused politicians to lose touch with their constituents and has encouraged them to represent interests that are not identical to those of their region. Reformers promote an old-fashioned notion that members of Congress gain a better sense of the sentiments of their constituents if they depend upon those constituents to finance their campaigns.

As a result, out-of-state money is often portrayed as tainted. "There is a perception, even among the politicians themselves, that in-state money is cleaner than out-of-state money," said Ellen Miller, executive director of the Center for Responsive Politics, a bipartisan group advocating campaign finance reform.

A poll conducted in 1990 by Greenberg-Lake, a well-known Washington, D.C., polling firm, showed that a majority of Americans would support legislation requiring congressional candidates to raise the bulk of their money from within their own districts or states.

But most members of Congress who depend upon out-of-state fund raising insist that there is simply not enough money in their home state to support a viable campaign. Sen. Tom Harkin, D-Iowa, who raised more than $3 million in out-of-state money, said he was forced to do so by political and economic forces within the state. "Iowa traditionally is not a state where you can raise money," said Lorraine Voles, spokesperson for Harkin. "To compete there, there's not enough money. Democrats are working people and farmers. Our fund-raisers in Iowa are $5 a head. Republicans have more money in Iowa."

Harkin, of course, also made good use of his out-of-state fund-raising contacts when he decided to run for the Democratic nomination for president in 1992. For him, like so many others, out-of-state fund raising served a dual purpose.

Some members of Congress from less populous states, particularly in the West, contend that they could raise more money from their own constituents if federal law did not limit to $2,000 the amount they can accept from individuals. Others told us that they raised out-of-state money in an effort to leave the in-state fund-raising field to state and local candidates.

Yet even the dwindling breed in Congress that still raises money primarily from hometown contributors sees fund raising as something more than simply collecting checks. For them, too, it is a way of getting to know the most influential people in the region and a way to make them feel as if they are playing an important part in the political process. For that reason, it is not unheard of for a candidate to spend nearly $2,000 to curry favor with a prominent citizen who, under law, can contribute no more than $2,000 to the campaign.

Former representative Steve Bartlett, R-Texas, for example, spent $140,116 to throw a single fund-raising party in 1989. Ticket sales amounted to less than $150,000, but the effort was worth it to Bartlett because the guest list was a who's who of Texas GOP politics. In 1991, Bartlett was able to use these contacts to assist himself in becoming mayor of Dallas.

On a much smaller scale, Sen. William S. Cohen, R-Maine, held a $5-a-head fund-raising event—what his aide Bob Tyrer called "a markdown special"—in a small Maine town, just to get to know the people there. "We started out saying we'd come in at $25 a head and were told that was too much," Tyrer recalled. "So, we said, 'How about $10?' Still too much. So we did it for $5. We did that to build our list. Once you're in with a contributor, you're in. It doesn't matter whether they give you a $250 check or five $50 checks."

Members of Congress frequently complain that fund raising is too time consuming. Some claim to devote as much as one-third to one-half of their time to raising money. But when you consider that fund raising often has a hidden agenda for those politicians seeking to expand their contacts, the time candidates devote to it may be more easily justified.

Fund raising still is a relatively inexpensive undertaking for some candidates. A few candidates spent hundreds of thousands of dollars on direct mail or lavish fund-raising parties, but they were not the norm. Just about 20 percent of all the money spent in the 1990 congressional election was devoted simply to raising more money, much of it paid to consultants who specialize in direct mail, telemarketing, or fund-raising events.

On average, Senate incumbents spent nearly $1.3 million on fund raising, while challengers spent about $327,000. In hot Senate races, where the winner got 60 percent or less of the vote, the average incumbent spent nearly $2.3 million to raise money, compared with nearly $478,600 for the challenger. In House races, fund raising cost the average incumbent about $69,000 in all races and $84,000 in hot races, compared with $11,732 for challengers in all races and $20,736 in hot races.

House incumbents did not cut back drastically on their fund-raising costs if they had no opponent. The average unopposed House member spent about $54,000 to raise money.

While direct-mail fund raising is said to have suffered a general decline in recent years, it continues to be popular with many members of Congress. It has become a staple in some hotly contested Senate races and a popular technique with many House members as well. In fact, some incumbents tried direct mail for the first time in 1990, apparently to escape the stigma that has increasingly been attached to PAC contributions. Telemarketing also appears to be an increasingly popular way to raise money among members of Congress.

In the field of direct-mail fund raising, Coyle, McConnell, & O'Brien and A. B. Data, Ltd., both of Washington, D.C., and Response Dynamics of Vienna, Va., were the leading participants. In the 1990 congressional election, Coyle had total receipts of nearly $3 million, A. B. Data brought in $2.3 million, and Response Dynamics tallied $1.9 million.

The senators who spent the most on direct-mail fund raising were: Helms, nearly $11 million; Phil Gramm, R-Texas, $4.2 million; John Kerry, D-Mass., $2 million; Paul Simon, D-Ill., $1.9 million; Rudy Boschwitz, R-Minn., $1.3 million; Harkin, $1.1 million; and Carl Levin, D-Mich., $1 million. In the House, the big spenders on direct mail were: Robert K. Dornan, R-Calif., $896,346, not including the money he spent through his 1988 committee to pay off his outstanding 1988 debts; Ronald V. Dellums, D-Calif., $358,566; Dannemeyer, $298,467; Lantos, $284,363; and Solarz, $268,272 (see Table 7-2).

Direct mail was especially appealing to those members of Congress who hate asking people for money. As direct-mail consultant Roger M. Craver of Falls Church, Va., explained, "You don't have to have a lot of events, you don't have to have a lot of cocktail parties, you can deal with humanity but you don't have to deal with people. You sit down and you write a letter and you mail it, you don't have to organize people, you don't have to sit and deal with them face to face. The individual idiosyncrasies don't enter into it."

Some candidates found that direct-mail fund-raising letters also could be used to deliver harsh attacks on their opponents without opening themselves to the criticism that negative television advertising usually generates. "It's kind of like a water moccasin," said Craver. "It's silent and it's deadly."

Solarz got into direct-mail fund raising in 1985 primarily because he no longer wanted to be dependent upon Jewish money from his district, which made him beholden to the pro-Israel lobby. Ostensibly, he did it in preparation for what he feared would be a bruising 1992 battle against another Democratic incumbent following reapportionment of the districts in New York. He also feared that his previous fund-raising base would not produce enough money.

However, Solarz acknowledged that the objectives of his direct-mail campaign far exceeded mere fund raising. "It's helpful in the sense that there are people out there that I can mobilize on behalf of legislation," he said. "When I'm trying to muster support for a particular legislative initiative, I call on them to contact their own congressmen or senators."

In 1990, for example, Solarz sent a letter to supporters across the country calling on them to lobby for legislation he had authored designed to make it easier for foreign-educated physicians to obtain licenses in the United States.

According to Michael Lewan, a former aide, Solarz developed his list of Asian-American donors by speaking at many ethnic events around the country, asking for the names and addresses of the participants in lieu of honoraria. He reinforced his name identification with these people by appearing frequently on ethnic cable television shows.

Because Solarz's lists were narrowly targeted to specific ethnic groups, his direct-mail costs were lower than most. He even categorized his donors by subgroups and mailed each subgroup letters discussing issues of particular interest to them, according to Lewan. "No one [subgroup] list is much more than several thousand names, so it's relatively inexpensive to print and put the postage on, as compared to, say, getting the *TV Guide* subscribers' list and mailing to it," he explained. By spending about $268,000 for direct mail in the 1990 cycle, Solarz raised $1.2 million, much of it from mail solicitations.

Most direct-mail campaigns are not as cost-effective as Solarz's. By and large, direct mail is an expensive undertaking—particularly for those who are prospecting from lists purchased from national organizations. Aides to Dellums recalled that he lost $45,000 on a single mailing when he first got into direct-mail fund raising.

There is no better evidence of the high cost of direct mail than Helms's campaign, which spent more than $11 million on fund raising, most of it for direct mail to like-minded conservatives around the country. Helms's direct-mail costs accounted for 61 percent of the money he spent to win the 1990 election. Likewise, while Dornan raised more than $1.6 million, his direct-mail costs ate up more than half his receipts.

In 1990, the rising cost of direct mail clearly made it a less attractive option than it was when some members of Congress first tried it. "Back when I began using direct mail in 1976, it was a tremendous way to raise money," Dornan said. "Stamps were 15 cents. The technology was cheap. But costs have gone up. You're not going to raise as much money with it now. I've never had as good a year as 1977-1978 in terms of my net."

The costs of direct mail have grown so large that direct-mail specialists have sometimes been accused of overcharging.

In 1989, Dornan ended his longstanding and sometimes stormy business relationship with the guru of conservative direct-mail fund raising, Richard A. Viguerie of Falls Church, Va., because he concluded that Viguerie's services were simply too expensive. Dornan also complained that Viguerie "was renting my lists out to the point of destroying them."

Most proponents of direct-mail fund raising say the benefits far outweigh the costs and other drawbacks. Dornan believes that without his powerful direct-mail list, he would have been challenged in

1990 by Ron Kovic, the disabled Vietnam War veteran and antiwar activist whose life was depicted in the 1989 film, *Born on the Fourth of July.*

In addition, many see direct mail as a way to circumvent one of the evils of congressional politics: PACs and $2,000 donors who later come seeking favors. Not only were Helms, Dornan, Solarz, and others strengthened politically by their broad support among $25 contributors, they also did not have to feel beholden to any particular donor. Their direct-mail fund-raising base freed them from the implied quid pro quo that came with every big contribution from a business executive. "You never hear from the small donor," said Dornan. "It gives you a tremendous sense of independence."

Some members of Congress, particularly those on the far right and left, undoubtedly have been forced to raise money through direct mail because their views were too extreme to appeal to the traditional sources of money. Dellums began using direct mail because his reputation as a liberal activist made him unpopular in the business community.

Yet direct-mail fund raising is not an option for every member, particularly those who would be considered middle-of-the-road. In 1988, for example, Rep. Matthew G. Martinez, D-Calif., experimented with direct mail and found that he could barely cover the cost of his postage, so he abandoned it in 1990.

Clearly, the most successful direct-mail fund-raising campaigns are those on the political extremes. Direct-mail experts firmly believe that effective fund-raising appeals must scare potential contributors, causing them to give money to prevent whatever evil outcome is threatened in the letter. Conservatives warn that the liberals are taking over the Congress; liberals caution against a conservative political tide.

On the right, Dornan, who sent a long letter to 25,000 of his contributors about every three weeks in 1990, wrote: "There are so many battles yet to be fought. The liberals are licking their chops." On the left, Dellums wrote letters discussing arms control issues and events in South Africa.

Some politicians shy away from direct mail because they do not want to take the extreme positions necessary to be successful. Even Dellums has been thinking of scaling back his direct-mail fund raising in the future, apparently because the one-time radical is gradually becoming a more mainstream politician and does not want to make extreme appeals for money. Rep. Patricia Schroeder, D-Colo., a renowned liberal, also prefers a toned-down message, even if it raises less money. That is why Schroeder's own press secretary wrote her fund-raising letters, instead of using a professional direct-mail fund-raiser.

"We don't like the 'white-water rapids' approach that most fund-raising consultants write—the 'Jesse Helms is coming, and if you don't give me some money I'll let him in your front door' approach," said Daniel Buck, Schroeder's chief of staff. "We also try to do things differently, play with the size to make it look more personal."

Some members of Congress have built their own in-house direct-mail fund-raising operations to save them the expense of hiring a consulting firm and to prevent their lists from being shared with other groups. Rep. George E. Brown, Jr., D-Calif., who helped to pioneer direct-mail fund raising during an unsuccessful 1970 Senate bid, has always relied on his own staff to do the work. "We do the targeting, pull the labels, and write the letters," explained a Brown aide. "Only then do we turn it over to someone else to produce and mail it. The returns come back in [to Brown's headquarters] and we do the caging ourselves. In 1990, we also wrote and mailed out the thank-you letters."

Another way that members of Congress use fund raising to build a national constituency is by holding fund-raising parties in cities all across the country. The most prominent members of Congress—usually committee chairmen, party leaders, and well-known celebrities such as Bradley, a former pro basketball star—find it is an easy way to raise money while at the same time laying the groundwork for a presidential campaign.

The vast majority of unknown members of Congress could not raise a dime by throwing a fund-raising party in New York City or Los Angeles. Most of them hold only two kinds of fund-raising parties: PAC fund-raisers in Washington, D.C., and fund-raisers for loyal contributors back home. Nevertheless, virtually every young, ambitious member of Congress aspires to having fund-raisers in Los Angeles and New York.

In the eyes of many, California is the best source of political money. Veteran members of Congress from California say they are under constant pressure to arrange fund-raisers in Hollywood or Bev-

A Sample of Bill Bradley's Fund-Raising Expenses

Site	Location	Date	Expenses
Meadowlands Hilton	Secaucus, N.J.	12/85	$ 40,472
Marriott Marquis	New York, N.Y.	06/86	26,145
Regal Rents	Culver City, Calif.	03/87	16,858
La Maison	Austin, Texas	04/87	3,047
Metropolitan Club	Chicago, Ill.	05/87	572
Marriott Marquis	Newark, N.J.	06/87	42,549
Hotel Meridian	Boston, Mass.	06/87	2,973
Mansion on Turtle Creek	Dallas, Texas	07/87	2,488
Commerce Club	Atlanta, Ga.	08/87	1,178
Banker's Club	Cincinnati, Ohio	11/87	727
Bayou Club	Houston, Texas	11/87	4,679
Meadowlands Hilton	Secaucus, N.J.	12/87	45,299
Racquet Club of Chicago	Chicago, Ill.	12/87	4,689
Marriott Marquis	New York, N.Y.	01/88	27,120
Fairmont Hotel	San Francisco, Calif.	05/88	2,057
Ocean Reef Club	Key Largo, Fla.	05/88	1,443
Loews Glenpointe Hotel	Teaneck, N.J.	12/88	74,986
Crescent Court Hotel	Dallas, Texas	03/89	2,620
Life's a Party	Van Nuys, Calif.	03/89	11,697
RSVP	St. Lake City, Utah	03/89	419
Worthington	Fort Worth, Texas	03/89	5,139
Waldorf Astoria	New York, N.Y.	04/89	176,905
Concordia Argonaut	San Francisco, Calif.	04/89	16,381
Loews Glenpointe Hotel	Teaneck, N.J.	05/89	24,850
New York Hilton	New York, N.Y.	06/89	44,271
Westwood Country Club	St. Louis, Mo.	08/89	2,357
Boston Harbor Hotel	Boston, Mass.	09/89	8,843
Greenville Hyatt	Winston-Salem, N.C.	09/89	601
Century Plaza Hotel	Los Angeles, Calif.	10/89	63,095
Casa Jurado	El Paso, Texas	10/89	1,104
Fairmont Hotel	Chicago, Ill.	10/89	38,615
Ramada Renaissance	East Brunswick, N.J.	11/89	70,742
Meiji-En	Philadelphia, Pa.	12/89	3,839
Taste Buds of Florida	Ponte Verda Beach, Fla.	01/90	1,709
2001 Club	Dallas, Texas	01/90	5,679
Club of 110 Tower	Ft. Lauderdale, Fla.	03/90	1,097
Grand Hyatt	New York, N.Y.	04/90	100,000
Concordia Argonaut	San Francisco, Calif.	04/90	8,848
Fisher Island Club	Miami, Fla.	05/90	4,394
Meiji-En	Philadelphia, Pa.	07/90	6,605
Lettuce Eat	Philadelphia, Pa.	09/90	3,403
Ramada Renaissance	East Brunswick, N.J.	10/90	43,955

erly Hills for their congressional colleagues. Rep. Henry A. Waxman, D-Calif., said he helped four Senate candidates and about twenty House members raise money in Los Angeles during the 1990 cycle. "I either held events or lent my name to help like-minded Democrats who were coming to L.A.," he said.

Bradley was the king of fund-raising parties in 1990 (see box, page 146). By our count, he held fifteen major fund-raising parties in New Jersey and New York and thirty-nine big events in such places as Boston, Chicago, Cincinnati, Atlanta, St. Louis, Philadelphia, Salt Lake City, Winston-Salem, N.C., and a number of cities in California, Texas, and Florida. No other member of Congress reported such a wide geographic mix. Among Bradley's many out-of-state fund-raising events was one $1,000-a-plate affair held at the Century Plaza Hotel in Los Angeles in 1989 that was cohosted by Michael Ovitz, head of Creative Artists Agency, and Michael D. Eisner, chief executive officer of Disney Studios. The party cost Bradley $63,095 and raised nearly $700,000.

Gramm distinguished himself by throwing the biggest, most expensive, and most lucrative fund-raiser of the cycle (see box, page 148). No party hosted by any other member of Congress could compare with the $500,000 "presidential gala" that the Texas senator held in December 1989 featuring President Bush. The event drew 4,000 people at ticket prices ranging between $100 and $1,000 and raised an estimated $2.4 million. The program also featured actors Charleton Heston and Chuck Norris. The costs included $278,191 for catering, $75,000 for the president's transportation, and $14,843 to rent the Astrodome. The fund-raising consultant who arranged the event received $63,500.

In the Senate, the leading spenders on fund-raising events were: Bradley, $2.5 million; Gramm, $1.3 million; and Simon, $1.1 million. In the House, the representatives who spent the most for fund-raisers were: Bartlett, $409,464; Levine, $237,320; Ileana Ros-Lehtinen, R-Fla., $232,376; and William H. Gray III, D-Pa., $213,511 (see Table 7-3).

Levine threw one high-priced fund-raiser in the 1990 cycle. His Beverly Hills party in June 1989 cost $73,258, including invitations, entertainment, flowers, food, and drink. About 1,500 people attended at $500 each, bringing the gross receipts for one night to $750,000.

Many members of Congress throw expensive fund-raisers intended

Phil Gramm's Presidential Gala

Item	Expenses
Catering	$278,191
Travel	75,000
Fund-raising consultant	63,500
Freeman Co.	34,174
Astrodome rental	14,843
Printing	5,657
Oakwood Apartments	3,917
Miscellaneous	1,570
Total	**$476,852**

primarily to impress contributors or attract new supporters. Such was the case with Dingell's annual party, dubbed the "Yack Event" because it was held in a local hockey rink called Yack Arena. It attracted about 2,000 guests who paid $25 a person. It raised only slightly more than the $31,485 he spent on invitations, food, drink, and entertainment.

Likewise, Rep. Dean A. Gallo, R-N.J., hosted a series of events that cost more than $200,000 to sponsor. "The old adage that you don't confuse fund raising with political events doesn't apply here," explained Peter McDonough, Jr., a longtime Gallo aide. "In off-years people don't come out to vote as much. Events are a way to compete for their attention. That's why we spent so much money on fund-raising events."

Candidates involved in particularly tough races usually received assistance in fund raising from party luminaries. President Bush, Vice President Dan Quayle, and members of Bush's cabinet traveled hundreds of thousands of miles in 1990 to appear at fund-raisers for Republican candidates. The most popular were Secretary of Labor Elizabeth Dole and Secretary of Transportation Samuel K. Skinner, who later became the White House chief of staff. Transportation costs were normally paid by the candidate.

Perhaps the one nonincumbent who got the most attention from

Republican party bigwigs in 1990 was Gary Franks of Connecticut, who would become the only black Republican in the House. Franks enjoyed fund-raising assistance from President Bush, Secretary of Health and Human Services Louis W. Sullivan, First Lady Barbara Bush, and Secretary of Housing and Urban Development Jack Kemp. When President Bush was forced to cancel a scheduled appearance at a Franks fund-raiser in September 1990, Secretary Dole filled in for him. Contributors who had purchased $250 tickets for the event received rainchecks that entitled them to attend another cocktail party two weeks later when Bush was able to appear.

Celebrity fund-raisers not only raise a lot of money, but they also generate what politicians like to call "free media"—or news stories in the local press. Kerry was clearly trying to generate some media attention with the huge fund-raiser he held two weeks before the election for a sellout crowd of 5,000 at the Wang Center for the Performing Arts in Boston. The entertainment included Robin Williams; Peter, Paul, and Mary; Stephen Stills; and Tom Chapin. Ticket prices ranged from $25 to $1,000, and the event grossed about $400,000.

For most candidates, their best campaign events are fund-raisers. Democrat Toby Moffett, who lost to Franks in Connecticut, remembered fondly his $10-a-head fund-raiser featuring former House Speaker Thomas P. "Tip" O'Neill, Jr., which was held at an Irish pub. After making his way to the stage of the packed pub, O'Neill grabbed the microphone and broke into "Give Ireland Back to the Irish." "The place went crazy," said Moffett. "I will never, ever forget it."

Most members of Congress hold their most lucrative fund-raisers in Washington, D.C., usually at one of several facilities run by the political parties, such as the National Democratic Club, the Capitol Hill Club, or the Ronald Reagan Center, or at a number of favorite restaurants located near the Capitol. These events are primarily for PAC representatives.

In the House, most committee chairmen demanded $500 contributions from those who attend their Washington fund-raisers. Most other House members could not get more than $250 to $350 from each guest. Virtually all senators were charging $1,000 a ticket for their fund-raisers.

For many candidates, fund raising was an expensive operation (see

Table 7-4). Both challengers and incumbents tend to hire consultants to arrange their Washington, D.C., events as well as many of the fund-raising parties back home. Steven H. Gordon & Associates of St. Paul, Minn., was the highest paid consultant on fund-raising events in 1990, with total billings of $524,877. The next three top consultants involved in hosting fund-raisers were all located in Washington: PM Consulting Corp., $502,905; Creative Campaign Consultant, $432,860; and Barbara Klein Associates, $302,817. Amy Zisook & Associates of Chicago ranked fifth with receipts of $294,156.

Many candidates used multiple fund-raising consultants, often one in every city where they held a fund-raiser. Simon may have set a record by hiring no fewer than nineteen fund-raising consultants. His total bill was more than $2.9 million. One of Simon's fund-raisers, Amy Zisook, who had been on a $12,500-a-month retainer throughout most of the campaign season, later filed suit saying Simon still owed her $42,750.

Washington, D.C.-based fund-raising consultant Mike Fraioli of Fraioli/Jost acted as a middleman between the campaign and the PACs. Among other things, he created informational packets about the campaign to send to the PACs. "It's a persuasion process," said Fraioli.

The success of a Washington fund-raising party is usually measured more by how much money it raises than whether the guests are having a good time.

One prominent lobbyist told us that he went only to the Washington fund-raisers held by powerful committee chairmen, such as Dingell. "At $1,000, it's a bargain," he said, because it gives him an opportunity to talk to many other important members of Congress as well. But like many lobbyists and PAC managers, he said he tried to avoid attending the endless stream of fund-raisers held by the lesser lights in Congress. "The first question I ask is, 'Do I have to come?' " he said. "They will usually say, 'No, just send a warm body.' If I do go at all, I just say hello to the member and leave. I'm in and out of there in five minutes. Or I send someone from our office."

Candidates are forever searching for new gimmicks to raise money and enliven their fund-raising parties. Sen. Pete V. Domenici, R-N.M., was the beneficiary of one of the more interesting fund-raisers of the 1990 season: a screening of the old Marx Brothers movie *A Night at the Opera,* with waiters dressed like the Marx Brothers.

Domenici aide Diana Dagget said it was a big success, primarily because it was different.

Frequently, PACs or big contributors throw their own fund-raisers for members of Congress. This is permitted under federal election law as long the expenses do not exceed the amount that the host can legally contribute to the campaign. These are known as in-kind contributions, because the donors are providing services instead of money.

For example, Democrat Harvey I. Sloane, who challenged Sen. Mitch McConnell, R-Ky., was the beneficiary of an in-kind dinner on April 21, 1989, cohosted by Democratic party fund-raiser Maurice Sonnenberg, authors Theodore Sorensen and Arthur M. Schlesinger, Jr., former New York City mayor John V. Lindsay, and former Health, Education, and Welfare secretary Joseph Califano, Jr.

In 1990, many PACs hosted in-kind fund-raisers for Sen. Jim Exon, D-Neb., who chaired the Armed Services strategic forces subcommittee. Among the organizations that threw fund-raisers for Exon were the American Trucking Association PAC, Phillip Morris PAC, Bell Atlantic, Allied Signal PAC, INTEL PAC, U.S. Telephone PAC, Nevada Resort Association PAC, U.S. West PAC, Burlington Northern PAC, LTV Aerospace PAC, and the Motion Picture Association PAC. It was an impressive list, but not entirely unusual for an incumbent senator believed to be facing a serious challenger. Even Sen. Al Gore, D-Tenn., who had no serious opposition in 1990, reported at least eleven in-kind fund-raisers held by PACs.

Money flows easily into the coffers of powerful incumbents, sometimes even to those who do not hold fund-raising events. Rep. David Dreier, R-Calif., who had one of the largest campaign bank accounts in the House, claimed to have received most of his contributions unsolicited. Dreier has never employed a fund-raising consultant.

"It's easy to raise money in Washington," enthused Schroeder's chief of staff. "The longer you're here the easier it is to depend on your committee assignments to help you raise money. People you don't know show up with checks. You don't have to ask."

Not surprisingly, challengers do not find fund raising as easy as incumbents find it. Even those few challengers who succeed must work very hard at raising money.

In Connecticut, Moffett recalled how his intense need for cash became a preoccupation. "Down the stretch we tried to raise some money every day," he said. "Almost every night, I'd attend three or four receptions in people's homes, each one with a price of $25 to $50 per person."

Republican Jim Nussle of Iowa rented two adjoining hotel meeting rooms for two days and carried on an intensive fund-raising marathon. Every thirty minutes a new group of about ten people would be ushered into one room, where Nussle would talk to them about himself. Then the candidate would move to the next room, where another group was waiting. An aide would then go into the first room and give them the pitch for money. "He just alternated between the two rooms all day long for two days," an aide recalled.

One of the most controversial challengers in 1990, David Duke, the former Ku Klux Klan leader who ran against Sen. J. Bennett Johnston, D-La., relied mostly on direct-mail fund raising, but he also collected large amounts of cash in buckets at rallies and sold thousands of dollars worth of Duke political paraphernalia to fund his campaign.

When it came to raising money, Democrat Harvey B. Gantt was the most successful challenger of 1990. He used a variety of clever techniques and benefited enormously from out-of-state contributors seeking to oust Helms from the Senate. After Helms took a stand against funding "obscene" art by the National Endowment for the Arts, Gantt persuaded famous artists to donate limited edition prints, which were offered as incentives to $1,000 donors. The art sale raised $1.3 million for Gantt and benefited contributors as well. When artist Robert Motherwell died, the value of the prints that he contributed soared.

As hard as it is for challengers to raise money, another bitter lesson awaits those winners who think their access to money will be dramatically improved once they become members of Congress. Rep. C. Christopher Cox, R-Calif., had a big campaign debt that he figured would be easy to pay off, but he found that it was no easier for an unknown House member to raise money than a challenger. It took him a long time to get over his self-consciousness whenever he asked someone for money. While he eventually learned to depersonalize the process, he said he will never really get used to "begging" for money.

"It is always difficult to raise money," Cox lamented. "It's like being a car salesman, except you're the car."

Table 7-1 The Top Twenty-Five Recipients in the 1990 Congressional Races: Out-of-State Individual Contributions

Rank	House		Senate	
	Candidate	Out-of-State Contributors	Candidate	Out-of-State Contributors
1	Richard A. Gephardt, D-Mo.	$297,765	Bill Bradley, D-N.J.	$6,933,962
2	Joseph P. Kennedy II, D-Mass.	287,894	Jesse Helms, R-N.C.	2,544,863
3	Sidney R. Yates, D-Ill.	253,977	Phil Gramm, R-Texas	2,278,940
4	Dick Swett, D-N.H.	226,400	John Kerry, D-Mass.	1,857,522
5	Les Aspin, D-Wis.	216,615	Carl Levin, D-Mich.	1,832,216
6	Mike Synar, D-Okla.	196,900	Paul Simon, D-Ill.	1,754,436
7	Newt Gingrich, R-Ga.	186,824	Tom Harkin, D-Iowa	1,554,637
8	Wayne Owens, D-Utah	182,190	Joseph R. Biden, Jr., D-Del.	1,340,255
9	Stephen J. Solarz, D-N.Y.	170,980	John D. Rockefeller IV, D-W.Va.	1,183,457
10	Ron Wyden, D-Ore.	140,771	Larry Pressler, R-S.D.	897,604
11	Jolene Unsoeld, D-Wash.	138,180	Mitch McConnell, R-Ky.	892,901
12	Robert K. Dornan, R-Calif.	137,246	Al Gore, D-Tenn.	841,418
13	Rosa DeLauro, D-Conn.	134,375	Howell Heflin, D-Ala.	814,540
14	Edward J. Markey, D-Mass.	130,500	J. Bennett Johnston, D-La.	774,298
15	James P. Moran Jr. D-Va.	122,700	Claiborne Pell, D-R.I.	686,958
16	Robert J. Mrazek, D-N.Y.	120,475	Max Baucus, D-Mont.	686,368
17	John P. Murtha, D-Pa.	117,825	David L. Boren, D-Okla.	608,371
18	David R. Obey, D-Wis.	111,797	Pete V. Domenici, R-N.M.	550,945
19	David E. Bonior, D-Mich.	107,727	Mark O. Hatfield, R-Ore.	505,868
20	John D. Dingell, D-Mich.	106,288	Hank Brown, R-Colo.	459,415
21	Helen Delich Bentley, R-Md.	102,813	Strom Thurmond, R-S.C.	458,701
22	Dan Burton, R-Ind.	101,552	William S. Cohen, R-Maine	423,675
23	Robert G. Torricelli, D-N.J.	94,700	Alan K. Simpson, R-Wyo.	408,960
24	Tim Roemer, D-Ind.	91,533	John W. Warner, R-Va.	363,804
25	Amo Houghton, R-N.Y.	90,600	Sam Nunn, D-Ga.	346,360

Note: Totals for the House are for the entire two-year cycle, including special elections; totals for the Senate are for the entire six-year cycle.

Table 7-2 The Top Twenty-Five Spenders in the 1990 Congressional Races: Direct-Mail Fund Raising

Rank	House		Senate	
	Candidate	Expenditures	Candidate	Expenditures
1	Robert K. Dorman, R-Calif.	$896,346	Jesse Helms, R-N.C.	$10,957,563
2	Ronald V. Dellums, D-Calif.	358,566	Phil Gramm, R-Texas	4,165,133
3	William E. Dannemeyer, R-Calif.	298,467	John Kerry, D-Mass.	2,000,601
4	Tom Lantos, D-Calif.	284,363	Paul Simon, D-Ill.	1,863,377
5	Steven Solarz, D-N.Y.	268,272	Rudy Boschwitz, R-Minn.	1,278,655
6	Newt Gingrich, R-Ga.	207,221	Tom Harkin, D-Iowa	1,133,417
7	Patricia Schroeder, D-Colo.	196,610	Carl Levin, D-Mich.	1,036,418
8	Jim Ramstad, R-Minn.	149,451	Strom Thurmond, R-S.C.	897,084
9	Gerry E. Studds, D-Mass.	146,301	David Duke, R-La.	887,426
10	Bernard Sanders, I-Vt.	130,469	Bill Bradley, D-N.J.	840,274
11	Les Aspin, D-Wis.	129,901	Daniel R. Coats, R-Ind.	680,799
12	George E. Brown, Jr., D-Calif.	126,102	Lynn Martin, R-Ill.	631,483
13	Chester G. Atkins, D-Mass.	95,653	Tom Tauke, R-Iowa	630,303
14	Bob Williams, R-Wash.	95,494	J. Bennett Johnston, D-La.	488,765
15	Elton Gallegly, R-Calif.	91,359	Harvey B. Gantt, D-N.C.	368,542
16	Marge Roukema, R-N.J.	91,149	Hal Daub, R-Neb.	315,545
17	Tom McMillen, D-Md.	90,234	Bill Cabaniss, R-Ala.	303,873
18	Cliff Stearns, R-Fla.	87,411	William S. Cohen, R-Maine	276,063
19	Peter H. Kostmayer, D-Pa.	84,673	Pete V. Domenici, R-N.M.	234,348
20	David F. Emery, R-Maine	82,935	Joseph R. Biden, Jr., D-Del.	221,900
21	Vin Weber, R-Minn.	81,186	Claudine Schneider, R-R.I.	192,465
22	Constance A. Morella, R-Md.	79,097	Hugh Parmer, D-Texas	173,225
23	Barbara F. Vucanovich, R-Nev.	74,687	Robert C. Smith, R-N.H.	158,738
24	Denny Smith, R-Ore.	72,497	Al Gore, D-Tenn.	143,684
25	H. James Saxton, R-N.J.	71,917	Bill Schuette, R-Mich.	137,498

Note: Totals for the House are for the entire two-year cycle, including special elections; totals for the Senate are for the entire six-year cycle.

Table 7-3 The Top Twenty-Five Spenders in the 1990 Congressional Races: Fund-Raising Events

Rank	House		Senate	
	Candidate	Expenditures	Candidate	Expenditures
1	Steve Bartlett, R-Texas	$409,464	Bill Bradley, D-N.J.	$2,499,461
2	Mel Levine, D-Calif.	237,320	Phil Gramm, R-Texas	1,334,683
3	Ileana Ros-Lehtinen, R-Fla.	232,376	Paul Simon, D-Ill.	1,140,802
4	William H. Gray III, D-Pa.	213,511	Lynn Martin, R-Ill.	875,893
5	Dean A. Gallo, R-N.J.	210,900	Rudy Boschwitz, R-Minn.	824,479
6	Barbara Boxer, D-Calif.	198,960	Jesse Helms, R-N.C.	458,536
7	Richard A. Gephardt, D-Mo.	184,264	Mitch McConnell, R-Ky.	433,306
8	Bill Alexander, D-Ark.	179,555	John D. Rockefeller IV, D-W.Va.	418,932
9	Tom Campbell, R-Calif.	170,672	Harvey B. Gantt, D-N.C.	358,379
10	Tom McMillen, D-Md.	148,507	John Kerry, D-Mass.	358,287
11	Charles B. Rangel, D-N.Y.	143,732	Hank Brown, R-Colo.	314,357
12	Ronald D. Coleman, D-Texas	141,777	Daniel R. Coats, R-Ind.	305,342
13	Douglas H. Bosco, D-Calif.	140,096	Harvey I. Sloane, D-Ky.	293,304
14	Dick Zimmer, R-N.J.	139,986	Bill Schuette, R-Mich.	292,260
15	Bob Hammock, R-Calif.	139,790	J. Bennett Johnston, D-La.	271,347
16	Joseph P. Kennedy II, D-Mass.	139,518	Claiborne Pell, D-R.I.	271,046
17	Bill Lowery, R-Calif.	138,811	Tom Tauke, R-Iowa	270,232
18	Helen Delich Bentley, R-Md.	138,222	Joseph R. Biden, Jr. D-Del.	241,534
19	Duncan Hunter, R-Calif.	138,132	Carl Levin, D-Mich.	235,533
20	Bob Clement, D-Tenn.	132,955	Patricia Saiki, R-Hawaii	222,331
21	Robert T. Matsui, D-Calif.	132,900	Hal Daub, R-Neb.	216,758
22	Matthew J. Rinaldo, R-N.J.	132,601	Howell Heflin, D-Ala.	214,008
23	Susan Molinari, R-N.Y.	131,952	Pete V. Domenici, R-N.M.	200,917
24	Bill Grant, R-Fla.	130,895	Al Gore, D-Tenn.	193,125
25	Wayne Owens, D-Utah	129,127	Jim Rappaport, R-Mass.	185,524

Note: Totals for the House are for the entire two-year cycle, including special elections; totals for the Senate are for the entire six-year cycle.

Table 7-4 The Top Twenty-Five Spenders in the 1990 Congressional Races: Total Fund-Raising Expenses

Rank	House		Senate	
	Candidate	Expenditures	Candidate	Expenditures
1	Robert K. Dornan, R-Calif.	$978,767	Jesse Helms, R-N.C.	$11,416,099
2	Ronald V. Dellums, D-Calif.	493,892	Phil Gramm, R-Texas	5,525,079
3	Steve Bartlett, R-Texas	409,464	Paul Simon, D-Ill.	3,742,993
4	William E. Dannemeyer, R-Calif.	359,056	Bill Bradley, D-N.J.	3,339,735
5	Newt Gingrich, R-Ga.	356,536	John Kerry, D-Mass.	3,131,989
6	Steven J. Solarz, D-N.Y.	353,277	Rudy Boschwitz, R-Minn.	2,368,119
7	Tom Lantos, D-Calif.	319,692	Lynn Martin, R-Ill.	1,534,643
8	Les Aspin, D-Wis.	278,586	Carl Levin, D-Mich.	1,495,442
9	Barbara Boxer, D-Calif.	259,999	Tom Harkin, D-Iowa	1,391,739
10	Tom McMillen, D-Md.	238,741	Tom Tauke, R-Iowa	1,312,147
11	Mel Levine, D-Calif.	237,320	Harvey B. Gantt, D-N.C.	1,288,932
12	George E. Brown, Jr., D-Calif.	236,504	Daniel R. Coats, R-Ind.	1,038,574
13	Ileana Ros-Lehtinen, R-Fla.	232,376	Strom Thurmond, R-S.C.	991,104
14	Patricia Schroeder, D-Colo.	230,459	David Duke, R-La.	892,496
15	Jim Ramstad, R-Minn.	215,687	J. Bennett Johnston, D-La.	760,113
16	William H. Gray III, D-Pa.	213,511	Hal Daub, R-Neb.	590,690
17	Richard A. Gephardt, D-Mo.	211,357	Mitch McConnell, R-Ky.	569,044
18	Dean A. Gallo, R-N.J.	210,900	Bill Schuette, R-Mich.	535,855
19	Tom Campbell, R-Calif.	193,681	John D. Rockefeller IV, D-W.Va.	489,206
20	Jim Ross Lightfoot, R-Iowa	185,696	Joseph R. Biden, Jr., D-Del.	463,434
21	Jill L. Long, D-Ind.	180,115	Bill Cabaniss, R-Ala.	446,138
22	Bill Alexander, D-Ark.	179,555	Pete V. Domenici, R-N.M.	435,265
23	Gary Condit, D-Calif.	176,223	William S. Cohen, R-Maine	382,789
24	Gerry E. Studds, D-Mass.	175,758	Harvey I. Sloane, D-Ky.	366,438
25	Vin Weber, R-Minn.	162,751	Hank Brown, R-Colo.	364,712

Note: Totals for the House are for the entire two-year cycle, including special elections; totals for the Senate are for the entire six-year cycle.

CHAPTER 8

Individual Donors
Money by the Bundle

Trial lawyers who paid $1,000 each to attend an elegant San Diego fund-raiser in September 1991 were understandably impressed by the lineup of top politicians assembled there: Senate Majority Leader George J. Mitchell, D-Maine, four other prominent Democratic senators, and five leading Senate candidates.

The host of this unusually high-powered party was William S. Lerach, an energetic San Diego attorney who specializes in class-action suits and a volunteer Democratic fund-raiser. Lerach is one of a growing breed of rich, politically active lawyers and business professionals who contribute large sums of their own money to congressional campaigns—sometimes more than the law allows—and who also collect big contributions for candidates from their friends and business associates.

Known as "bundlers" or "rainmakers," these collectors of large donations are rapidly replacing political action committees (PACs) as the leading source of special-interest money for America's politicians. Ever since PAC contributions began acquiring an unsavory public image, members of Congress have come to depend increasingly on bundlers to provide the cash they need to keep their personal political machines in operation.

Bundling is the "hot new idea" in campaign financing circles, according to University of Virginia political scientist Larry Sabato. "That's where the real influence is. It's with the gatherers—the people who collect $100,000 at a shot."

There is no way of knowing precisely how much money flows into congressional politics through bundling. But Citizens Action, a nonprofit consumer organization interested in campaign finance reform, has estimated that contributions from large individual donors reached $164 million in the 1990 cycle, exceeding the amount contributed by PACs.

As a bundler, Lerach was an unqualified success. His September 1991 party raised $190,000 for the Democratic Senatorial Campaign Committee, and that was only one of many such fund-raising efforts that he has undertaken for congressional candidates. He also persuaded members of his law firm, Milberg, Weiss, Bershad, Specthrie, & Lerach, to contribute a combined total of about $218,000 to various candidates in the 1989-1990 cycle (see box, page 159).

Lerach is more than just a bundler of other people's money. In the 1989-1990 campaign cycle, he also contributed at least $74,000 of his own money to congressional candidates. In 1990, in fact, he exceeded the legal limit of $25,000 a year by giving away a total of $58,000 to various candidates. He also persuaded his relatives to make contributions, bringing the total contributions made in the Lerach name to $107,000 in 1990.

According to Federal Election Commission (FEC) records, more than sixty people—including Lerach—exceeded the $25,000 annual limit on contributions to congressional candidates in either 1989 or 1990, and some of them in both years (see Table 8-1). In addition, these contributors and hundreds of others took advantage of loopholes in federal law to give away millions more in soft money contributions that were not monitored by the FEC. Their contributions far exceeded the intent of the post-Watergate amendments to federal election law, which still technically impose a limit of $2,000 on individual contributions to a single candidate.

Lerach's record of personal contributions and his fund-raising activities illustrate how contributors have circumvented the post-Watergate reforms, which were intended to limit the influence that rich individuals could have on the political system and the legislative process.

By all accounts, Lerach's contributions, combined with his prodigious bundling, have given him considerable influence among leading Democratic senators in Washington, D.C. In 1991, he played a key role in persuading Congress to enact legislation reversing a Supreme Court decision that imposed a strict statute of limitations on class-

Contributions by the Law Firm of Milberg, Weiss, Bershad, Specthrie, & Lerach to Federal Candidates and Party Organizations in 1989-1990

Given to:	Amount
Sen. Alan Cranston, D-Calif.	$27,000
Sen. Joseph R. Biden, Jr., D-Del.	13,750
Sen. Bill Bradley, D-N.J.	13,650
John Inelli, D-Pa.	11,000
Sen. John Kerry, D-Mass.	10,000
Sen. Arlan Specter, R-Pa.	10,000
Sen. Howell Heflin, D-Ala.	7,250
Sen. John D. Rockefeller IV, D-W.Va	6,000
Rep. John Conyers, Jr., D-Mich.	5,000
Stephen Georgiou, D-Calif.	3,500
Ted Muenster, D-S.D.	3,500
Harvey B. Gantt, D-N.C.	2,200
Sen. Al Gore, D-Tenn.	2,000
Baron P. Hill, D-Ind.	2,000
Harry Lonsdale, D-Ore.	2,000
Rep. Nita M. Lowey, D-N.Y.	2,000
Sen. Claiborne Pell, D-R.I.	2,000
Sen. Lloyd Bentsen, D-Texas	1,500
Rep. William J. Hughes, D-N.J.	1,500
Jim Bates, D-Calif.	1,000
Sen. David L. Boren, D-Okla.	1,000
Rep. Gerry Sikorski, D-Minn.	1,000
Rep. Mike Synar, D-Okla.	1,000
Rep. Edward F. Feighan, D-Ohio	500
Democratic Senatorial Campaign Committee	77,250
National Assn. of Securities and Commercial Law Attorneys PAC	9,000
Democratic Congressional Campaign Committee	1,250
Golden Eagle Club of San Diego	650

Note: Totals include contributions made by attorneys working for the law firm of Milberg, Weiss, Bershad, Specthrie, & Lerach and, where identifiable, their spouses.

action stockholder suits. Lerach was not only the leading proponent but also one of the the chief beneficiaries of the legislation.

The bill was introduced by Sens. Richard H. Bryan, D-Nev., and Alan Cranston, D-Calif., just two months before these two senators joined Mitchell as honored guests at Lerach's fund-raiser. Lerach, Bryan, and Cranston all insisted that there was no connection between the fund-raiser and the bill. Byran said he did not even talk to Lerach about the matter until after the bill had been introduced. Cranston acknowledged that Lerach had persuaded him to cosponsor the Bryan bill, but added that Lerach's contributions were irrelevant to his decision.

It is impossible to believe that Lerach saw no connection between the fund-raiser and the Bryan bill. In a letter he wrote in August 1991, inviting other trial lawyers to the party, Lerach suggested that his guests should use the occasion to discuss the statute of limitations issue with the influential senators. "You don't often get a chance to spend an evening with [five] members of the United States Senate," Lerach wrote in the letter. "Most importantly, this evening will give us an opportunity to support and express our views to some of the most influential members of the Senate who are in a position to protect the rights that we fight for on a daily basis and must preserve."

Whether or not Lerach's contributions were instrumental in shaping the legislation, the story vividly illustrates why PAC contributions are no longer viewed as the premier instrument for business lobbying in Washington, D.C. While a corporate PAC can give no more than $10,000 to a single candidate, there is no limit on the amount of bundled individual donations a candidate can receive from the executives of a single firm or a single industry. Furthermore, while PAC contributions carry the taint of special-interest money, bundled individual contributions are still viewed in many circles as being better than PAC contributions.

Some members of Congress, such as Sens. John Kerry, D-Mass., David L. Boren, D-Okla., and Rep. Edward J. Markey, D-Mass., refused to accept PAC contributions but still accepted bundled donations from top executives of a single corporation. Kerry, for example, received $46,146 from seventy people in four Massachusetts law firms during the 1989-1990 cycle.

Bundling meets the needs of senators who feel they must raise thousands of dollars every week toward their reelection. Cranston, who raised and spent more than $11 million in his 1986 reelection campaign, said that as a busy senator he no longer had enough time to raise contributions of as little as $2,000 from individuals. "Large sums are necessary to be successful," Cranston said. "There was not time to raise them . . . in small denominations from a lot of people."

Because bundlers can provide more money than PACs, it is understandable that they can garner more influence in Congress than PACs.

A few years ago, a prominent Washington lobbyist was casting about for what he described as "grass-roots" lobbying support for an important bill. After asking around, he obtained the name of a man who might be able to bring pressure to bear on a key senator. When the lobbyist asked why this man was being recommended for the task, he was told simply: "This guy just raised $1 million for the senator."

"Now that's really grass-roots influence," the lobbyist concluded.

The most notorious bundler of all was Charles H. Keating, Jr., the former owner of Lincoln Savings & Loan, headquartered in Irvine, Calif. Five senators for whom Keating raised large amounts of money—Cranston, Donald W. Riegle, Jr., D-Mich., Dennis DeConcini, D-Ariz., John Glenn, D-Ohio, and John McCain, R-Ariz.—all insisted they were not influenced by the contributions that the thrift executive bundled together for them. Yet Keating freely acknowledged that his purpose in raising the money was to persuade these senators to intervene with federal regulators on his behalf.

Even though Cranston refused to acknowledge any quid pro quo between Keating's contributions and his willingness to provide assistance for Lincoln, there is no question that the senator's aides saw a clear connection between the two. Memos written by Cranston's chief fund-raiser, Joy Jacobson, indicated that she felt that big contributors such as Keating were entitled to the senator's assistance in matters before the federal government. In one memo dated January 2, 1987, Jacobson even named several contributors who she said "have been very helpful to you who have cases or legislation matters pending with our office who will rightfully expect some kind of resolution."

Another well-known bundler in Republican fund-raising circles was Rabbi Milton Balkany of New York, whose generosity and hard work on behalf of the GOP was acknowledged each year when party officials invited him to offer a prayer at the president's annual fund-raising dinner. During the Reagan administration years, Balkany used his influence with White House Chief of Staff Donald Regan to obtain a $1.3 million community development grant for a Jewish school he supported. By his own account, Balkany asked Regan for the grant during one of their regular meetings at the White House. Regan not only agreed but also arranged for a White House car to take the rabbi over to the Department of Health and Human Services, where the grant was hastily okayed by top administration officials.

Bundling is all the more insidious because there is no requirement in the law for bundlers to disclose their fund-raising activities. While PAC contributions are easily identified in FEC records as special-interest money, bundled checks are reported only as unrelated, individual contributions. For that reason, it has been extremely difficult for reporters and other analysts to trace bundling activity through public records.

While most bundling activity is undisclosed, some patterns are apparent. For example, FEC records show that the nation's top securities, law, and lobbying firms are the biggest bundlers. Many of these firms operated PACs as well as highly successful bundling operations. The companies whose executives contributed the most in the 1989-1990 cycle were Goldman Sachs & Co., $744,866; Salomon Brothers, $708,150; General Electric, $657,306; Morgan Stanley, $654,671; Baer, Sterns & Company, $634,185; Time-Warner Inc., $567,875; Aiken & Gump, $491,503; and Fluor Daniel Inc., $448,809.

Hollywood is another major source of bundled money for congressional candidates. Executives of Walt Disney Co. contributed $477,391 to congressional candidates and other political committees in the 1989-1990 cycle—$393,872 in individual donations from top corporate executives and the remainder through their PAC. Most other movie studios were bundling large contributions to congressional candidates as well. In 1990, only Paramount executives appeared to be giving more money through their PAC than through bundled individual donations.

In the movie industry, bundling is fast becoming part of the corporate culture. "It's not a policy—it's a custom that's developed," explained Joe Shapiro, Disney senior vice president and general counsel. Shapiro was one of the many studio executives who solicited contributions from coworkers on behalf of members of Congress. Sometimes his coworkers mailed their own contributions to the candidate, but frequently Shapiro gathered up their checks and mailed them in a single envelope. "If you set out to raise $6,000 for Sally Smith, you collect all the checks and then mail them out all at once," he said.

Tim Boggs, vice president of public affairs and PAC chairman at Warner, offered a similar explanation of how bundling works within his organization: "It's like when you go around your office collecting for the United Way or any other charity. You wait until you have a bunch of checks, and then you send them in."

Hollywood fund-raising parties are an integral part of the bundling system. Top movie executives such as Disney CEO Michael Eisner and MCA's longtime chairman, Lew R. Wasserman, often invite other studio executives to their homes for fund-raising parties. A few corporate executives are then designated to collect the checks. Even those who do not attend the fund-raisers often make contributions afterwards, either to the designated bundler or directly to the candidates.

Rep. Tom McMillen, D-Md., a former professional basketball star who has enjoyed considerable support from Hollywood, recalled receiving numerous checks from movie industry people even after a scheduled Los Angeles fund-raising party for him was canceled.

In the 1990 election cycle, Hollywood's favorite politician appeared to be Sen. Bill Bradley, D-N.J., who received at least $78,040 from Disney executives and the Disney PAC and more than $850,000 in individual contributions from California. Bradley's popularity among movie people was based in large part on his glittering past as a New York Knicks basketball star and his future promise as a potential presidential contender. Eisner was known to be "territorial" about hosting all Hollywood fund-raisers for Bradley, a personal friend.

In its quest for more influence in Washington, D.C., Disney also has provided substantial financial support to a handful of California Democrats, including Reps. Mel Levine, Howard L. Berman, and Vic Fazio. In 1991, these three lawmakers were deeply involved in an abortive effort by Disney to win $395 million in federal funds for a highway project that would have benefited a proposed expansion near Disneyland in Anaheim, Calif. The proposed project proved to be politically embarrassing for the representatives when it was revealed that federal funds were going to be set aside to help one of the richest private corporations in the nation.

As a result of Hollywood's incredible generosity to politicians, California is regarded in national political circles as a kind of money Mecca. As California Treasurer Kathleen Brown put it, "California

has traditionally been the ATM machine for national candidates."
But as sometimes happens in politics, the state's reputation as a haven
for money-hungry office seekers has been somewhat exaggerated.
First of all, there is so much competition for Hollywood money that it
is not available to many lesser-known candidates. Secondly, New
York—not California—was the nation's premier exporter of campaign cash in the 1990 cycle.

In 1990, individuals living or working in only two elite ZIP codes
on Manhattan's Upper East Side—10021 and 10022—accounted for
a total of more than $3 million in large contributions of $200 or more
to congressional candidates. These contributors included many top
corporate leaders, members of prestigious law firms, and a few fabu-
lously wealthy individuals such as John W. Kluge, owner of Metro-
media; fashion designer Liz Claiborne and her husband, Arthur
Ortenberg; real estate magnate Donald J. Trump; and leveraged
buyout specialists Henry R. Kravis of Kohlberg, Kravis, & Roberts,
and Ronald O. Perelman, owner of Revlon cosmetics.

By comparison, the most generous West Coast ZIP code—90210
in Beverly Hills—came in at less than $1 million in total contributions
during the 1990 cycle.

Members of Congress typically get acquainted with New York
business executives by visiting their offices in Manhattan, usually for
a breakfast, luncheon, or "issues forum" in which they can discuss the
matters pending in Washington, D.C. Not until the end of the meeting are the participants asked to contribute to the campaign or to
solicit money from their friends and business associates. Those who
agree to raise money often do so by holding cocktail parties where the
candidate will make an appearance.

The New York fund-raising scene is oriented more around business
policy than the cause-oriented approach used to collect contributions
in Los Angeles. "Most of the senators and congressmen just love to
come to New York, not only because they can raise a lot of money
here but also because they usually learn something here," observed
one veteran Democratic fund-raising consultant, who regularly ush-
ers senators around Manhattan.

New York contributors are impressed by competence; Los Angeles
contributors are impressed by commitment to issues. As one Democratic
official put it: "In New York you have to come across as smart, and in
Los Angeles you have to be prepared to come across as an expert."

In Washington, D.C., three ZIP codes encompassing Georgetown and the K Street corridor where most lobbying offices are located accounted for nearly $2.2 million in contributions from individuals in 1990, proving once again that many lobbyists now write personal checks to the candidates as well as giving through PACs.

In all these prime fund-raising areas, Democrats fared better than Republicans, even though the GOP is normally more closely identified with wealthy interests. Of course, there are more Democrats in Congress and by virtue of being in the majority party they also chair all the committees that oversee business interests.

In the two top ZIP codes in Manhattan, for example, Democrats reaped $2.2 million, compared with $929,618 for the Republicans. Republicans tended to dominate fund raising in wealthy suburbs and smaller cities, such as Midland, Mich., home of Dow Chemical Co., where Republican candidates raised $396,000, compared with only $8,000 for Democrats.

Much of the money coming from these top ZIP codes was collected by bundlers. One trademark of bundled contributions is that they sometimes go to members of Congress who have nothing in common with the contributors. In such instances, the contributor likely has been contacted by a business associate who supports the candidate, and the contributor agrees to give in order to curry favor with that particular business associate, not necessarily to gain influence with the candidate. In this way, an elaborate web of business or personal relationships is spun around political fund raising.

In some cases, prominent members of Congress even act as bundlers for other candidates. During Senate Select Ethics Committee hearings into the Keating affair, DeConcini acknowledged that his chief fund-raiser had been bundling cash for Riegle, who apparently was expected to reciprocate. Strong ties between members of Congress are forged through such reciprocal fund-raising activities.

Normally, contributors are more interested in gaining favor with the collector than the recipient of the money. A Washington lobbyist said he responds enthusiastically whenever he receives a telephone call from a high-ranking congressional leader asking him to contribute to another GOP candidate, even if he knows nothing about the candidate. He contributes because he wants to preserve his good relationship with the party leadership. As he put it, "The only question I ask is: 'Where do I send the check?'"

Bundling is only one technique used to circumvent restrictions on contributions. Another entirely legal maneuver that contributors frequently use is to give money in the names of their relatives, usually spouses or children. Citizen Action estimated that $30.6 million flowed to congressional candidates during the 1989-1990 cycle through relatives of top business executives. Nearly $20 million was donated by women who listed their occupation simply as housewife. It is not at all unusual to find in FEC records that an eighteen-year-old college student has contributed $5,000 to the PAC of the corporation where his or her father is employed.

The Gallo wine-making family, for example, had no corporate PAC. But Gallo family members contributed more than $294,000 to candidates in 1989-1990, including twenty separate $1,000 checks that went to Cranston on a single day, April 13, 1989.

Soft-money contributions are another option open to contributors who have already given the maximum $25,000 a year permitted under federal law. Soft money is usually funneled through state parties in order to escape federal restrictions. Donations to state parties frequently include direct contributions from corporate and union treasuries, which are prohibited from giving directly to federal candidates under federal law.

The growth of soft money contributions has been a boon to the treasuries of state party organizations. As a result, state party leaders strongly defend the practice on grounds that it strengthens the two-party system. But an increase in their treasuries should not be mistaken for a real resurgence in state parties.

Although soft money was intended to be used only for state and local elections, it is no secret that members of Congress encourage contributors to make soft-money donations that help them win reelection. Since state party organizations are not required to report their receipts to the FEC, there is no way of knowing how much soft money was contributed to assist in congressional races in 1990. But the national parties reported receiving more than $25 million in soft-money contributions during that period.

Forty contributors gave $100,000 or more. Atlantic Richfield Co. contributed $303,360 in soft money to the Republican and Democratic national party organizations in the 1989-1990 cycle. Mary C. Bingham, matriarch of the Bingham newspaper family, contributed $280,000 to the Democratic National Committee (DNC). The United

Steelworkers Union contributed $222,550 to the DNC as well.

After the election, the Republicans charged that a $250,000 soft-money contribution from Bingham to the DNC had been funneled back into Kentucky to produce a television ad designed to assist Democrat Harvey I. Sloane in his unsuccessful bid to unseat Sen. Mitch McConnell, R-Ky. Before making the DNC contribution, Bingham had already made the maximum possible individual contribution to Sloane.

Because of the growth in this type of donation, reformers have focused on trying to enact restrictions on soft-money contributions. Meanwhile, a proliferation of other types of contributions has gone virtually unnoticed. Kent C. Cooper, the FEC official primarily responsible for public disclosure of contributions, estimated that members of Congress have devised nearly fifty other ways to collect money legally from rich contributors and circumvent the intent of federal election law.

Cooper called these various methods "the many pockets of a politician's coat." They include legal defense funds, voter registration drives, ballot recount accounts, "testing the water" funds, independent expenditures, travel aboard corporate or personal jets, foundations, book deals, employment of family members, scholarship funds, library funds, redistricting funds, caucus funds, local district committees, state-level PACs, and leadership PACs. A single individual contributor could give to all these funds without violating the law.

By 1990, at least thirty-two members of Congress were raising money through their own PACs. In addition, Democrats charged that House Minority Whip Newt Gingrich, R-Ga., was trying to circumvent federal law by using money raised by GOPAC, a nonfederal political action committee he established to influence federal elections.

While some were trying to skirt the law in a variety of clever ways, other contributors were blatantly violating it by contributing more than $25,000 to federal candidates and federal PACs during a single calendar year. Some violators claimed they were unaware of the law. Others knew the law well enough to realize that it was not being properly enforced by the FEC and that the fines for such a violation were normally minimal. FEC enforcement records in 1990 contained no evidence that the FEC had ever imposed any serious fines for contributions in excess of the $25,000 limit.

According to FEC records, Michael L. Keiser, president of Recycled

Paper Products of Chicago, the nation's fourth largest greeting card manufacturer, made $95,750 in campaign contributions to federal candidates, party organizations, and PACs during 1990—almost four times the legal limit. That would make him the biggest violator of the $25,000 limit during the 1989-1990 election cycle (see Table 8-1).

Of course, not all the contributors whose names appear in FEC files as having given more than $25,000 were knowingly violating the law. A few of them probably were the victims of reporting errors and other commonplace glitches in the complex campaign finance disclosure system. But by failing to investigate these cases, the FEC sent a clear signal to contributors that there is no reason to adhere to the law.

FEC Chairman Joan R. Aikens insisted that her agency did not have sufficient resources to monitor contributions by individuals. She also acknowledged that contributors who are found to have given more than the legal limit are often permitted to reallocate their contributions to different years to bring themselves into compliance with the law. But in keeping with the FEC's policy of secrecy, such settlements are never announced.

Of the more than sixty contributors whose annual donations exceeded $25,000 in the 1989-1990 cycle, most were successful business executives or lawyers such as Lerach who had the benefit of expert legal advice on the intricacies of the federal election laws. These wealthy business people are the very contributors that Congress had in mind in 1974 when it rewrote the federal election laws in order to restrict giving by individuals to $25,000 a year.

Although a lawyer himself, Lerach professed to be unaware of that law. "I just started to give money in the 1989-1990 election cycle," he said. "I'm a little confused about these cycles. . . . Obviously if you put all the numbers together, they appear to be over the limit."

No matter what barriers are erected to stem the flow of money into congressional campaign treasuries, clever minds will surely think of new ways to get around them.

Bundling would be restricted in one way or another under virtually every proposal that has been considered in recent years for campaign finance reform, but no law is likely to eliminate the practice entirely. All Americans, no matter what their corporate affiliation, have a constitutional right to make personal political contributions, even in consultation with friends and business associates.

Table 8-1 Contributors Exceeding the $25,000 Federal Contribution Limit

		Contributions in	
Name	City	1990	1989
Michael L. Keiser	Chicago, Ill.	**$95,750**	$24,000
William S. Lerach	San Diego, Calif.	**58,000**	16,000
Marvin Schwan	Marshall, Minn.	**51,655**	23,650
Mrs. Stanley Stone	Milwaukee, Wis.	**45,870**	17,555
Roy H. Cullen	Houston, Texas	**42,800**	**26,055**
Elsie H. Hillman	Pittsburgh, Pa.	**39,820**	19,250
Arthur B. Belfer	New York, N.Y.	**36,880**	**39,615**
Satiris Kolokotronis	Sacramento, Calif.	**39,500**	2,000
Stephen Schutz	La Jolla, Calif.	**39,500**	20,000
Joseph J. Bogdanovich	Long Beach, Calif.	**38,950**	**31,000**
Susan Schutz	La Jolla, Calif.	**38,500**	20,000
Charles Harrington	Wilmington, Del.	**38,280**	20,126
Stanley Hirsh	Studio City, Calif.	**38,100**	**30,000**
Kuei Yu	Kings Park, N.Y.	21,990	**38,050**
Henry J. Casey	Portland, Ore.	**37,725**	**25,250**
Bennett Lebow	New York, N.Y.	**37,500**	20,000
Norman V. Kinsey	Shreveport, La.	**37,350**	24,250
John P. Chase	Boston, Mass.	30,340	**37,330**
John C. Camp	Washington, D.C.	**36,328**	8,998
Henry H. Slack	Peapack, N.J.	21,500	**36,000**
Mary C. Bingham	Glenview, Ky.	**35,900**	15,750
Elinor Goodspeed	Washington, D.C.	**35,830**	10,350
Mrs. Wesley West	Houston, Texas	**34,525**	20,335
Maura Morey	Tiberon, Calif.	**34,500**	**26,600**
A. D. Hulings	Bayport, Minn.	**34,300**	18,000
Roger Milliken	Spartanburg, S.C.	**33,400**	13,000
Frederick W. Field	Los Angeles, Calif.	**32,750**	13,825
James R. Houghton	Corning, N.Y.	**32,500**	13,750
Morton Mandel	Shaker Heights, Ohio	5,500	**32,500**
Henry J. Evertt	New York, N.Y.	**32,200**	22,000
Robert N. Rose	New York, N.Y.	5,000	**32,000**
Steven Grossman	Chestnut Hill, Mass.	**31,000**	**26,450**
Richard Devos, Sr.	Grand Rapids, Mich.	**30,750**	24,340
Cloud L. Cray, Jr.	Atchison, Kan.	**30,240**	23,740
Edith Everett	New York, N.Y.	**30,000**	5,250
Vonnie M. Davidson	Los Angeles, Calif.	**29,840**	0

(table continues)

Table 8-1 *(continued)*

		Contributions in	
Name	*City*	*1990*	*1989*
John C. Whitehead	New York, N.Y.	**29,500**	5,000
Mrs. Julius E. Pierce	Miami, Fla.	19,500	**29,275**
Geraldine Lebow	New York, N.Y.	**29,250**	20,000
Lewis Rudin	New York, N.Y.	**29,140**	**28,000**
Robert Morey	Tiberon, Calif.	**28,000**	20,250
John Torkelsen	Princeton, N.J.	**28,000**	20,000
James F. Keenan	Aiken, S.C.	4,500	**28,000**
Susie Field	Los Angeles, Calif.	**27,750**	21,000
Joseph C. Canizaro	New Orleans, La.	**27,750**	10,000
John W. Kluge	New York, N.Y.	**27,750**	1,000
Yong C. Kim	Fremont, Calif.	13,000	**27,575**
Monty Hundley	New York, N.Y.	1,000	**27,500**
Harvey Friedman	Miami, Fla.	**27,450**	7,265
Mark B. Dayton	Wayzata, Minn.	22,750	**27,100**
Richard J. Dennis	Chicago, Ill.	22,000	**27,000**
Phillip B. Rooney	Hinsdale, Ill.	**26,975**	25,000
Hamlet T. O'Hanian	Los Angeles, Calif.	21,455	**26,769**
John Mascotte	New York, N.Y.	**26,750**	20,000
Mrs. R. H. Hargrove	Shreveport, La.	**26,567**	11,320
Albert J. Dwoskin	Fairfax, Va.	**26,100**	18,500
Paul Tudor Jones	New York, N.Y.	**26,000**	24,000
Jerome Kohlberg, Jr.	New York, N.Y.	**26,000**	0
Ernest Hubbell	Kansas City, Kan.	**25,895**	20,970
Robert Rubin	New York, N.Y.	**25,750**	21,000
Diane T. MacArthur	Bethesda, Md.	**25,475**	19,000
Ellen St. John Garwood	Austin, Texas	**25,417**	18,650

Note: Totals in bold indicate contributors in excess of the $25,000 limit established in 1974 by Congress.

Source: Computer analysis of Federal Election Commission contribution records, *Los Angeles Times,* September 15, 1991.

CHAPTER 9

Political Action Committees
Taking All the Blame

I n his first campaign for Congress in 1988, Rep. Glenn Poshard, D-Ill., succeeded in persuading a number of big political action committees to support his candidacy.

"In 1988, I came to Washington, D.C., and I went from PAC to PAC to PAC," recalled Poshard, a former Illinois state legislator. "At every stop, they asked me to fill out a questionnaire: 'On House Bill X, will you vote yes or no?' You not only have to pledge to support their position on these bills, but you have to sign your name to them."

After Poshard was elected, he slowly came to regret the pledges he had made on some of his PAC questionnaires. After studying the issues more carefully, he found that some of his PAC commitments were not consistent with the policies he favored to solve the nation's problems. He began to dread the days when he would be called upon to make good on those preelection PAC pledges.

"Now the bell rings in your office at 11 a.m. Tuesday morning and now you understand how it affects the nation," he explained. "Your guts start being torn apart because you signed a form a year ago during the campaign saying you'd vote the other way. Now you understand the issue and it comes in conflict with what you told them you would do a year ago. This is a rage inside you."

"You walk onto the floor and you know that if you vote their way, they will announce it in their PAC newsletters, and next time you won't even have to beg for money," he continued. "Or you can do what in your heart you think is right. That happened to me three or four times in a row and I told my AA [administrative assistant], 'I can't do this anymore.' I'm not going to take any PAC funds. I want to be free to vote how I want to vote."

Poshard's experience is not unusual. While not all PACs force candidates to sign pledges in exchange for contributions, incumbents frequently find that as a consequence of their fund-raising efforts they have taken political positions that make them feel uncomfortable or put them in conflict with their constituents.

In recent years, PACs have been unfairly singled out as the bogymen of American politics. In truth, PAC contributions are no more corrupting than contributions from rich, favor-seeking individuals. PAC contributions are probably less troublesome than bundled, individual donations because they are strictly limited and fully disclosed to the public. Yet there is no question that PACs exist for one purpose: to buy influence with members of Congress.

Occasionally, a member of Congress responds to pressure from PACs by deciding to forswear PAC funding in all future elections, as Poshard did. But not many of them do.

In all, only a small minority of the members of Congress—including Poshard—do not accept PAC money. In the Senate this includes David L. Boren, D-Okla., John Kerry, D-Mass., and Herb Kohl, D-Wis. In the House this includes Bill Archer, R-Texas, Chester G. Atkins, D-Mass., Anthony C. Beilenson, D-Calif., Philip M. Crane, R-Ill., Bill Goodling, R-Pa., Bill Gradison, R-Ohio, Andrew Jacobs, Jr., D-Ind., Jim Leach, R-Iowa, Edward J. Markey, D-Mass., Romano L. Mazzoli, D-Ky., William H. Natcher, D-Ky., Ralph Regula, R-Ohio, and Mike Synar, D-Okla.

While the list is short, it grows a little longer every year as the reputation of PACs and special-interest money worsens. Many of those who join the list of PAC opponents use it at election time to battle the growing anti-incumbent feeling in the electorate. When Mazzoli stopped taking PAC money for that reason in 1990, he found he could easily expand his small contributor base and win with less money.

"It's doable," said Charlie Mattingly, Mazzoli's chief of staff. "You can pull away from campaigns based on interest groups. You can run without the lavish budget we're all used to. You can disprove the myth that elections are won by thirty-second television spots."

For Poshard, the decision to do without PAC money was a particularly wrenching one since he knew that redistricting would put him in a contest against another Democratic incumbent in 1992. Without PAC money, however, he figured he could cast himself as a reformer—a strategy that enabled him to defeat Rep. Terry L. Bruce, D-Ill., in the 1992 Democratic primary.

"We feel that this is an issue before the public right now," Poshard said. "I don't care if there's a well-financed opponent who comes along. We have to determine what's right for us. I think the people would respect my position. I can use that as well as if I had another $400,000 in the bank. My position is on the cutting edge."

Forced to decide whether or not they will take PAC money, some members of Congress have chosen a middle course—placing a limit on the percentage of PAC money they will accept. In most cases, these lawmakers support legislation that would limit PAC financing.

Rep. Fred Upton, R-Mich., adhered to his legislative proposal to limit PAC funding to 40 percent of the total receipts. He also insisted that virtually all his contributions—from PACs as well as individuals—came from inside Michigan. Upton held PAC fund-raisers, but they were—according to Joan Hillebrands, his press secretary—"few and far between."

Rep. H. James Saxton, R-N.J., said he donated any PAC contribution that conflicted with his political philosophy to charity.

Still, Upton, Mazzoli, Saxton, and Poshard were clearly out of step with the overwhelming majority. Most House and Senate members—even some who share Poshard's qualms about the commitments that PACs are seeking for their contributions—simply made their peace with a pervasive system that would ultimately work to their advantage.

Some of the leading recipients of PAC money in 1990 were the most outspoken critics of PAC funding. Sen. Mitch McConnell, R-Ky., a longtime opponent of PACs, received more than $1.3 million from them for his 1990 race. Before Rep. Hank Brown, R-Colo., was elected to the Senate, he sponsored a bill that would have outlawed PAC contributions. But in 1990, Brown raised nearly $1.4 million from PACs for his Senate campaign.

Even though the dramatic surge in PAC activity over the last two decades began to level off in 1990, PAC contributions to incumbents were still on the rise. Congressional candidates raised nearly $150 million from PACs in the 1990 cycle, and $117 million of it went to incumbents. The amount of money involved in Senate campaigns is so high that PACs provide only 22 percent of it. In the House, more than half of those elected in 1990 obtained at least 50 percent of their receipts from PACs.

In 1990, Sen. Phil Gramm, R-Texas, received more than $1.8 million from PACs, more than any other member of Congress. Sens. Tom Harkin, D-Iowa, Paul Simon, D-Ill., Max Baucus, D-Mont., and Jim Exon, D-Neb., each received $1.5 million or more from PACs. In the House, the leading PAC recipients were House Majority Leader Richard A. Gephardt, D-Mo., with $762,687 and David E. Bonior, D-Mich., with $728,055. Reps. Jill L. Long, D-Ind., John D. Dingell, D-Mich., Jolene Unsoeld, D-Wash., Peter Hoagland, D-Neb., Pete Geren, D-Texas, Robert T. Matsui, D-Calif., Glen Browder, D-Ala., Butler Derrick, D-S.C., Wayne Owens, D-Utah, Robert H. Michel, R-Ill., and William H. Gray III, D-Pa., each received more than $500,000 (see Table 9-1)

Members of Congress rely on PACs for the simple reason that it is easy money. Rep. Henry A. Waxman, D-Calif., said that he accepts PAC money because he has better things to do with his time than raising money from small, individual donors. "I don't want to spend my time raising money," he said. "My goal is to raise the amount you need in the least amount of time possible."

Waxman's aide, Philip Schiliro, noted that because the California Democrat chaired the House Energy and Commerce Subcommittee on Health and the Environment, he received money from many PACs without even holding a fund-raiser. "PACs will hold a meeting once or twice a year and decide who to give their money to," he said. "They try to gear their giving to an event, but if you don't have one, they give it anyway."

PAC fund raising is cost-effective. Generally, members of Congress who spent the least money on fund-raising activities depended the most on PAC money. Rep. Joel Hefley, R-Colo., for example, raised most of his funds at two PAC fund-raisers held at the headquarters of the American Trucking Association in Washington, D.C. He spent only $13,132 to raise $135,707—and that included $6,967 for a fund-raising consultant, Tucker and Associates of Washington, D.C.

Some recipients claim that they have no alternative but to raise money from PACs. This is particularly common with members from poor areas of the country where political contributions are scarce.

"We have a tough time raising money," said Krysta Hardin, an aide to Rep. Charles E. Hatcher, D-Ga., and staff director of the House Agriculture subcommittee on peanuts and tobacco. "All our contributions come from agriculture interests. We try not to hit people hard at any one time." Hatcher held PAC fund-raisers in Washington, D.C., and Atlanta, where he attracted executives from many Georgia-based agricultural companies.

In the eyes of the PAC managers, all incumbents are not created equal. As a result, they do not have the same access to PAC money. Party leaders and committee chairmen found it much easier to raise PAC money than the others.

Even though Hatcher was a ranking member of an economically important subcommittee in Congress, his PAC receipts totaled no more than $211,150. Hardin acknowledged she was jealous of the high-ranking, well-known members of Congress who seem to have an endless source of PAC cash.

"When I look at those guys with all that money, I say 'I would love to have a piece of that action,' " she said. "The guys on the Ag Committee, they try, but they just can't match that kind of money."

Under federal law, almost any group of citizens can band together to create a PAC. The group may include people with similar ideological views, employees of a corporation, or members of a labor union. In 1990, there were 4,677 registered federal PACs, including about thirty PACs established by members of Congress to support other candidates.

PACs can collect contributions of up to $5,000 a year from each PAC member and contribute up to $5,000 in each primary and each general election to a single candidate. In 1990, the nation's richest PAC, the Teamsters' Democratic Republican Independent Voter Education Committee, dispensed nearly $10.6 million, $2.3 million of which was directly contributed to federal candidates.

In addition to making contributions, PACs can make unlimited independent expenditures on behalf of candidates, as long as they do not coordinate their efforts with the candidate. AutoPAC, a group of foreign car dealers that some Democrats have accused of being a front for Japanese auto manufacturers, has been the acknowledged leader in this field. In 1990, AutoPAC spent almost $600,000 in the final two weeks before the election on behalf of Rep. Robert C. Smith, R-N.H., who was elected to the Senate, and Sen. Rudy Boschwitz, R-Minn., who lost.

Smith was a chief beneficiary of independent expenditures in 1990. According to the FEC, more than $516,000 was spent independently to help him win reelection. Others who realized substantial benefit from independent expenditures included Sen. Jesse Helms, who had $218,500 spent on his behalf; Sen. J. Bennett Johnston, who benefited from more than $278,000 in independent expenditures; and Boschwitz, who had nearly $254,000 spent on his behalf. But for Helms, independent expenditures were a mixed blessing. Nearly $405,000 was spent independently to defeat Helms. Likewise, Johnston's opponent, David Duke, had $293,088 spent against him by independent groups.

In addition to independent expenditures, some PACs specialize in providing in-kind services to candidates, such as polling or loaning out their facilities for fund-raising parties. Rep. Dave Nagle, D-Iowa, received polling assistance valued at $4,446 from the Realtors PAC.

In exchange for their PAC contributions, business and labor executives expect access to members of Congress and some degree of cooperation on issues important to their industries. It is not an iron-clad bargain, however. "We don't expect them to vote 100 percent our way," insisted Al Spivak, the Washington, D.C., spokesman for General Dynamics, whose PAC made $369,631 in contributions to federal candidates in 1989-1990.

It is somewhat easier for members of Congress to reject requests for help from PACs than it is to say "no" to individuals who have raised large sums of money for them. It is also easier for them to vote against PAC contributors on high-profile issues than it is on issues that receive no public attention. Rep. Norm Dicks, D-Wash., who received $240,055 from PACs in the 1990 election, said that decisions on major issues are usually based on ideological or parochial considerations, not on PAC contributions.

But as Poshard's tale demonstrates, even though PACs do not expect complete cooperation, they do try to exert heavy-handed influence over lawmakers, particularly the new members of Congress who are the most vulnerable to their tactics. A high-ranking member such as Waxman need not fear losing the funding of PACs if he refuses to vote their way on a few issues, but members with less seniority clearly feel more beholden to the PACs that helped elect them.

Rep. Charles Wilson, D-Texas, a recipient of nearly $440,000 in PAC donations in 1989-1990, said members of Congress usually solicit contributions only from PACs whose agenda they support. As he put it: "I think any fair-minded person knows that when anybody gives you $10,000 in PAC contributions, they're not doing it because your breath smells good. . . . When you actively solicit money from special-interest groups, you are implying you support them. The idea that you announce your candidacy and these people come running to you because of your splendid record of public service—well, if you believe that, you ought to talk to somebody about buying a bridge. If you go out and aggressively solicit Jewish money, it's clearly implicit that you're going to support Israel. If you vigorously solicit money from wheat farmers, it's implied you're going to support wheat subsidies. And it's the same with defense contractors. People who say differently are not telling it like it is."

Members of Congress also solicit contributions from PACs whose views are consistent with those of their constituents. Nevertheless, PAC contributions can undermine the relationship between lawmakers and their constituents. When their funding comes primarily from national PACs and not from the people back home, they are likely to be more attuned to PAC interests and less sensitive to shifts in hometown sentiment.

For their part, PAC managers note that they seldom have to beg candidates to accept their money. On the contrary, they usually are inundated with solicitations for money from members of Congress. "It's more like extortion than bribery," said one PAC manager.

Critics of the current campaign finance system argue that PACs unfairly favor incumbents over challengers, particularly the entrenched incumbents. In 1990, while incumbents received nearly $117 million from PACs, challengers got only $15.6 million. On average, House incumbents received $213,485 from PACs while challengers averaged no more than $22,561.

PAC preferences for incumbents were clearly described in the pages of the *1990 PAC Workbook,* which the Democratic Congressional Campaign Committee (DCCC) distributed as a $100 in-kind donation to Democratic candidates across the country. The workbook listed all the prominent PACs and explained the individual characteristics of each. Virtually every PAC listed in the book was said to prefer giving to incumbents.

PACs should not bear the brunt of criticism for the current campaign finance system, especially when large amounts of special-interest money also are flowing to candidates through bundled individual donations. When compared with bundled donations from top executives, PAC contributions can be considered the lesser evil. As Larry Sabato of the University of Virginia wrote in his book, *Paying for Elections:* "Many of the charges made against political action committees are exaggerated and dubious." *

PAC contributions normally are derived from small contributions given by employees of a company or members of a labor union. They do, in fact, serve their original purpose: allowing small donors to join together to support candidates favorable to their industry or point of view. In 1989, according to the National Association of Business Political Action Committees, the average corporate PAC had 799 contributors who gave an average of $121.50 a year. By comparison, bundled individual contributions are seldom less than $1,000 each.

Unlike bundled individual contributions, PAC contributions are fully disclosed in reports to the FEC. Every two years, the FEC even issues a four-volume report on PAC activities. In fact, it is because of the intense scrutiny given to PACs by the FEC that they have come in for so much criticism.

Indeed, scrutiny of PAC contributions by the FEC and the press has made them much less desirable. Whenever members of Congress accept PAC contributions, they know their constituents are likely to read about them in the newspapers. Whenever they accept bundled individual contributions, even from the same source, they can be almost certain that the money will go unnoticed by the news media. Finally, it is not true that PACs give only to incumbents. PACs contribute heavily in open seat races and even bestow money on an occasional challenger, much as any ordinary individual contributor would do under the same circumstances.

In Wisconsin, Democrat Jerome Van Sistine, who challenged Republican Rep. Toby Roth, was more successful with PACs than Roth because he had the support of a wide range of labor and liberal groups. Seventy-five percent of Van Sistine's money came from PACs while Roth received only 52 percent of his money from PACs.

Even though the DCCC's *PAC Workbook* noted repeatedly that while most organizations favored incumbents, it also listed PACs that

* Larry J. Sabato, *Paying for Elections: The Campaign Finance Thicket* (New York: Twentieth Century Fund Paper, 1989), 10.

were not averse to helping an occasional challenger. For example, the American Academy of Ophthalmology Political Committee was described as follows: "PAC is growing in size. Normally aligns itself with friendly incumbents, but will support challengers if there is strong local support."

In 1990, Democrat Jim Bacchus managed to raise nearly half of his $877,500 campaign war chest from PACs for his open seat race in Florida. His administrative assistant, Linda O. Hennessee, said he did it primarily by calling upon many real estate brokers, insurance agents, and other local business people and persuading them to intercede for him with their industry PACs in Washington, D.C.

"People don't understand PAC fund raising," she said. "They think the way to do it is to go to the NRCC [National Republican Congressional Committee] or the DCCC and say, 'We need PAC money.' It doesn't happen that way. If you want to raise money, you start at home. PAC fund raising is bottom up, not top down." In addition, Public Citizens' Congress Watch, in a study of fifteen races where challengers defeated incumbents in 1990, found that PACs frequently gave to both sides. In California, thirty-seven PACs contributed to both Rep. Chip Pashayan, R-Calif., and his successful challenger, Democrat Calvin Dooley. Pashayan got $74,572; Dooley received $57,900. Since PACs primarily are seeking access to lawmakers, they can be expected to support challengers such as Dooley who appear to have a reasonable chance of winning.

Gregg Ward, an officer of the National Association of Business Political Action Committees, a lobbying group for PACs on campaign finance reform issues, said he has been puzzled by the complaint that PACs favor incumbents. "It would seem that would be a basic, protected right of political expression," Ward said. "What's most difficult to accept, however, is why PACs are singled out for this criticism when it is true for all other categories of political donors. No one is suggesting, for example, that we punish individual contributors for giving mainly to incumbents." *

To many voters, however, abolishing PACs looks like a simple prescription for reforming the campaign finance system and eliminat-

* Gregg Ward, testimony on behalf of the National Association of Business Political Action Committees, House Campaign Finance Reform Task Force, May 28, 1991.

ing the advantage that incumbents appear to have in congressional elections. The popularity of PAC reform has spawned numerous legislative proposals. In the Senate, where PAC contributions average only 25 percent of an incumbent's receipts, both the Republican and Democratic leadership were on record in 1991 in favor of banning PACs. In the House, where candidates depend more heavily upon PACs, a majority voted to limit PAC funding to $200,000 per election—a figure that was exceeded by more than 200 congressional candidates in 1990. Neither of these provisions made it into law.

Why would these politicians vote to cut off one of their primary sources of funding? Some of them genuinely believe that PAC funding is undermining representative democracy. Some were responding to fears that PACs have spawned an anti-incumbent sentiment in the land. Some of the Congress members who voted to limit PAC funding were doing so on the assumption that the bill would never pass or be signed into law by the president.

Even if PACs were eliminated, members of Congress still would enjoy a steady flow of special-interest dollars into their campaigns. Without a shift to public financing of congressional elections, the elimination of PACs would prompt a sharp increase in bundled individual donations from executives of corporations and other organizations. Without PACs, special-interest political contributions would simply go underground.

Table 9-1 The Top Twenty-Five Recipients in the 1990 Congressional Races: PAC Donations

	House		Senate	
Rank	Candidate	Expenditures	Candidate	Expenditures
1	Richard A. Gephardt, D-Mo.	$762,687	Phil Gramm, R-Texas	$1,812,176
2	David E. Bonior, D-Mich.	728,055	Tom Harkin, D-Iowa	1,748,081
3	Jill L. Long, D-Ind.	687,532	Paul Simon, D-Ill.	1,714,221
4	John D. Dingell, D-Mich.	625,727	Max Baucus, D-Mont.	1,659,933
5	Jolene Unsoeld, D-Wash.	624,498	Jim Exon, D-Neb.	1,500,057
6	Peter Hoagland, D-Neb.	615,587	Howell Heflin, D-Ala.	1,488,876
7	Pete Geren, D-Texas	607,901	J. Bennett Johnston, D-La.	1,461,940
8	Robert T. Matsui, D-Calif.	582,964	John D. Rockefeller IV, D-W.Va.	1,424,813
9	Glen Browder, D-Ala.	547,750	Bill Bradley, D-N.J.	1,399,393
10	Butler Derrick, D-S.C.	542,789	Carl Levin, D-Mich.	1,381,047
11	Wayne Owens, D-Utah	541,232	Hank Brown, R-Colo.	1,370,808
12	Robert H. Michel, R-Ill.	519,161	Tom Tauke, R-Iowa	1,369,278
13	William H. Gray III, D-Pa.	516,953	Mitch McConnell, R-Ky.	1,327,043
14	Philip R. Sharp, D-Ind.	498,599	Rudy Boschwitz, R-Minn.	1,323,584
15	Roy Dyson, D-Md.	497,700	Daniel R. Coats, R-Ind.	1,216,837
16	John P. Murtha, D-Pa.	496,920	Lynn Martin, R-Ill.	1,203,894
17	Frank Annunzio, D-Ill.	478,891	Al Gore, D-Tenn.	1,147,982
18	Gary Condit, D-Calif.	472,603	Mark O. Hatfield, R-Ore.	1,050,983
19	Jack Brooks, D-Texas	459,444	Larry Pressler, R-S.D.	1,000,247
20	John Bryant, D-Texas	458,721	Patricia Saiki, R-Hawaii	958,540
21	George E. Brown, Jr., D-Calif.	454,935	Ted Stevens, R-Alaska	954,946
22	Thomas J. Manton, D-N.Y.	452,323	Jesse Helms, R-N.C.	950,958
23	Vic Fazio, D-Calif.	451,245	Pete V. Domenici, R-N.M.	891,637
24	Jim Moody, D-Wis.	450,704	Claiborne Pell, D-R.I.	881,512
25	Byron L. Dorgan, D-N.D.	449,050	Daniel K. Akaka, D-Hawaii	847,059

Note: Totals for the House are for the entire two-year cycle, including special elections; totals for the Senate are for the entire six-year cycle.

CHAPTER 10

Reform

A Different Idea

This book lays to rest some myths about elections: that television advertising rates are responsible for the rising costs of campaigning, that politicians are helpless to control costs, that candidates amass large campaign war chests either because they need them or to scare off potential opponents, that campaign contributions are strictly limited by law, and that special-interest money is helping to rebuild the political parties.

Unfortunately, the proposals that have been offered in Congress for campaign finance reform have been based, in part, on these flawed concepts of how the American political system works. Proposals for public financing of congressional elections are predicated on the commonly held notion that candidates spend the bulk of their campaign funds to communicate with voters. But the case for public financing is undermined by our findings that less than half of their campaign funds are spent on traditional campaign activities.

If candidates are squandering campaign funds on personal luxuries or investing the money in political empire building, why should American taxpayers be subsidizing such antidemocratic extravagance?

Proposals for cut-rate television are based on the mistaken assumption that television advertising is primarily responsible for rising congressional campaign costs. But television costs account for only about one-third of the cost of campaigning, and they also appear to be declining. As long as average members of Congress spend about two-thirds of their campaign funds on overhead, fund raising, polls, and other costs, why should broadcasters be forced to subsidize congressional campaigns?

Likewise, lawmakers have been reluctant to crack down on soft money because they contend that it is helping to revive state and local parties. But the parties will never be strong as long as the candidates are raising millions of dollars for themselves and simply passing along some of the money to state and local party leaders. The state and local parties will not have an important role in the electoral process until they reclaim a central role in fund raising for all candidates.

When Congress finally enacts campaign finance reform—as it eventually must—the authors of that legislation must begin with a clear understanding of how money is distorting the American electoral process. Otherwise, they risk making a deplorable situation even worse.

Two elements of the current system are most troubling: (1) too much special-interest money is available to politicians, and (2) too much secrecy surrounds the financing of elections. If any reform is to succeed, it must drastically reduce the amount of money spent in elections and bring the entire system into the open for public scrutiny.

The objectives of any reform legislation passed by Congress should be to limit the growing influence of special interests, to restrict the money that politicians can spend, to provide more opportunity for challengers, to force incumbents to dismantle their permanent political machines, and to prevent campaign treasuries from being used as personal slush funds.

SPENDING

Campaign spending should be limited to campaigns. Advertising, yard signs, balloons, rallies, phone banks, and get-out-the-vote efforts are the things that should be funded with campaign contributions.

Members of Congress should not be permitted to spend their contributions to build gold-plated, permanent political machines with year-round offices, a fleet of automobiles, a full-time staff, and all the other trappings of a thriving medium-sized business. Nor should they be permitted to use their campaign contributions for personal expenses.

So far, the spending patterns of candidates have been virtually overlooked in any discussion of campaign finance reform, even though spending is an important part of the equation. Candidates will continue to amass larger and larger war chests unless their spending is restricted in some way.

Most existing reform proposals to restrict spending would impose an aggregate limit. In most cases, the proposed limit would far exceed what an average candidate currently spends. While the American electoral system would surely benefit from some limit on campaign spending, any aggregate limit might create new, unforeseen difficulties.

Given the huge disparity in true campaign costs from region to region, a single limit would surely be too restrictive in some locations and too permissive in others. Under the Supreme Court's decision in *Buckley v. Valeo,* aggregate spending limits would necessarily be voluntary. Aggregate spending limits also might discourage candidates from seeking contributions from small, hometown donors, since that sort of fund raising is more expensive than relying on special interests.

Instead of imposing an aggregate limit, Congress should limit campaign spending by simply setting down strict guidelines that would prohibit candidates from spending their contributions on purchases deemed to be outside the realm of legitimate campaign costs.

The following expenditures should not be funded with campaign contributions: clothing, club memberships, babysitting, family portraits, vacation costs, apartments, automobiles for family members, charitable donations, college scholarships, endowed chairs, congressional office expenses, donations to other candidates, and augmenting the salaries of congressional staff workers.

Even legitimate campaign expenditures—rent for a campaign headquarters, campaign salaries, travel expenses, automobile leases, consulting fees, polling costs—should be restricted, perhaps to the years in which elections are held. All candidates should be required to shut down their campaign organizations during the off-years. They should be prohibited from carrying over any more than a limited amount of campaign funds—perhaps, no more than $50,000—from election to election. Candidates should be required to return all excess funds to contributors on a pro rata basis, as Sen. Sam Nunn, D-Ga., currently does.

Incumbents should be prohibited from simply raising money to cover their legal bills whenever they get into trouble. They also should be required to disclose publicly how their campaign funds are invested.

Under these rules, campaigns would still be permitted to operate in a free market without artificial restrictions. No legitimate campaign expenditure would be off limits. No candidate would be limited by anything but his or her ability to raise money and appeal to the voters. Competitive races would still be expensive; noncompetitive races would not.

Candidates under such a system would not raise much more than they needed because returning the money would be too much trouble. Incumbents would still have some advantage, as they always will. But the opportunity for challengers would be improved because they would no longer have to compete with multimillion-dollar permanent political machines. And contributors could be assured that their money would be used for legitimate campaign purposes.

In order for a system like this one to work, however, candidates must be required to accurately report their expenditures to the Federal Election Commission (FEC). They would no longer be permitted to report vaguely itemized expenditures such as "constituent services," "campaign consulting," or "entertainment."

In fact, the FEC should adopt a standard list of acceptable expenditures and give each one a code number, much as we did in devising our own computer analysis of campaign spending. This would not only simplify reporting by congressional candidates, but would also aid political analysts who wish to study campaign spending patterns in the future. Such a system would also enable the FEC to live up to its commitment to require candidates to fully disclose their campaign financing.

CONTRIBUTIONS

Public financing of elections would no doubt cure many of the ills of the current system. But public financing is out of the question until members of Congress can persuade the taxpayers that they would not squander the money. None of the existing proposals for public financing call for better accountability of spending by the candidates.

Perhaps the simplest way to restrict private funding of elections is to merely enforce the intent of current law by imposing strict limits on all contributions, including soft money.

No federal candidate should be permitted to solicit contributions in excess of $2,000 from an individual or $10,000 from a political committee. No contributor should be permitted to give more than $25,000 in a single year. No exemptions should be granted for any reasons, not even to fund state party get-out-the-vote efforts.

If the limits on contributions were strictly enforced, the Congress could even raise current contribution limits. The value of the dollar has declined substantially since these original limits were established in the 1970s. There would be less incentive for contributors to forge loopholes in the law if these limits were raised periodically.

In addition, Congress should prohibit House members from soliciting contributions in off-years. Senators should be prohibited from raising money during the first four years of their term. Some members of Congress already observe these guidelines voluntarily.

To strengthen the Republican and Democratic parties, party organizations should be allowed to raise money in off-years when candidates are restricted from doing so.

No new limitations are necessary on PAC contributions, but bundlers should be forced to abide by the same rigorous disclosure rules as PAC managers. Bundlers should be required to report their fundraising activities to the FEC or all contributors should be required to tell the FEC the name of the person who collected their check.

Without disclosure of bundling, voters will never know the true source of influence that is being brought to bear on lawmakers whenever they accept bundled contributions.

ENFORCEMENT AND DISCLOSURE

The FEC should be transformed by Congress into an independent, nonpartisan agency with full investigatory powers. At the minimum, the commission should conduct random audits of some campaigns, hire a trained field staff to conduct investigations, and cooperate with other investigatory agencies.

FEC officials have allowed the abuses of election laws that have been outlined in this book to go unchecked. Not only have they not enforced the law, but they have also failed to live up to their pledge to use public disclosure to bring voluntary compliance.

Most of the information in this book was obtained from FEC files, but not without several years of sustained effort and considerable expense. In congressional elections, the FEC has focused on monitoring PAC contributions. Not until 1990 did the agency provide the public with the same computerized access to individual contributions that it offered for PAC donations. Even now, no effort is being made to put campaign spending information on line.

The FEC has an obligation to make campaign spending information as available to the public as is the information about contributions. It has a duty to force candidates to disclose the actual purchases they make with campaign funds and to reject all reports from candidates that use vague descriptions designed to mask the real purpose of the expenditure.

At the same time, Congress should reject legislation that would require the FEC to computerize data on contributions under $200. This is nothing but a mischievous proposal designed to overburden the FEC and slow down the current pace of public disclosure of large contributions. Among other things, it would likely delay until after election day the publication of the preelection reports that candidates must file disclosing their last-minute contributors and expenditures.

The FEC also must lift the shroud of secrecy that surrounds its investigative proceedings. Under most circumstances, the commission provides no public notice of any investigation until it has been completed. Aggrieved parties who bring complaints to the FEC go for years without knowing if the case is being investigated or ignored.

Few federal agencies operate under such tight secrecy. The FEC's procedures succeed both in overprotecting politicians who abuse the system and in bringing unnecessary embarrassment to those who are falsely accused of wrongdoing.

REFORM IS POSSIBLE

As long as politicians make decisions that affect American industry, money and politics will be indivisible in the United States. No matter what kind of a system is created to limit their influence, special interests will eventually find a way around it. Even after nearly two decades of public financing of presidential elections, private money still is a growing source of funding in the quest of major party nominees for the White House.

It is possible to create a system for financing congressional elections in which members of Congress are less likely to be corrupted by money, a system in which the acceptance of money does not necessarily impart the impression that the politician is beholden to the contributor. It is possible to enact reforms that will limit the amount of money that can be spent on congressional elections and to smooth out many of the distortions that money has wrought in the electoral process.

Index

The page numbers in **bold** indicate tables and boxes. Congressional district numbers are shown in parentheses.